Rethinking Sustainable Development

This book demonstrates falsified economic performance of global economies when the environment is not recognised as a capital, and when the ecosystem is overlooked towards sustainable development.

Seck begins with an analysis of standard macroeconomic framework and policy practice. He argues, with reference to environmental accounting literature, that environmental capital must form an integral component of economic measurement. This paves the way for an alternative environmental-macroeconomics framework for policy analysis that promotes sustainable development. The book demonstrates how environmental capital can be measured with reference to select OECD countries and provides a methodology for analysing how macroeconomic goals are related to a steady-state economy. Seck then concludes with a summary of the conflict between current economic growth and ecosystem preservation, and outlines possible policy improvements and directions for research.

Rethinking Sustainable Development is an invaluable reference for policymakers as well as researchers and students of environmental economics, sustainable development, and macroeconomics.

Seck TAN is Associate Professor at the Singapore Institute of Technology. He researches on environmental economics with reference to valuation of environmental goods and services. Seck is an applied economist with broad research interests in policy analysis and recommendation towards sustainable development.

Routledge Studies in Public Economics and Finance

The Challenges of Public Procurement Reforms
Edited by Annalisa Castelli, Gustavo Piga, Stéphane Saussier and Tünde Tátrai

Public Financial Management in the European Union
Public Finance and Global Crises
Marta Postuła

Public Goods and the Fourth Industrial Revolution
Inclusive Models of Finance, Distribution and Production
Edited by Maria Płonka

The Privatisation of Knowledge
A New Policy Agenda for Health, Energy, and Data Governance
Massimo Florio

Rethinking Sustainable Development
Economic Integration and Public Policy
Seck TAN

For more information about this series, please visit: www.routledge.com/Routledge-Studies-in-Public-Economics-and-Finance/book-series/LICPUBECONFIN

Rethinking Sustainable Development

Economic Integration and Public Policy

Seck TAN

Routledge
Taylor & Francis Group
LONDON AND NEW YORK

First published 2024
by Routledge
4 Park Square, Milton Park, Abingdon, Oxon OX14 4RN

and by Routledge
605 Third Avenue, New York, NY 10158

Routledge is an imprint of the Taylor & Francis Group, an informa business

British Library Cataloguing in Publication Data
A catalogue record for this book is available from the British Library

ISBN: 978-0-367-43341-3 (hbk)
ISBN: 978-1-032-77201-1 (pbk)
ISBN: 978-1-003-00255-0 (ebk)

DOI: 10.4324/9781003002550

Typeset in Galliard
by Newgen Publishing UK

Contents

Figures

Tables

Preface

With the understanding that the fatal flaw of current policies of growth and development is due to a lack of understanding of the finite nature of the environment, this book argues that policy intervention via policy co-creation and policy co-production must be deployed to ensure that ecosystem-centric policies are implemented that will promote sustainable development.

This book is organised as follows. Chapter 1 provides an introduction to this study and a synoptic description of the standard macroeconomic framework and policy practices that stem from the utilisation of such a framework. Chapter 2 stresses the debate between growth and development with the natural ecosystem as a bedrock for stabilisation policies. Chapter 3 reviews the challenges posed by standard macroeconomic framework when environmental capital is not internalised and paves the way for proposing an alternative environmental-macroeconomics framework for policy analysis. Chapter 4 addresses the measurement of environment as a capital and its utilisation with reference to selected Organisation for Economic Co-operation and Development (OECD) economies, namely, Australia, Canada, Germany, Japan, Korea, New Zealand, the United Kingdom, and the USA from 1990 to 2021. Chapter 5 compares economies' steady states between the standard macroeconomic framework and the environmental-macroeconomics framework where the capacity of an economy can be overstated in the absence of environmental capital. Chapter 6 presents a methodology for analysing how macroeconomic goals are affected by steady states with significant findings of policy ranges when the environmental-macroeconomics framework is adopted. Finally, the book concludes with a summary of the research directed at sustainable development and public policy with directions for future studies.

Acknowledgements

Writing this book had been an enjoyable and painstaking process and I savoured each and every moment of triumphs and setbacks. The process was undoubtedly made to be enjoyed.

I would like to thank Professor Dodo Jesuthason Thampapillai, for without his encouragement and guidance, I would certainly not have embarked on this career path and commence on this journey of academic research. I also owe Professor Mike Howlett deep gratitude for his advice and unwavering support in my first pursuit of the book proposal and writing.

I would like to thank the anonymous reviewers for their feedback on the book proposal and the team at Routledge, including Lam Yongling (Ex-Editor for Economics and Business) for her vote of confidence in my research specialisation and Kendrick Loo (Current Editor) and Chelsea Low (Editorial Assistant) for their patience and heroics as I complete my first book project.

Many parts of this book were written at airports and cities around the world. From Oslo Airport, Gardermoen, to Rome–Fiumicino International Airport "Leonardo da Vinci" to Félix Houphouët Boigny International Airport to Tan Son Nhat International Airport, I had been extremely lucky to have met and interacted with concurring international researchers.

Last, and never the least, I am grateful to my parents and sister for their affection and support. And daughter dearest, Ariane Tan.

1 The Standard Macroeconomic Framework and Economic Performance

1.1 Introduction

The main aim of macroeconomic policy is stabilisation. That is, to close or reduce gaps relating to output, employment, and inflation both in the short run and the long run. The main issue raised in this study is that the standard macroeconomic framework currently in use does not adequately represent these gaps. The contention is that these gaps are better represented by the adoption of an environmental-macroeconomics (EM) framework. The superiority of the EM framework rests on the inclusion of environmental capital (KN) as an integral component of the economy. As a result, the use of the EM framework facilitates the choice of policies that safeguard KN and uphold the principles of sustainability. Selected policy interventions must fulfil the requirement of minimal damage to the environment whilst economic growth is maintained. Therefore, the main objective of this study is to demonstrate both "why" and "how" current practices of policy formulation must change by recourse to the utilisation of EM frameworks. The main outcome of this study is the demonstration of methods for deriving a distinct set of stabilisation policies that addresses not only output, employment, and inflation but also sustainability with respect to steady-state equilibrium. The policy implication in relation to this study is to close the gaps relating to output, employment, and inflation. Hence, the key determinant for formulating stabilisation policies is the difference in the magnitude of the gaps when the EM framework is used as opposed to the standard macroeconomic framework.

A brief review of standard concepts in macroeconomics is considered next. This review facilitates the illustration of "why" and "how" environmental and natural resource variables can influence macroeconomic processes.

1.2 Standard Macroeconomic Framework

The economic model of aggregate demand and aggregate supply (AD-AS) is used to analyse economic fluctuations for most economies. Aggregate demand (AD) is the quantity of goods and services that households, firms, and the

DOI: 10.4324/9781003002550-1

government would want to buy at each price level. Aggregate supply (AS) is the quantity of goods and services that firms would choose to produce and sell at each price level. AD and AS are combined to determine the equilibrium level of output and price for the economy. An economy can fluctuate, for example, it can grow, contract, or stay the same. Its performance is measured by the growth rate of output produced in a given time period. In addition, policymakers would also be interested in the levels of unemployment and inflation for the same time period to avoid any macroeconomic in-balances. Thus, the level of output, unemployment, and inflation are key indicators that determine the health of an economy. Based on the AD-AS model, there are three basic macroeconomic policy areas of intervention: the level of aggregate output, unemployment, and inflation.

Unemployment

Economists' definition of full employment could include existence of unemployment in terms of frictional and structural categories. This level of unemployment is an economy's natural rate of unemployment. There are other types of unemployment, namely, frictional, structural, and cyclical. Frictional unemployment occurs because the labour market is always in a state of flux and is dependent on the structure of the labour market (Dornbusch et al., 2008). Frictional unemployment refers to people who are between jobs or looking for their first job. Such a scenario is also termed voluntary unemployment. This unemployment is dependent on labour turnover and the time taken to match the appropriate worker to an appropriate job. Selected economies may provide unemployment benefits to people who have been laid off. These unemployment benefits may increase frictional unemployment, as the unemployed can choose to remain unemployed or take their time to look for the ideal job. Although deterioration in frictional unemployment may be unintentional, such benefits can improve the ability of economies to match workers to the most appropriate job (Mankiw, 2004), and a certain level of frictional unemployment is essential to the smooth running of a rapidly changing dynamic economy (Frank and Bernanke, 2009). Structural unemployment occurs when the unemployed do not have the skills necessary to take advantage of employment opportunities. In this scenario, there is a mismatch between the needs of the workers and the requirements of the job vacancies. Unemployment of a structural nature is affected by job location and worker's skill sets. Job vacancies may exist, but they are in a region different from that of the unemployed, and workers may be under- or over-qualified for available jobs, resulting in a mismatch. Alternatively, discrimination can also prevent a worker from getting a job, even when the worker is qualified because employers may practice discrimination against a select group of people. An employer may advertise a position to fulfil the hiring process even though an internal candidate is certain to fill the position. An external advertisement might, however, fulfil the legal requirement to search internally and externally for the best candidate.

Structural unemployment can also be a result of impediments to employment, such as minimum wages and/or unions' demands to keep wages above market equilibrium. Higher wages can affect the structure of the labour market and add to more unemployment. As an economy fluctuates between expansion, stagnation, and contraction, there will be similar fluctuations in unemployment around the natural rate of unemployment. This type of unemployment is termed cyclical unemployment. Cyclical unemployment is the difference between the actual rate of unemployment and the natural rate of unemployment. This occurs when demand for labour is low and can also be termed as involuntary unemployment. Zero cyclical unemployment can occur when an economy experiences minimal economic fluctuation. However, an economy will always experience positive frictional and structural unemployment even when there is equilibrium in the labour market. Therefore, an economy will realistically never obtain zero unemployment as there will always be people between jobs, new entrants to the workforce, and a mismatch of workers' skill sets with job requirements. This is particularly evident with globalisation, ease of immigration, and improved technology; technological advancement can translate into a lower dependence on labour and a higher level of productivity.

Inflation

Inflation is defined as the overall increase in prices and is primarily a result of an increase in the quantity of money. Historically, the relationship between money and prices is theorised by the quantity equation. The quantity equation of money states that the money stock multiplied by the velocity of money equals the price level multiplied by income. If the velocity of money and income are assumed to be fixed, any changes in the money stock will also change the price level. As the measurement of the variables (money stock and price level) is usually in percentage terms, it can be concluded that the rate of growth of the money stock equals the rate of inflation. When prices rise, the value of money falls; and when prices fall, the value of money rises. Hence, the value of money is measured by the price level, and the price level is determined by the demand for and supply of money.

Demand for money can be broadly classified as transactive, precautionary, or speculative. Firstly, money is demanded for purposes of making transactions as it is a medium of exchange for goods and services. A higher price level will increase the demand for money as it is now of a lower value; that is, a greater amount of money is required to purchase the same amount of goods and services. Secondly, money is demanded as a precautionary measure to meet unexpected circumstances. Money is held as cash to make unanticipated payments. However, the holding of credit cards is likely to reduce the demand for precautionary money. Lastly, money is demanded for speculative purposes, according to the expected returns and risks involved. When there is an increase in expected returns on interest-bearing assets, there is less money demanded. In this case, money would be much better off invested in interest-bearing assets. A high interest rate increases the cost of holding money. Thus, the interest rate is the opportunity cost of holding money.

The supply of money can be controlled by the central bank through open-market operations and reserve requirements (Mankiw, 2004). Open-market operations refer to activities in which the central bank issues bonds or purchases bonds from the public. The objective is to manipulate an economy's money supply. When the central bank issues bonds, the money supply falls as the public's money is used to purchase these bonds. However, when the central bank purchases bonds, the money supply rises as money flows to the market from the purchase of the bonds. Reserve requirements are regulations set by the central bank on the minimum amount of reserve that financial institutions must hold against deposits. The money supply falls when the reserve ratio is higher and rises when the reserve ratio is lower. The central bank can use these tools to influence the money supply. Success in influencing the money supply is dependent on the credibility and performance of the economy. When households have confidence in the financial institutions, they will deposit more money. When an economy is growing, financial institutions will be more willing to lend as capital is easily obtained. The opposite is true when households have less confidence and when an economy is contracting. At equilibrium, the overall level of prices would be at a level at which money demand equals money supply. The overall price level of an economy is also termed inflation.

Inflation can be classified into two categories, namely, demand-pull and cost-push. Demand-pull inflation occurs when prices are "pulled-up" by excess demand for goods and services. There is too much money chasing too few goods and services. Cost-push inflation occurs in the absence of any excess demand for goods and services and is caused purely by supply-side disturbances. Prices are pushed upwards by increasing costs of production, such as, increased wages, producer mark-ups, and increased interest rates, and exogenous shocks, such as, pandemic and war. In the short-run analysis of the AD-AS framework, increasing aggregate expenditure at low levels of economic activity and spare capacity can increase production and employment with negligible increases in price levels. However, price increases will not be negligible when an economy is operating at levels of economic activity close to or at its capacity. When an economy is close to or at its capacity in the long run, increases in AD will not result in increases in production because as an economy approaches capacity, firms will not be able to meet demand as there are limited resources available for production. There will be greater demand chasing a fixed supply. These bids increase the prices of the goods and services. Thus, any increase in AD will only result in increasing prices when an economy is close to or at its capacity. This is demand-pull inflation. Similarly, for an economy operating close to or at its capacity, production output is unlikely to increase. There are fewer resources available for production. The use of these limited resources is likely to come at a higher price as competition for the resources bids the cost upwards. This translates to cost-push inflation, in which changes to AS will only result in higher prices. An economy can also experience higher prices earlier when capacity contracts in the long run. This can occur when there is a reduction in the labour force, an aging population, or when productivity falls. Thus, cost pull inflation can be attributed to decreases in AS, as well as to a contraction of the economy.

Unemployment and Inflation

In the short run, unemployment can be caused by a downward shift of AD or an upward shift of AS. In the long run, unemployment is greatly dependent on the production capacity of the economy. If there is no spare capacity, unemployment will rise as capacity is close to being fully utilised with no allowance for further employment. Unemployment can also rise when an economy faces real wages that are too high. Policies to increase AD will not reduce unemployment. Instead, policies should aim towards lowering real wages to reduce unemployment. Both unemployment and inflation are interdependent indicators as they relate to the fundamental question of macroeconomics, that is, the aggregation of economic activity. In other words, they determine the degree to which productive resources are used for aggregate output in relation to potential output. Ideally, an economy should have zero unemployment and inflation within a range of between 2% and 3%, with a matching level of aggregate output. But the reality is far from ideal. Unemployment and rising prices exist in all economies. And high inflation will not be tolerated by central banks for measures will be taken to curb inflation by slowing output growth and raising unemployment. Inflation targeting is a commitment by the central bank to maintain stability of the general price level. As long as unemployment is within an acceptable level and inflation is within a targeted band, both macroeconomic indicators can be managed with intervention. Stabilising policies help predict output growth and the corresponding price level changes, which are critical to a stable macroeconomic environment.

The relationship between unemployment and inflation can be explained by the Phillips curve – where there is an inverse relationship between unemployment level and the rate of inflation. That is, a lower level of unemployment will bring about a higher level of inflation for an economy and vice-versa. While this trade-off between unemployment and inflation holds true in the short run, it does not offer a comprehensive solution to the complex issues faced by economies in the long run. This is because prices are sticky in the short run and flexible in the long run. However, if this inverse relationship between unemployment and inflation is assumed to be stable, policy intervention in the form of monetary and/or fiscal can be used to stimulate an economy by controlling unemployment and managing inflation. A higher level of inflation can be tolerated as this would lead to a lower level of unemployment at equilibrium. An economy at equilibrium will display a gap from its steady-state equilibrium. This gap is known as the income gap. The duration of economic slowdown, high unemployment, and inflation should also be considered and thus explains the trade-off and difficulty in formulating policy interventions.

1.3 Economic Performance

Level of Aggregate Output and Policy Interventions

Fluctuations in AD can lead to greater fluctuations in aggregate output, unemployment, and inflation. There are stabilising policies that governments can undertake to manage AD (Stegman and Junor, 1993). The policies are aimed at stimulating AD during periods of high unemployment and acting to restrict AD when the economy is at its productive capacity and generating inflationary pressures. The discretionary fiscal interventions of expenditures and tax revenues are clearly warranted by the government. This is because tax revenues are required to finance national defence, education, health care, and infrastructure. However, such direct government intervention may provide no sustainable reduction in unemployment because the effect of changes to the true structure and behaviour of the economy will take time. For example, when tax revenue is reinvested in the infrastructure of an economy, AD will increase due to increases in investment in the short term. However, the returns to the economy will only be felt in the longer term, when capacity of the economy is increased. Samuelson and Nordhaus (2001, 2009) attributed the shortcomings of fiscal intervention to timing, politics, and macroeconomic theory. Timing refers to time taken to recognise a shock, to formulate a response, and for the legislative approval of a budget. Politics refers to the ease of cutting taxes as opposed to raising them. Lastly, macroeconomic theory refers to temporary tax changes that do not affect lifetime income. Intervention is not always necessary as there is a built-in component of automatic stabilisers that can be used to stabilise the economy. These counter-cyclical effects are a result of fluctuations in the economy with no government intervention. When real output increases, government expenditure will decrease, and taxes will increase. As an illustration, a fall in unemployment reduces benefits spending, and this reduces the budget deficit during an economic expansion. A higher level of employment is likely to bring about a greater level of tax receipts and lower government expenditures. Economic growth is likely to be controlled as AD is likely to be reduced, minimising the risk of inflation. However, automatic stabilisers may not be as effective as previously thought because consumer-expectations and business-expectations may change. External economic influences may lead to changes in expectations, especially if uncertainties and risks exist. Alternatively, the government can rely on the central bank to use monetary policy to address the stability of the economy. This is an indirect intervention through the use of interest rates, primarily to target inflation in the economy. There must be a right amount of monetary stimulus or restraint. For simplicity, interest rates are assumed to be set by the central bank. This assumption is critical as Taylor and Williams (2009) found macroeconomic models of monetary policy evaluation could not reconcile the spread between central banks' interest rates and market interest rates set by commercial banks. Frank and Bernanke (2009) proposed that to make sensible policy, central banks must have an idea of the inflation rate they would like to achieve. Similarly, Chari et al. (2009) echoed that some form of inflation target with well-defined escape clauses is what most macroeconomists are comfortable with. The success of monetary policy depends on the policymaker's commitment and on keeping both interest rates and inflation low on average. Central banks announce a numerical target for inflation to increase credibility and better anchor inflation expectations. This keeps inflation within a band and helps to maintain a desired employment level. To ensure credibility of the use of monetary policy, central banks have been given more independence. They are insulated from short-term political considerations and allowed to take a long-term view of the economy (Frank and Bernanke, 2009). However, if the shock is of a supply-side nature, monetary policy will not help with addressing unemployment because policies dealing with labour supply and productivity are not within the jurisdiction of the central bank. A fiscal-monetary mix can also be used, depending on the relative strength of the fiscal and monetary policies and their effects on the different sectors of the economy (Samuelson and Nordhaus, 2001, 2009). Thus, to manage AD fluctuations, fiscal and monetary policies or a combination of a fiscal-monetary mix can be used to keep AD and output at equilibrium.

When an economy is at its natural rate of unemployment, policies will have marginal or no influence on employment. Such interventions can only result in inflation (in the long run), generating further inflationary pressures. Given that the level of aggregate output is explained in reference to the natural level of output determined by the productive capacity of the economy, it is critical that the productive capacity of the economy be correctly determined. The productive capacity of the economy is dependent on the production process. The production function in most economic textbooks (Antonovics et al., 2015; Begg et al., 2014; Dornbusch et al., 1995; Frank, 2003; Pindyck et al., 2006; Mankiw et al., 2008; Blanchard, 2009; Frank and Bernanke, 2009; Blanchard and Sheen, 2013; Mankiw, 2020; Frank et al., 2021) considers labour (L) and manufactured capital (KM) to be the only factors of production. The price of labour is the wage paid to each unit of labour. And the amount of labour can be determined through demand and supply in the labour market. KM refers to goods used in future production. They can be priced as rent, assuming that it is not owned and supply is fixed. With technological advancement, the rent can be discounted for depreciation. Thus, both L and KM can be priced easily through their respective markets. However, production does not rely only on L and KM but also on the natural environment. For example, air, land, and water are essential requirements for the production process.

Internalisation of KN

There are a few authors who have considered natural environment inputs to production. Frank (2003) discussed natural resources as inputs in production. The discussion was focused on the awareness of renewable and exhaustible (non-renewable) resources, and the transition from exhaustible to renewable energy sources. Frank's collaboration with Bernanke and other scholars in later textbooks (Frank and Bernanke, 2009; Antonovics et al., 2015; Frank et al., 2021) presented the production function to include technology and land. However, the numerical illustration focused only on L and KM. Mankiw et al. (2008) included L, KM, natural resources, and technology in their production function. Similar to Frank and Bernanke (2009) and Frank et al. (2021), the numerical illustration focused on L and KM based on their returns to scale. As per Frank (2003), their natural resource discussion was limited to renewable and non-renewable resources. Most authors discussed the natural environment but did not proceed further to incorporate natural resources into the production function. They stopped short of accounting for natural resources and attributed economic growth to non-resource factors. Although resources are recognised as a necessity for production, the amount of resources used can be small because L and KM can be substituted in sufficient quantities. Perhaps, a justifiable analysis of the natural environment as inputs to production was made by Samuelson and Nordhaus (2001, 2009). They divided factors of production into three categories: land, L, and KM. Land and L are the primary or original factors of production. Land can be a derived demand as it depends on the product produced. KM was added only as the produced factor of production and can be categorised as structures, equipment, and inventories. A United Nations (2012) report had identified nature (as well as capital and labour) as a capital and it includes land, forests, fossil fuels, and minerals as a wealth asset. Thus, investments towards production should consider natural capital as a factor of production.

If the production process takes into consideration the natural environment, using up more of the KN will reduce the capacity of an economy. The economy will contract, resulting in greater unemployment at current market wages. This overstates the capacity of the economy as the true capacity of the economy has been appreciated. In turn, this will generate inflationary pressures as there are fewer resources to go around within the economy. Hence, an inclusion of KN in the standard macroeconomic framework might generate greater unemployment and higher prices. Thus, the policy implication is to close the gaps relating to output, employment, and inflation. And the key determinant for formulating stabilisation policies is the difference in the magnitude of the gaps when the EM framework is used as opposed to the standard macroeconomic framework. Consider a vineyard operating in a wine county. The grapevines (roots) require water from the soil to grow. Minerals from the water are absorbed by the vines, providing the necessary nutrients for growth. Thus, water acts as both a sink and a source. The ideal water required is nature's water and explains why a lake or a water catchment is located not far from the vineyard. The first step in winemaking is the harvesting process. Grapes, twigs, and vines have to be separated as only the grapes will be crushed for their juice. The twigs and vines can be returned to the soil as organic fertilisers. They serve to retain moisture in the soil. This reduces the water intake (from the water catchment) required by the grapevines. It is the inorganic fertilisers that pollute the water and the polluted water will in turn affect the growth of the next bunch of grapes. This will affect the quality of wine and bottle sales for the vineyard, and thus may result in a lower quantity of wine being bottled. In addition, these combined factors can lead to the closure of the vineyard in the long run with unemployment for the vineyard staff; no doubt a simplistic example but the potential of such a scenario becoming a reality cannot be disregarded if the KN (the water catchment in this example) is not properly maintained.

1.4 Conclusion

Managing the economy involves concern about the level of aggregate output, unemployment, and inflation. These are the concerns to promote economic growth and further raise the material standard of living. Beyond recession, increase in unemployment, and rising inflation, steps should also be taken to ensure that the malfunctioning of the natural environment does not impose greater costs on and disruption to the economy. Macroeconomic policies aim to stabilise an economy in the short run and to maintain a steady state of economic growth and employment in the long run. Traditional methods of macroeconomic policy formulation consider the state of an economy but exclude the state of KN. Therefore, the challenge of macroeconomic frameworks will depend on the recognition afforded to KN aside from the traditional factors of L and KM to ensure the effectiveness of policies. The standard frameworks discussed above pave the way for alternative frameworks in the rest of this book. There are challenges to the standard frameworks, which are demonstrated in the next two chapters of EM literature review.

The book is structured as follows. The first chapter provides an introduction to this study and a synoptic description of the standard macroeconomic framework and relative implementation of policy practices. The next two chapters address the challenges of the standard frameworks towards sustainable development and implications on economic performance; these challenges are demonstrated in the literature on environmental accounting and the EM model. This literature is classified on the basis of materials that (a) focus on concepts and paradigms and (b) extend the conceptual/dogmatic premises to empirical applications. These chapters address questions that arise in the context of recognising KN in the standard macroeconomic framework and help to pave the way for proposing an alternative EM framework for policy analysis. Chapter 4 addresses the measurement of KN and its utilisation with reference to selected Organisation for Economic Co-operation and Development (OECD) economies, namely, Australia, Canada, Germany, Japan, Korea, New Zealand, United Kingdom, and the USA. Chapter 5 provides a comparison of the economies' steady-state equilibrium between the standard macroeconomic framework and the EM framework. Chapter 6 presents the methodology for analysing how macroeconomic goals are affected by the steady-state equilibrium and highlights significant findings of policy ranges when the EM model is used as opposed to the standard macroeconomic model. These chapters underline the importance of EM frameworks when used in macroeconomic policymaking. Finally, this book concludes with a discussion on sustainable development and public policy, and a summary of the research with directions for future research.

References

Antonovics, K., Bernanke, B., Frank, R. (2015), *Principles of Economics*, McGraw-Hill Higher Education, New York.

Begg, D., Vernasca, G., Fischer, S., Dornbusch, R. (2014), *EBOOK: Economics*. McGraw Hill.

Blanchard, O. (2009), *Macroeconomics – Fifth Edition*, Pearson Education, Sydney, Australia.

Blanchard, O., Sheen, J. (2013), *Macroeconomics – Australasian Edition*, Pearson Higher Education, Sydney, Australia.

Chari, V. V., Kehoe, P. J., McGrattan, E. R. (2009), "New Keynesian models: Not yet useful for policy analysis", *American Economic Journal: Macroeconomics*, 1(1), pp. 242–266.

Dornbusch, R., Fischer, S., Kearney, C. (1995), *Macroeconomics – Australian Edition*, McGraw-Hill Book Company, Sydney, Australia.

Dornbusch, R., Fischer, S., Startz, R. (2008), *Macroeconomics – Tenth Edition*, McGraw-Hill Book Company, New York, United States of America.

Frank, R. H. (2003), *Microeconomics and Behaviour – Fifth Edition*, McGraw-Hill Higher Education, New York, United States of America.

Frank, R. H., Bernanke, B. S. (2009), *Principles of Economics – Fourth Edition*, McGraw-Hill Irwin, New York, United States of America.

Frank, R. H., Bernanke, B. S., Antonovics, K., Heffetz, O. (2021), *Principles of Economics – Eight Edition*, McGraw-Hill, New York, United States of America.

Mankiw, N. G. (2004), *Principles of Macroeconomics – Third Edition*, Thomson South-Western, Cincinati, OH.

Mankiw, N. G. (2020), *Principles of Economics*, Cengage Learning, Boston, United States of America.

Mankiw, N. G., Wilson, P., Quah, E. (2008), *Principles of Economics: An Asian Edition*, Cengage Learning, Singapore.

Pindyck, R. S., Rubinfeld, D. L., Koh, W. T. H. (2006), *Microeconomics – An Asian Perspective*, Prentice Hall, Singapore.

Samuelson, P. A., Nordhaus, W. D. (2001), *Economics – Seventeenth Edition*, McGraw-Hill Book Company, New York, United States of America.

Samuelson, P. A., Nordhaus, W. D. (2009), *Macroeconomics – Nineteenth Edition*, McGraw-Hill Higher Education, Maidenhead, The United Kingdom.

Stegman, T., Junor, B. (1993), *Introductory Macroeconomics*, Harcourt Brace Jovanovich, Sydney, Australia.

Taylor, J. B., Williams, J. C. (2009), "A black swan in the money market", *American Economic Journal: Macroeconomics*, 1(1), pp. 58–83.

UNU-IHDP, UNEP (2012), *Inclusive Wealth Report 2012 – Measuring progress toward sustainability*, Cambridge: Cambridge University Press.

2 Sustainable Development and Implications on Economic Performance

2.1 Introduction

Sustainable development [as defined by Brundtland et al. (1987)] points to development that meets the needs of the present without compromising the ability of future generations to meet their own. However, sustainable development denotes different perspectives to different audience; and for development to be truly sustainable, growth must be inclusive and demands equal attention to the tri-nexus of economy, society, and the environment. Unfortunately, this is far from reality. In an effort to continue growing, economies pedestalise economic progress where attention is skewed towards economic performance with an intentional lack of attention to the environment.

This chapter highlights the difference between economic growth and economic development as a precursor for a healthy understanding of sustainable development. For the purpose of this book, sustainable development shall focus on debates between the twin-nexus of economy and the environment. As the environment is both a source and a sink, care ought to be taken for it to be accorded as a capital in macroeconomic modelling. However, pricing and valuing the environment as a capital has its debates which presents challenges for recognising environment as a capital in the standard macroeconomic framework. This rationalises the argument for a revised environmental-macroeconomics (EM) framework as the basis for formulating stabilisation policies with strong implications on economic performance.

2.2 Economic Growth versus Economic Development

Economic growth is expanding the community with natural endowments, such as land and other resources towards a better standard of living via improved economic performance. On the other hand, economic development is enhancing liveability, for instance, culture and heritage, education, employment, safety, and community development. Growth relies on extracting finite resources to progress the economy whilst development works with resources that have already been extracted to maintain a standard of living. Georgescu-Roegen

DOI: 10.4324/9781003002550-2

(1970, 1971) and Daly (1977) argued that more economic growth would entail more production and consumption activities to satisfy human wants. Kolstad and Krautkraemer (1993) pointed out a dynamic link between the environment, resource use, and economic activity. While resource use, especially of energy sources, yields immediate economic benefits, it also has a negative impact on the environment but this downside is observable only in the long run. England (2000) explored the relationship between capital accumulation and economic growth and between capital accumulation and the natural world. He found that modern growth models were silent about the natural foundation of production. Land was not considered as an asset, raw materials were not considered as commodities, and no energy was required to drive the production process. However, if an economy is to grow by consumption, nature must play an important role.

Growing by consumption may not necessarily represent a greater level of well-being. Manner and Gowdy (2010) explored the usage of consumption as a proxy for well-being, but challenges by behavioural research have found that well-being is a function of much more than economic consumption. There are other factors that affect well-being; and Rothman (1998) found that consumption is the principal driving force behind environmental impacts. Hence, economic growth (at least through consumption) has failed to explain well-being as well as the degradation of the environment. This may put a population's well-being at risk should the environment continue to be neglected as economies grow. However, the environment must be kept intact so as to provide future generations with a set of life opportunities undiminished relative to present opportunities (Howarth, 1997).

Vide paper by Boersema (2011), a simple explanation is that every person impacts the earth's natural resources to some extent. To achieve a sustainable world, population figures need to be stabilised at a given point. However, as people live longer due to better health care and services, the world's resources are straining to support an aging population (Boersema, 2009). To be sure, the world's population cannot continue growing indefinitely. And Boersema (2009) argues that there is a limit to population growth, in terms of the earth's capacity. The danger of the earth's capacity being exceeded in the future due to population growth cannot be discounted. In fact, in Case et al. (2005) the argument is that population pressures have built up to the point that land has run out! An earlier argument from Ehrlich (1968) is that population size is the most significant factor in determining environmental impact. He had even argued for a formula in the following form:

$$\text{Environmental Impact (I)} = \text{People (P)}*\text{Measure of Affluence (A)}*\text{Technology (T)}$$

According to Dietz and Rosa (1994) and Boersema (2009), this is an analytical formula which describes the interaction of the variables in a quantitative way. However, this formula (like many others) is not without limitations.

Arrow et al. (2004) reconciled the conflicting intuitions of consumption (towards economic growth) by using both ecological and economic insights to raise questions that might not have been raised. Consumption increases the use of natural resources, reflecting a higher demand from a growing world population. It also reflects growth, or per capita output, and consumption. According to Arrow et al. (2004), with the increase in the use of natural resources, an increase in investments has also been witnessed. The implicit assumption is that the entire utilisation of natural resources goes to investment (I). However, a large part of this utilisation also contributes towards consumption (C). Despite stresses on the natural resource base, such investment was necessary to ensure higher (or at least similar) real living standards in the future. In addition, there are other ways to compensate for the diminishing of natural resources, for example, through incremental boosting of manufactured capital and human capital, and technological advances. Therefore, Arrow et al. (2004) argued that it was unnecessary to account for the environment in macroeconomic frameworks when an economy is growing. After all, there are other measures, such as the ecological footprint that measures the resources necessary to produce the goods and services an individual or population consumes. Notwithstanding, namely, the ecological footprint being a plausible measure for sustainability, Fiala (2008) critiqued it as an ineffective proxy and argued for better measures of sustainability. His focus was on abandoning composite indicators and directing examination of two issues for sustainability, namely, land degradation and carbon dioxide aggregation. Despite his emphasis on land degradation and carbon dioxide aggregation, it is neither the degradation (consumption) nor the aggregation (production) that derives satisfaction. According to Boulding (1949), satisfaction occurs when there is no degradation or aggregation, that is, when an economy has reached a steady-state equilibrium.

Steady state, as defined by John Stuart Mill (1857), is a "stationary state" of zero growth in population and physical stock coupled with a continuous improvement in technology and ethics. Steady state is not an end in itself but merely a situation with restriction on any further growth in population and production. In Daly's (1996a) words, this is the concept of sustainable development.

2.3 Sustainable Development

Sustainable development is where virgin natural resources are no longer necessary for the progress of an economy (beyond economic growth). Growth is dependent on the extraction of finite resources to progress the economy whilst development works with resources that have already been extracted to maintain a standard of living. From a scientific angle, sustainable development can be explained by the two laws of thermodynamics. The first law of thermodynamics states that matter cannot be created nor destroyed; it can only be re-arranged (Wagner, 1891; Guggenheim, 1985). Matter is re-arranged as the environment provides material for energy input and absorbs waste. The second law is when energy is transformed from a state of low entropy (high energy) to that of high entropy (low energy) to do work. When an economy consumes, matter goes through phases of arrangement and re-arrangement. These phases use up the available energy levels with no recycling option. Consumption involves a rearrangement of energy within the economy as well as the environment (Daly, 1997). As a result of this non-recycling, some of the matter will become residual waste. The combination of the two laws results in absolute scarcity of resources (Daly, 1991) and such scarcity implies that the ecosystem must be used in an efficient manner to allow for sustainability. On 8 November 2011, Daly blogged on www.neweconomics.org that the first and second laws of thermodynamics should be called the first and second laws of economics (Daly, 1996b).

Given that the ecosystem is finite, non-growing, and materially closed; the economy depends on the ecosystem for its sink and source function, which is the bedrock for environmental macroeconomic analyses (Hanley et al., 1997). Valuing the environment provides an understanding of the economy as a sub-system and allows an appreciation for the close-knit relationship between the sub-system and ecosystem. Attaching a price serves to offer some form of provision towards the depletion of the environment as a capital but does not address the accumulated degradation of the ecosystem. Continued degradation may compromise the services provided by the ecosystem and internalising the cost of degradation is one way towards sustainable development.

Once growth is allowed to progress beyond sustainable development, there will be two immediate trade-offs: (1) regeneration of renewable natural resources of an economy and (2) the environment's assimilative capability of waste absorption. This demonstrates the close-knit relationship between economic activities and the natural environment. As discussed earlier, Daly first highlighted this in 1994 – the natural world is an ecosystem that is finite, non-growing, and materially closed (Daly, 1996a). Arrow et al. (1995) led ten other academic economists to make the similar point that the environmental resource base is finite. In addition, they made two other points: there are limits to the carrying capacity of the planet; and economic growth will not cure falling environmental quality. This close-knit relationship demonstrates that the environment acts as a sink when economies grow, and that environmental degradation is a result of economic growth. This is a contradiction to a later claim by Arrow et al. (2004) that there is no need to account for the environment in macroeconomic frameworks when an economy is growing, but rather the environment only needs to be accounted for at steady state. Hence, exponential growth cannot go on forever in a finite world (Boulding, 1966). Instead, it is the improvement in liveability and standard of living in terms of culture and heritage, education, employment, safety, and community development that can be sustainable.

Over the past decades, scholars (selected) had made attempts to discuss and provide frameworks for measuring sustainability – see Norton and Toman

(1997), Moffatt and Hanley (2001), and Pezzey and Toman (2005). The trend has been skewed towards theoretical debates as opposed to empirical work, as ideological pre-convictions appear to triumph over a greater ability to identify future limits to growth (Pezzey and Toman, 2005). Similarly, Ferng (2014) argued for both planetary boundaries and impacts of international trade documented for ecological footprint to be a suitable tool for measuring sustainable development. Cavender-Bares et al. (2015) combined both economics and ecology for appeal to a wider audience of sustainability analytical framework.

Hanley et al. (1999) had reviewed the policy need for indicators of sustainable development but concluded that there is no available macroeconomic measure of sustainability. Even though there is no single measure for sustainability, Randall (2008) argued that weak sustainable options suffice for now to ask more out of the status quo. Gray (2010) added that the challenge is a nuanced understanding of what sustainability actually is and what it represents empirically. Whilst Portney (2015) demonstrates the associated concepts of sustainability applied in various contexts, it is not without controversies. From an economic perspective, sustainability is the reversal of economic growth that had been extracting essential ecosystem services (Caradonna, 2014) and exhausting finite resources. Related concepts of growth, limits, scale, and substitutability were discussed by Goodland (1995) across different paths but remained focused at the goal of environmental sustainability. This was supported by Giovannoni and Fabietti (2013) where opportunities do abound in an integrated approach to reporting sustainability (or sustainable development). Therefore, the impacts of economic activities on the ecosystem ought to be carefully analysed.

Caradonna (2014) offered a history of sustainability in his book and gathered evidence of writings with the words sustainable or sustainability since 1900. For close to eight decades (1976 to be precise), there were no books on sustainable or sustainability. But from 1989, there was an exponential surge of titles in the field and the rise remains strong over the next three decades. The writing by Brundtland et al. (1987) should be credited as well as writings from international scholars. Undoubtedly, there may also be a change in attitudes and habits of consumption choices informed by the writings. The idea of sustainability dates back to ancient times but its vocabulary is three decades old (Thiele, 2016). Thus, it is little wonder that Thiele's (2016) book targeted students and built on Stone (2010) that students are part of the natural world – who will protect and maintain the environment as rightful future owners. And as Scoones (2007) summarises, the idea of sustainability should not be underestimated as a powerful and influential meeting of ideas and politics.

Barring the debates of sustainability, a transition to sustainable economic development implies different development paths from present and involves a transition from current business-as-usual practices to a nuance form of environmental-friendly path. Two key challenges remain: one, assigning a fair monetary value to an environment proxy; and two, the ease of internalising environmental degradation into selected macroeconomic frameworks. These are critical challenges as they are vital towards the formulation of sustainable development policies.

2.4 The Environment

The environment is both a source and a sink. It is a source as it provides oxygen to support living things and a sink for carbon emissions. For example, plants absorb carbon dioxide (sink) and emit oxygen (source) during photosynthesis. There are also parts of the environment that are not in the ecosystem but are used as a sink for carbon emissions. An example is the stratosphere which does not support life, but the presence of ozone invaders harms the environment. Ecosystem consists of a set of living things (the living environment of flora and fauna) and their habitats (a non-living environment of airshed, soil, and water). For development to be sustainable, the ecosystem must be maintained and protected. This is because natural endowments are finite resources, and once they contribute to growth they cannot be utilised for another purpose.

The general well-being for an economy does not depend solely on economic performance as the environmental health should also be considered. For instance, living things will not function normally and this can impact an economy's progress when the air is polluted. Although there is universal acceptance that clean air is a pre-requisite for the well-being of an economy, there is no universally accepted measurement of environmental degradation due to the type of good and a non-existent market. The good by nature is a public good, that is, it is non-excludable and non-rivalrous. Non-excludable implies that consumers cannot be barred from accessing and consuming a good without payment. And non-rivalrous refers where the consumption of a good does not prevent others from consuming nor does it reduce the availability for consumption. These compounding characteristics contribute to a non-existent market for public goods as it would not be possible to properly cost and quantify leading to market failure.

There is an increasing call to move away from cost–benefit analysis and environmental impact assessment and to value natural resource stocks, land, and ecosystems (Azqueta and Sotelsek, 2007). There are two explanations for this: (i) to enable capital depreciation and value changes over time and (ii) to bestow social wealth to adequately plan changes in land use. But there remain problems with the ecological legitimation of "environment as capital approach" – this according to Harte (1995). The Natural Capital Committee (2013) offered a framework for measurement and valuation of natural capital to embed natural capital in the UK's Environmental Accounts with the aim of managing social wealth. This is strong evidence to Harte (1995) where various environmental possibilities are valued in terms of their potential contribution to human well-being.

Due to the nature of the good and failure of the market, the environment has often been proxied by the airshed, carbon emissions, energy consumption, forest cover, soil, and water quality. The environment has also been discussed extensively by El Serafy (1991) as a capital in a production process and accounted for as an income flow. Whilst his early discussions centred on accounting and absorptive capacity (El Serafy, 1981) of the environment, El Serafy's piece in 1991 formalised environment as a capital with Thampapillai et al. (1998) arguing for the same even when technology appeared to offset the scarcity of environment as a capital. Further, environment as a capital will allow an economy to function within its real productive capacity (Thampapillai et al., 1998). A method to estimate the income impact of the "El Serafy" approach in El Serafy (2002) made relevant the acknowledgement of the environment as a capital and its significant impacts on policy analyses.

An important aspect of applied policy analyses is the valuation of environment as a capital at the macroeconomic level. Repetto and Baliga (1997) provided the basis of soil valuation and identified a link between environment and health. Health is used as a benchmark for the quality of the environment. Mendelsohn (2002) and Falk and Mendelsohn (1993) developed a basis and framework for air quality measurement. Vincent (1999, 2000) focused on forestry assessment. Qu et al. (2023) utilised an integrated macroeconomic framework and proxied fish stock as an indicator of environmental well-being. Applications of environment as a capital in macroeconomic framework are also evident in Thampapillai (2002) and Thampapillai et al. (2005), using the framework of the above three authors Falk, Mendelsohn and Vincent to develop policy analyses and further developing into environmental macroeconomics frameworks (Thampapillai, 2012; Thampapillai and Sinden, 2012; Thampapillai and Ruth, 2019).

The inclusion of environment in macroeconomic frameworks was first proposed by Thampapillai (1993) to illustrate how environmental constraints can be explicitly incorporated into selected macroeconomic frameworks. An environmental cost function was developed and used in the adaptation of the following frameworks: the Harrod–Domar (H-D) growth model, the IS-LM model, aggregate supply, and the Keynesian expenditure (AD) model. Each framework has advantages and disadvantages.

The H-D growth model is one with emphasis on increasing savings to invest in efficient forms of capital towards economic growth. However, it does not consider interest rates, which are the price of investment. One model that considers interest rates is the IS-LM model. In this model, interest rates can shift decisions on current consumption and investment. Low interest rates would favour investment and do not contribute to sustainability because investment requires environmental inputs. The ambiguity of interest rates is attributed to the lack of information on environmental costs and the absence of such costs in National Income Accounting (NIA). An attempt to incorporate environmental measurement into macroeconomic analysis was made by Thampapillai and Uhlin (1994). Development of concepts and frameworks should begin by modifying the NIA to represent the role of the environment in an economy. One proposed example would be for environmental investment and an allowance for depreciation to be included in net national product (NNP). This proposal justifies conceptualising the natural environment in the aggregate as a capital asset and treating it the same way as traditional building and machinery assets.

Thampapillai and Uhlin (1997) discussed the concept of considering the natural environment as a capital asset for sustainable income, incorporating the model justification in Thampapillai (1993) and the measurement of environmental costs in national income in Thampapillai and Uhlin (1994). This extended the treatment of the natural environment as an asset in a simple Keynesian (AD) framework towards the determination of sustainable income. Their analysis included the derivation of sustainable income paths and an evaluation of wages and technology/management policies. Both the derivation and evaluation jointly achieved full employment and sustainable income. Therefore, a measure of inclusive (real) progress should integrate environmental aspects to economic performance. Sustainable development points to the importance of economic and environmental well-being and ensures that they are factored into public policy formulation.

With the twin-nexus of economy and the environment at its core, the EM framework offers an essential basis for the ecosystem in an economy's performance, that is, growth and development. Growth is expanding the community using land and other natural resources, whereas development is thought of as improving liveability. Developmental paths are transitional as an interim stage towards the future by adding and creating value in an economy. A signal for transition (development) becomes apparent when spare capacity in an economy is close to full utilisation. Therefore, development must occur within the realms of the natural ecosystem and be considered sustainable only when a system has its loop close.

2.5 Conclusion

It is a common belief that pricing a resource allows the environmental damage to be purchased as the cost of damage is embedded in the purchase. This belief is false as accumulated degradation inflicted on the environment remains in the ecosystem. Moreover, pricing the environment may not address the challenges of optimality and sustainability. Valuation of the environment serves two broad objectives: it offers some form of provision towards the depletion of the environment as a capital and allows an appreciation for the close-knit relationship between a sub-system and the ecosystem.

Following the brief review, two key challenges are observed. Firstly, environment is ignored because there is no universally agreed-upon method of valuation; and secondly, a standard macroeconomic framework may not accommodate sustainable development without environmental internalisation and allowance for the depreciation of the environment towards the formulation of sustainable policies. With the internalisation of environmental capital in standard macroeconomic frameworks, policies should include sustainable options to preserve the environment.

It is the aim of this book to add to this body of literature.

In the book *Slow Death by Rubber Duck* by Smith and Lourie (2009), the human body was used as an analogy to the environmental sink where the toxins humans consume from their daily routines remain in the body and pose long-term health risks. On a wider scale of the environment, most of us know and are more than aware that the environment is "sick" and its function as an environmental source may be compromised. The analogy made to the human body may help account for the extent of the "sickness", but this will not convince policymakers the value of environment in sustainable development. Quantifying the know and aware may be difficult to accept for some. Hence, the options are: (i) price the environment like a capital in order to appreciate the relationship between sub-system and ecosystem and (ii) ensure ease with which any selected proxy of environmental degradation can be internalised into macroeconomic frameworks towards the formulation of sustainable development policies.

References

Arrow, K., Bolin, B., Costanza, R., Dasgupta, P., Folke, C., Holling, C. S., Jansson, B. O., Levin, S., Mäler, K. G., Perrings, C., Pimentel, D. (1995), "Economic growth, carrying capacity, and the environment", *Science*, 268, pp. 520–521.

Arrow, K., Dasgupta, P., Goulder, L., Daily, G., Ehrlich, P., Heal, G., Levin, S., Mäler, K. G., Schneider, S., Starrett, D. Walker, B. (2004), "Are we consuming too much?", *Journal of Economic Perspectives*, 18(3), pp. 147–172.

Azqueta, D., Sotelsek, D. (2007), "Valuing nature: From environmental impacts to natural capital", *Ecological Economics*, 63(1), pp. 22–30.

Boersema, J. J. (2009), "Environmental Sciences, Sustainability, and Quality" in Boersema, J. J., Reijnders, L. (eds), *Principles of Environmental Sciences*, Springer, Dordrecht/Berlin, pp. 3–15.

Boersema, J. J. (2011) "Does the population issue still have a valid place on the environmental agenda?" in Kroeze, C., Boersema, J. J., Tellegen, E., Cremers, A. (eds), *Technology and Sustainability*, Techne Press, the Netherlands, pp. 9–16.

Boulding, K. (1949), "Income or Welfare?", *Review of Economic Studies*, 17, pp. 77–86.

Boulding, K. (1966), "The economics of the coming spaceship earth", in Jarrett, H. (ed), *Environmental Quality in a Growing Economy*, Baltimore, MD, Johns Hopkins University Press, pp. 3–15.

Brundtland, G. H., Khalid, M., Agnelli, S., Al-Athel, S., Chidzero, B. (1987), *Our Common Future*, United Nations, New York, United States of America.

Caradonna, J. L. (2014), *Sustainability: A History*, Oxford University Press, Oxford, The United Kingdom.

Case, K. E., Quigley, J. M., Shiller, R. (2005), "Comparing wealth effects: The stock market versus the housing market" Working Paper W01-004, University of California at Berkeley.

Cavender-Bares, J., Polasky, S., King, E., Balvanera, P. (2015), "A sustainability framework for assessing trade-offs in ecosystem services", *Ecology and Society*, 20(1): 17.

Daly, H. E. (1977), *Steady-State Economics: The Economics of Biophysical Equilibrium and Moral Growth*, W.H. Freemann and Company, San Francisco, United States of America.

Daly, H. E. (1991), "Towards an environmental macroeconomics", *Land Economics*, 67(2), pp. 255–259.

Daly, H. E. (1996a), *Beyond Growth*, Beacon Press, Boston, United States of America.

Daly, H. E. (1996b), "Comment: Is the entropy law relevant to the economics of natural resources scarcity? – Yes, of course it is!", *Journal of Environmental Economics and Management*, 23, pp. 91–95.

Daly, H. E. (1997), "Georgescu-Roegen versus Solow/Stiglitz – Forum", *Ecological Economics*, 22, pp. 261–266.

Dietz, T., Rosa, E. A. (1994), "Rethinking the environmental impacts of population, affluence and technology", *Human Ecological Review*, 1, pp. 277–300.

Ehrlich, P. R. (1968), *The Population Bomb*, Ballantine, New York, United States of America.

El Serafy, S. (1981), "Absorptive capacity, the demand for revenue, and the supply of petroleum", *Journal of Energy & Development*, 7, p. 73.

El Serafy, S. (1991), "The environment as capital", *Ecological Economics: The Science and Management of Sustainability*, pp. 168–171.

El Serafy, S. (2002), "The 'El Serafy' method for estimating income from extraction and its importance for economic analysis", A Synoptic Paper.

England, R. W. (2000), "Analysis – Nature caporal and the theory of economic growth", *Ecological Economics*, 37, pp. 425–431.

Falk, I., Mendelsohn, R. (1993), "The economics of controlling stock pollutants: An efficient strategy for greenhouse gases", *Journal of Environmental Economics and Management*, 25(1), pp. 76–88.

Ferng, J. J. (2014), "Nested open systems: An important concept for applying ecological footprint analysis to sustainable development assessment", *Ecological Economics*, 106, pp. 105–111.

Fiala, N. (2008), "Measuring sustainability: Why the ecological footprint is bad for economics and bad environmental science", *Ecological Economics*, 67, pp. 519–525.

Georgescu-Roegen, N. (1970). "The economics of production", The Richard T. Ely Lecture, *American Economic Review*, 60, pp. 1–9.

Georgescu-Roegen, N. (1971), *The Entropy Law and the Economic Process*, Harvard University Press, Cambridge, Massachusetts, London, The United Kingdom.

Giovannoni, E., Fabietti, G. (2013), "What is sustainability? A review of the concept and its applications", in Busco C, Frigo M, Riccaboni A, Quattrone P (eds). *Integrated Reporting: Concepts and Cases that Redefine Corporate Accountability*, Springer, pp. 21–40.

Goodland, R. (1995), "The concept of environmental sustainability", *Annual Review of Ecology and Systematics*, 26(1), pp. 1–24.

Gray, R. (2010), "Is accounting for sustainability actually accounting for sustainability … and how would we know? An exploration of narratives of organisations and the planet", *Accounting, Organizations and Society*, 35(1), pp. 47–62.

Guggenheim, E. A. (1985), *Thermodynamics: An Advanced Treatment for Chemists and Physicists*, North-Holland Publishing, the Netherlands.

Hanley, N., Shogren, F. J., White, B. (1997), *Environmental Economics in Theory and Practice*, MacMillan Press, The United Kingdom.

Hanley, N., Moffatt, I., Faichney, R., Wilson, M. (1999), "Measuring sustain ability: A time series of alternative indicators for Scotland", *Ecological Economics*, 28(1), pp. 55–73.

Harte, M. J. (1995), "Ecology, sustainability, and environment as capital", *Ecological Economics*, 15(2), pp. 157–164.

Howarth, R. B. (1997), "Sustainability as opportunity", *Land Economics*, 73(4), pp. 569–579.

Kolstad, A., Krautkraemer, V. (1993), "Natural resource use and the environment", in Kneese, A.V., Sweeny, J. L. (eds), *Handbook of Natural Resource and Energy Economics*, Elsevier, The Netherlands.

Manner, M., Gowdy, J. (2010), "The evolution of social and moral behavior: Evolutionary insights of public policy", *Ecological Economics*, 69(4), pp. 753–761.

Mendelsohn, R. (2002), "Environmental economics and human health", *Environmental Health Perspectives*, 110, A118–A119.

Moffatt, I., Hanley, N. (2001), "Modelling sustainable development: Systems dynamic and input–ouput approaches", *Environmental Modelling & Software*, 16(6), pp. 545–557.

Mill, J. S. (1857), *Principles of Economics*, Parker, The United Kingdom.

Natural Capital Committee (2013), The State of Natural Capital: Towards a framework for measurement and valuation, UK Government, UK.

Norton, B. G., Toman, M. A. (1997), "Sustainability: Ecological and economic perspectives", *Land Economics*, 73(4), pp. 553–568.

Pezzey, J., Toman, M. A. (2005), "Sustainability and its economic interpretations", Simpson, R. D., Toman, M., Ayres, R. U. (eds), *Scarcity and Growth: Natural Resources and the Environment in the New Millennium*, pp. 121–141, Taylor & Francis, New York, The United States of America.

Portney, K. E. (2015), *Sustainability*, MIT Press, New York, The United States of America.

Qu, Y., Hooper, T., Austen, M. C., Papathanasopoulou, E., Huang, J., Yan, X. (2023), "Development of a computable general equilibrium model based on integrated macroeconomic framework for ocean multi-use between offshore wind farms and fishing activities in Scotland", *Applied Energy*, 332, 120529.

Randall, A. (2008), "Is Australia on a sustainability path? Interpreting the clues", *Australian Journal of Agricultural and Resource Economics*, 52(1), pp. 77–95.

Repetto, R., Baliga, S. (1997), "Pesticides and immunosuppression: The public health risks", *Health Policy and Planning*, 12(2), pp. 97–106.

Rothman, D. S. (1998), "Environmental Kuznets curves-real progress or passing the buck? A case for consumption-based approaches", *Ecological Economics*, 25, pp. 177–194.

Scoones, I. (2007), "Sustainability", *Development in Practice*, 17(4–5), pp. 589–596.

Smith, R., Lourie, B. (2009), *Slow Death by Rubber Duck*, Alfred A. Knopf, New York, United States of America.

Stone, M. K. (2010), "A schooling for sustainability framework", *Teacher Education Quarterly*, 37(4), pp. 33–46.

Thampapillai, D. J. (1993), "Environmental macroeconomics: Some conceptual considerations", Uppsala, Sweden.

Thampapillai, D. J. (2002), *Environmental Economics – Concepts, Methods and Policies*, Oxford University Press, South Melbourne, Australia.

Thampapillai, D. J. (2012), "Macroeconomics versus environmental-macroeconomics", *The Australian Journal of Agricultural and Resource Economics*, 55, pp. 1–16.

Thampapillai, D. J., Uhlin, H-E (1994), "On the Measurement of Environmental Depreciation in Macroeconomic Analysis", Sweden.

Thampapillai, D. J., Uhlin, H-E (1997), "Environmental capital and sustainable income: Basic concepts and empirical tests", *Cambridge Journal of Economics*, 21, pp. 379–394.

Thampapillai, D. J., Wanden, S., Larsson, M., Uhlin, H-E (1998), "The environment in macroeconomic analyses – comparisons between Sweden and the US", *Australasian Journal of Regional Studies*, 4(2), pp. 349–362.

Thampapillai, D. J., Sinden, J. (2012), *Environmental-Macroeconomics, Environmental Economics: Concepts, Methods and Policies*, Oxford University Press, Melbourne, Australia.

Thampapillai, D. J., Ruth, M. (2019), *Environmental economics: Concepts, methods and policies*, Routledge, The United Kingdom.

Thampapillai, D. J., Thangavelu, S. M., Quah, E., Padaya, P. M. (2005), "The internalization of environmental capital in a Keynesian model of income determination: Revised approaches to public policy", in Ashiabor, H., Deketelaere, K., Kreiser, L., Milne, J. (eds), *Critical Issues in Environmental Taxation – International and Comparative Perspectives: Volume II*, Richmond Law & Tax Ltd., New York, United States of America. pp. 85–95.

Thiele, L. P. (2016), *Sustainability – Second Edition*, John Wiley and Sons, New York, United States of America.

Vincent, J. R. (1999), "A framework for forest accounting", *Forest Science*, 45(4), pp. 1–10.

Vincent, J. R. (2000), "Green accounting: From theory to practice", *Environment and Development Economics*, 5(1&2), pp. 13–24.

Wagner, A. (1891), "Marshall's principles of economics", *The Quarterly Journal of Economics*, 5(3), pp. 319–338.

3 The Case for an Environmental-Macroeconomics Framework

3.1 Introduction

The challenge of standard macroeconomic frameworks lies in its inability to encompass environment as a capital. These gaps will be established here in this chapter on the literature in environmental accounting and environmental macroeconomics. This literature is categorised as (i) focus on concepts and paradigms and (ii) extend the conceptual/dogmatic premises to empirical applications. Identifying concepts and paradigms supports the rationale for economies growing indefinitely (as it offers no consideration for environment as a capital). Whilst this is true, it also highlights the flaw that economies can grow indefinitely with no allowances made for the degradation of the environment. And by extending such premises to empirical functions, it makes real a false perception on economic performances determined by standard macroeconomic frameworks.

Analyses of this nature highlight the need for a revised macroeconomic framework that would recognise environment as a capital – that of the environmental-macroeconomics (EM) framework. On the basis of the literature, an elementary EM framework would be proposed and help pave the way for policy analysis. This chapter presents a literature review of EM with relevant literature on this topic broadly classified into two groups, namely, (i) literature on environmental accounting and (ii) literature on EM analyses. The chapter will follow with (i) and subsequently by (ii). Under (ii), there are two sub-categories, namely, (a) conceptual/theoretical analyses and (b) applied policy analyses.

3.2 Environmental Accounting

This section presents a literature review on environmental accounting.

The close relationship between the economy and the environment suggests that environmental damage caused by the economic system must be constantly managed and mitigated. But most of the literature has been predominantly based on microeconomic analyses. Microeconomic analysis is about optimisation, that is, maximising benefits and minimising costs. For example,

DOI: 10.4324/9781003002550-3

Dixon et al. (1997) presented areas where microeconomic analyses are applied through the improvement of the pricing system and correcting market failures using various valuation techniques; and the damages they do to the environment. Microeconomic analysis looks at one time period and does not address inter-generational equity as future time periods are not considered. Optimality indicates how much of an economy's resources to consume and at what prices with an assumption that markets can solve allocation problem by providing symmetric information and regulated incentives. But the problems of optimal scale and optimal distribution are not solved as there are conflicting values of allocation, distribution, and scale (Daly, 1996). In addition, microeconomic analyses failed to account for the economic performance of the economy – which can only be achieved with macroeconomic analyses.

However, even a comprehensive review of environmental economics by Cropper and Oates (1992) in the *Journal of Economic Literature* failed to include environmental considerations in macroeconomic analyses. The focus should lie on the analysis which can better represent the intimate relationship between the economy and the environment, that is, macroeconomic analyses. Beyond the standard macroeconomic indicators, the analysis should include the performance of the environment to demonstrate this intimate relationship between the economy and the environment. This was one of two concerns highlighted by Daly (1993). According to him, there are two concerns: (1) the relationship of the economy and the environment; and (2) the relationship of the economy to ethics. This review will focus on the former, the relationship of the economy, and the environment.

The World Bank (according to Daly) has acknowledged conflicts between growth and the environment; growth being seen as the solution to poverty, and environmental degradation being viewed to be mainly a consequence of poverty. By failing to account for the environment, economic growth may have been misrepresented. However, one cannot deny that political influence may make ignorance of the environment a matter of convenience that can be further aided by a continual denial in the accounting for the environment in macroeconomic frameworks. Daly raised a key point during his farewell speech at the World Bank in 1994 that it is not always possible to measure and value environmental damages.

Any effort in measuring and valuing environmental damage – to provide information on the interaction between the economy and the environment so that natural and environment resources can be more effectively managed (Sève, 2002) – although recognised in national accounting systems, tends to be incomplete with respect to environmental issues, as illustrated in the following accounting systems: (1) the United Nation's System of National Accounts (SNA) and (2) Natural Resource Accounting (NRA)/Green Accounting. NRA measures environmental degradation and resource depletion, and the results obtained are used to adjust the conventional gross domestic product (GDP). However, data availability and issues relative to this method of estimation remain a cause for contention (Statistics New Zealand, 2002). In addition, Harris and Fraser (2002) found that various models of work in this field are not well-integrated, linkages barely exist in some and in others there are significant conflicts. There is an increasing disparity between what matters to people and what is included in or excluded from GDP. Hence, any further increases in GDP (growth), unless carefully managed, will only make matters worse (Booth, 2004). Although scholars had offered some credibility to NRA in the context of Australia (Young, 1993) and sustainable development indicators (Alfsen and Greaker, 2007), NRA remains dogged with challenges since inception. A closer scrutiny shows that NRA was only applied in New Zealand (Janice, 1990), Norway (Lone et al., 1993), and India (Gundimeda et al., 2007), with a research progress review by Zhong et al. (2016) in the literature.

Thus, the focus will be on United Nation's SNA (1993) as it has shown significant progress towards accounting for the environment since its inception in 1953. Building on what El Serafy (1981, 1991) had written about accounting (1981) for the environment and it being a capital (1991); and accounting for environmental assets (Repetto, 1992) prior 1993, the United Nation's SNA (1993) has also attracted several criticisms and suggestion for improvements. See Heston (1994) where continual questioning will encourage improvement of the system. But most notable of all would be Holub et al. (1999) where the authors suggested for classification of human-induced environmental degradation and compiling a range of environmental indicators that can be aggregated across methods and scales, as well as an expanded coverage of intangible assets by Moulton (2004). And there had been updates on the development of SNA with a history of national accounting (Vanoli, 2005) highlighting the controversies and acknowledging the environment as a factor of production. The concept of extending the production boundary of SNA to account for ecosystem services was also further enhanced by Eigenraam and Obst (2018).

The SNA took a decade and evolved to the System of Environmental-Economic Accounting (SEEA-2003) to account for sustainable development (Bartelmus, 2007) and detail valuation for natural resources with the environmental-economic accounts. The SEEA-2003 with its environmental statistics seeks comparability with international economic statistics (Smith, 2007) and to measure weak and strong sustainability – though not with clear guidelines (Dietz and Neumayer, 2007). Application of the revised SNA framework had been used to value water in the Netherlands (Edens and Graveland, 2014) and Iran (Bagheri and Babaeian, 2020); and negative forestry impacts in Guatemala (Banerjee et al., 2019). Although the SEEA-2003 was able to offer environmental solace five decades since 1953 when the UN SNA was first endorsed, it is unable to accept monetary valuation of environmental degradation as "modelling" (Bartelmus, 2007) and must be left to "experimental" ecosystem accounts (Bartelmus, 2014). Thus, further revision of the SEEA is necessary for the proclaimed objective of assessing sustainable development (Bartelmus, 2007).

Further revision of the SEEA-2003 for a comprehensive system (as opposed to limited statistical standard) is necessary (Bartelmus, 2014). The revised SNA morphed to a System of Environmental-Economic Accounting Ecosystem Accounting (SEEA EA) which provides measurement on the extent and condition of ecosystems, and quantifying ecosystem services (Edens et al., 2022). EA is encouraged for use in policy and decision-making processes in both public and private sectors to further its methodological development (as the SEEA EA and its potential applications remain relatively unknown in the scientific community). The SEEA-2003 accounted for sustainable development (Bartelmus, 2007) whilst the SEEA EA described ecosystems and services they offer to an economy (Edens et al., 2022). In both variants of accounting, SNA is the constant as the bedrock of environmental accounting and environment as a capital. Hence, a greater understanding of the dexterity which the SNA possesses is warranted.

United Nation's System of National Accounts

The SNA was officially endorsed in 1953 for international use with the earliest version worked out by the United Nations after World War II to estimate national income through the medium of national accounting. It consisted of an integrated set of macroeconomic accounts, a balance sheet and tables based on internationally agreed-upon concepts, definitions, and classifications and accounting rules (United Nations, 1993). Because of its nature at inception, it serves to measure the level of employment and the value of output produced. This is one way to track how an economy has performed and progressed over time. It also serves to forecast and project the state of an economy in future time periods. Various revisions to the SNA have been made, resulting in a specific version in 1968, an updated version in 1993, SEEA in 2003, SNA in 2008, and SEEA EA in 2021. As it is the most comprehensive macroeconomic standard, it also serves as the main reference point for statistical standards of balance of payments, financial, and government finance statistics. However, the SNA up to now has given little or no information on how the environment is affected as a result of economic growth. Hecht (2005) offered a summary as to why the SNA must be reviewed to accommodate environmental degradation as follows:

i Natural assets, such as forests, fisheries, and land, are treated differently from manufactured assets, such as, factories and machinery. Like manufactured assets, depreciation should also be taken into account for natural resources, as they are continually being used up during economic growth. This view stemmed from an earlier approach by Repetto et al. (1989) and Repetto (1992), in which depreciation of natural capital was deducted from net national products (NNPs)
ii Defensive expenditures (expenditures on environmental protection) should not contribute to GDP as such expenditures do not add to

well-being. It is an expenditure that prevents the population from being worse off. Daly (2007) shared the same view

iii GDP and other macroeconomic indicators should be modified to accom modate the measurement of welfare

iv The value of environmental goods and services should also be included, even though some of these goods and services may not have been transacted through a market

Because of the SNA being deficient with regard to information on economic growth vis-à-vis the environment, the revised *Handbook of National Accounting: System of Integrated Environmental and Economic Accounting* (SEEA-1993) was an attempt at environmental accounting. SEEA is a satellite system of the SNA as it brings together economic and environmental information to measure the contribution of the environment to the economy and the impact of the economy on the environment. The discussion of concepts and methods for SEEA-1993 did not come to a final conclusion and was left as an "interim" version. According to Hecht (2005), this was because it was too conceptual to be implemented with ease. In addition, the discussion for revising the SEEA-1993 failed to involve key stakeholders. The key stakeholders (who were excluded) included the economists who had done significant conceptual work on environmental accounting, environmentalists who pushed for the inclusion of environmental accounting, and representatives from the developing world (Hecht, 2005). In response to increasing policy demands, the United Nations Statistical Division agreed to mainstream environmental-economic accounting, and a revised satellite system was developed a decade later, in 2003. The revised SEEA-2003 will be the statistical standard for environmental-economic accounting as SNA is the statistical standard for economic accounts (United Nations, 2008). The SEEA parallels the SNA structure but builds on it by constructing both physical and monetary accounts to address environmental issues as well as forecasting the future availability of environmental resources (Hecht, 2005). It has been designed for decision-making and policymaking across industrial structures and at different stages of a nation's economic development. More importantly, it has been geared towards international recognition, similar to how the SNA was originally conceived. Work was in progress to revise the SEEA-2003 version, with a timeline for publication in 2012 (United Nations, 2008). Based on the SNA-2008, the goals (selected) of the SEEA are to encourage the adoption of standard classifications in environmental statistics, bring a new dimension to environmental statistics by applying the economic accounting traditions linking stocks and flows, and identify use and ownership of, and hence responsibility for, environmental impacts. Furthermore, there must be some form of accounting for how environmental degradation impacts the national income of an economy. A chapter was devoted to this in SEEA-2003, and the SNA-2008 considered this to be one of three main sections when accounting for the environment. The following discussion examines the revised SEEA-2003 in detail.

According to the revised SEEA-2003, natural capital is generally considered to comprise of three principal categories: natural resource stocks, land, and the ecosystem. Natural resources refer to resources drawn into the production process to be converted into goods and services. Land acts as a sink to absorb the unwanted by-products of production and consumption. The ecosystem serves as a habitat for all living beings. Solow (1974a, 1974b) argued that there is, in principle, no "problem" as produced and human capital can be substitutes for natural capital. In this instance, income generated is constant, and natural capital can depreciate subject, however, to being replaced by other forms of capital. Besides Solow (2005), others have also argued that the extent of substitutability is limited (Hecht, 2005). This group of researchers has argued that capital will only be of value when complemented with another form of capital. In such instances, capital is maintained independent of other capital to ensure that income generated is constant (when capital is used together). There is a set of "precautionary principles" to ensure that capital is maintained (Hecht, 2005). Firstly, renewable resources should not be used beyond their natural regeneration; secondly, non-renewable resources should only be used prudently to ensure that future generations continue to have access to the same resource; thirdly, sink functions should not be used beyond their assimilative capacities; lastly, environmentally deteriorating activities should be avoided.

Notwithstanding the inclusion of contribution of the environment to the economy in the revised SEEA-2003, there are still some issues associated with measuring the environment that require further fine-tuning. Some of these issues are highlighted in selected chapters of the revised SEEA-2003 and will be discussed in turn together with the wider scholarly literature. Chapters 3 and 5 of the revised SEEA-2003 deal with the modus operandi for accounting for natural resources, economic activities, and products related to the environment. When a resource is extracted and used to produce a good or service of economic value, an identity can be derived to account for the flows. Recognising the environment can also be represented by expenses associated with maintaining the environment. Accounting for the flows recognises the environmental impact, but it fails to account for reductions of the environment's assimilative capacity as a sink. This is not in agreement with the third point of the "precautionary principles" from Hecht (2005), that is, not using the environment sink beyond its assimilative capacity. In Chapter 7, asset accounting can be practiced by measuring the stock of the asset at the start of an accounting period and at the end of the period. An asset is usually productively limited to one specific usage at a time, notwithstanding its capacity for use in competing ways. For example, if water were used as a source for drinking, the assimilative capacity for water as a sink would be reduced.

The discussion then revolves around: When should an asset be used for income generation, and when should the same asset be preserved for maintaining the sink? This is a critical question as assets are often scarce and have competing uses. Income has traditionally been used to measure an economy's well-being, besides being a guide to the maximum amount of consumption by an economy without compromising future expenditures. To ensure that the income is not fully consumed, depreciation is subtracted from income to obtain NNP. One consideration for such subtraction is the depletion of natural capital (Daly, 1996). Natural capital can be defined as capital required for industrial production and can be categorised as non-renewable or renewable. Depleting the renewable capital means reducing stocks available for consumption. A reduction in consumption might possibly help to maintain the stock level, but this does not ensure a sustainable level of income. Depletion of the non-renewable resources means that the resource is not available for future consumption or usage. Extraction of non-renewable resources should not contribute to income as the resource will eventually be completely extracted and is fully depreciated (Brekke, 1997). Ideally, there should be some form of measurement to account for its permanent loss, but the need to adjust accounts for environmental and ecological losses depends on the development stages of individual economies. Developed economies have liquidated most of their natural wealth in the developing process. Their domestic products are now derived mainly from secondary and tertiary production. However, developing economies would depend on primary production. Exchanges are made through the sale of assets, as opposed to value-added services. Economies at their development stage will make no attempt to distinguish between renewable and non-renewable assets. Therefore, the discussion on whether it was income from revenue or income from the sale of assets (or an allowance for depletion) would not have been a priority for developing economies.

When measuring the income of an economy, the SNA's model balance sheet recognises land, minerals, timber, and environmental resource as economic assets included in a nation's capital stock, but the income and product accounts do not (Hanley et al., 1999). Hicks (1946) defined income as "the maximum value which can be consumed during a week and still expect to be as well off at the end of the week as was in the beginning". El Serafy elaborated this and proposed the user cost approach to compute the Hicksian income. The "El Serafy Method" (first published in 1981) suggests that only part of the proceeds from the sale of resource assets can be considered income (El Serafy, 2002). His illustration was such that not all revenues accrued by oil-exporting nations can be calculated as income. After all, there is depletion to the stock of the asset – which is irreversible. And no allowance is made for that. Hecht (2005) made this similar point when considering resource accounting. As economies continue to grow and consume, the environment is degraded, and there is a need to account for this. The expenditure that goes towards protecting and maintaining the environment should only be considered once, as an earlier expenditure would have accounted for the degradation that has already occurred. In fact, it is also possible that expenditures to maintain the environment could contribute to further environmental degradation.

Price signals are typically used to aid in the discussion of whether an asset should be used or preserved. However, as Chapter Nine of the revised

SEEA-2003 shows, the non-existence of a market and price implies that there is no procedure in place to measure the costs and benefits of using or preserving an asset. Market prices reflect the relative scarcity of individual resources but do not measure the absolute scarcity of resources in general. Hence, income derived in this manner does not necessarily correspond to well-being. Perhaps, a better choice for an objective measurement of well-being might be consumer surplus. Consumer surplus is the difference between the maximum price an individual is willing to pay and the price paid. Unfortunately, consumer surplus is not included in the calculation of National Income Accounting. In the absence of markets, there are other factors that can be considered to contribute to national income, for example, the life of an asset, the resource rent it provides, and the discount factor that can be used to value future returns at the present time.

The challenges faced when measuring national income are no different from those for measuring environmental degradation. Valuation techniques (with time taken into consideration) may be a better estimation than the use of traditional statistical methods because degradation is a cumulative continuing process in a time continuum, not a one-off occurrence in one particular time period. An option is to base such valuation of the asset on the principle of replacement cost, or the willingness to pay (WTP). The replacement cost is simply the cost of replacing a damaged environmental asset, and WTP is the amount to be paid for an environmental benefit. In both instances, there is no market to attach a price to the cost or benefit, and even if a market exists, the economic framework may not always be practical for valuation (Ison et al., 2002). A no market scenario seems a convenient excuse not to account for and value a natural resource. But the absence of a market is only one of many considerations. For example, there are other considerations, such as valuing a mobile underwater resource (fisheries) or considering if there is a spatial component provision (land and water) (Hecht, 2005). A discussion of a popular valuation method is illustrated in the following as it provides a "shadow price" for resources that are non-market tradable.

When one considers the environment as a consumption good, valuing environmental damages based on WTP is termed the contingent valuation (CV) method. The CV method is the most widely used method as other valuation methods are unable to identify and measure passive or non-use values of biodiversity (Nunes and can den Bergh, 2001). This is evident with its application in various scenarios of environmental valuation (Carsons, 2007). According to Thampapillai (2002), it is a popular method because it is easy to apply and has a wide range of contextual applicability. However, the estimation of WTP can demonstrate biasness, such as in the case of preserving the Kariba lake shore in Zambia (Thampapillai et al., 1992); in this example there were respondents who were willing to contribute in excess of 50% of their income, whilst there were others who were unwilling to contribute. Knetsch (1994) argued that the correct measure for CV should be the sum total compensated to individuals for the environmental damage. This is the willingness to accept

(WTA), an amount which will normally be far larger than WTP. Outcomes of such nature demonstrate that WTP biasness may be inherent in nature, leading to inappropriate environmental policies and distorted incentives as losses are valued more than gains. It is argued that loss schedules might be implemented faster, provide deterrence incentives, and predict incurable outcomes, and hence are deemed as more appealing and more just than dependence on rational behaviour. Another study by Sinden (1994) found that the estimation of values for un-priced goods and services usually meets several objections. However, valuations serve to account explicitly for factors that are otherwise overlooked, implicitly valued, and often wrongly valued. Thus, the consistency in the findings across the body of valuation studies adds more value than the findings from each individual study.

No depreciation estimate, even in terms of a universally agreed-upon valuation method, can be considered as truly accountable. It can be argued that the existence of a market may be the key as prices can be rightfully determined. However, the fundamental goal is to ensure that there is some form of allowance allotted to the depletion of natural capital in the existing SNA. Adjustment towards a measure of true income (sustainable NNP) is a good start towards subtracting expenditures that do not reflect any increase in the net product available for consumption without eventual impoverishment (Daly, 1996).

According to Daly (1996), the error of implicitly counting natural capital consumption as income is customary in three areas: SNA, evaluation of projects that deplete natural capital, and international balance of payments accounting. The first area is on its way to being “greened”. Daly’s (1996) suggestion is to restructure national accounts to measure the costs and benefits of growth, such that comparison is allowed for finding the optimal scale of the macroeconomy. However, optimality is based on the assumptions made in the economic calculations for integrating the environment (Amin, 1992). Although Stavins (2007) encouraged market-based environmental instruments to test whether social benefits exceed total social costs, there are differing views. Specifically, Daly (1991) has suggested that markets can function to better allocate resources only through the provision of necessary information and incentives. This is because incentives or punishments can alter and drive behaviour, and markets do not solve the problems of sustainable scale (this is not widely appreciated) or optimal distribution (this is widely recognised). Hence, the challenge is to determine how to internalise external environmental costs and arrive at prices that reflect the full social marginal opportunity costs. Stimulating growth beyond a market-determined level makes macro-level comparison of costs and benefits necessary because application of public policy to stimulate aggregate growth must depend on a comparison of costs and benefits at the macro level, and the social benefits of growth must exceed social cost. The second area underscores the need to count “user cost” as part of the opportunity cost of projects that deplete natural capital or sink capacity. As such, the true rate of return on a project would be calculated on the basis of the income component from the sale of depleted natural assets as net revenue. The third area deals with non-sustainable exports as sales of capital assets and not simply as export income. Nations that export natural capital may seem to have a surplus when, in fact, they have a serious deficit. Thus, Daly (1996) suggests that instead of one account, Gross National Product (GNP), there should be three accounts for each basic magnitude: a benefit account to measure the value of accumulated services, a cost account to measure the value of depletion and pollution, and a capital account as an inventory of the accumulation of stocks for the economy.

Chapter Ten of the revised SEEA-2003 examines environmental adjustments to the flow accounts and demonstrates how depletion and degradation of environmental assets can be incorporated into GDP – "greened-economy modelling". Consumption of fixed capital is deducted from GDP to give a measure of net domestic product, thus, preserving a capital base. In line with preservation, a similar deduction should also be considered and made towards the consumption of natural capital. The controversy lies in the discussion on valuing non-priced degradation. An easy solution is to account for the physical quantity as opposed to monetary valuation. However, do all forms of degradation require valuation? Thus, accounting for the degradation can only be carried out when it is clear what needs to be counted. The incorporation of adjustments for degradation is still a work-in-progress, and it is this calculation of the adjustments that continues to be in debate. Although the SEEA-2003 (issued by the United Nations, the European Commission, the International Monetary Fund, the Organisation for Economic Co-operation and Development, and the World Bank) represented a major step forward in the development of environmental-economic accounting, it did not provide unique recommendations to several issues. As Hecht (2005) suggested, SEEA was developed parallel to, and aims to be compatible with, the SNA framework. It is unlikely that the SEEA is adequate for green macroeconomic indicators measurement. Hence, a range of measures that go beyond the SEEA and SNA is necessary to supplement the conventional macroeconomic indicators for considerations of output, welfare, and sustainability.

The above discussion on selected chapters of the revised SEEA-2003 hopes to emphasise some of the issues which need to be considered before further progression. An Indonesia example by Repetto et al. (1989) showed how the standard income could continue to rise when the natural resource is being degraded. That is because the natural resource stock has not been taken into account. And the OECD has not fully reconciled the measurement and accounting of KN in GDP. Even though there are significant gaps to be filled, accounting for the environment has certainly shown progression as it is now being considered for the mainstream. However, debates continue, and viewpoints differ for the accounting of environment. There is no one complete universal system which addresses the urgent need of measuring and accounting for environmental damage.

There have been a few noticeable attempts to measure and account for the environment. France attempted the most ambitious accounting system to date with patrimony accounting which encompasses the three basic dimensions of natural environment: economic, ecological, and social. President Clinton had also committed resources for developing environmentally adjusted accounts during his term. But like France's initiative, it did not enjoy implementation success (Dixon et al., 1997). Statistics Netherlands (2009) used the future-oriented approach – also known as capital-based approach to measure the natural resources (one of four themes; the other three being economic, human, and social) available to a society. However, as Stiglitz et al. (2009) described: The issue is indeed complex, more complex than the already complicated issue of measuring current societal well-being or economic performance. Although there continue to be hurdles, several economies remain persistent towards a sustainable measure. For example, every Ministry in Norway will separate their environmental expenditures known as the Green Budget in the State Budget and the private sector is also required to incorporate green expenditures or investments (Muller et al., 2011). The framework to integrate external damages into national economic accounts by Muller et al. (2011) is differentiated as it estimated the value of air pollution emissions, rather than simply reporting the quantity of emissions. Traditional accounts do not measure externalities of non-market sectors and therefore net national output is inflated. Beyond the limitations faced by the framework, there are also staffing issues for the efficient running of setting up an appropriate databank. There are many areas where economic valuation of environmental impacts should be improved. This will help to measure and value elements of improved human welfare and progress that cannot be captured by GDP alone (OECD, 2012).

As a concluding illustration to this accounting section, consider the context of natural disasters. Natural disasters are becoming increasingly prevalent. Disaster is not a result of nature or an act of God; rather, it is the result of human actions. Take the demand for wood-based products (consumption), which causes deforestation. Deforestation can result in landslides and eventual loss of lives. This production decision has exerted stress on nature. This decision considers labour and machinery required to produce the desired output, but it does not take into account the natural environment as a source of input. Cannon (1994) attributed this to nature not being adequately integrated into social and economic systems. A technical explanation given by Hecht (2005) is that conventional accounts include only the marketed forest products that have a price, for example, timber. Consumers acquire the wood-based products, but the environmental sink loses its capability as a result of fewer trees. Hence, even if accounts were constructed to value the natural capital, it would not be easy to evaluate the natural capital (Daly, 2007). A successful development of national green accounting framework must lead to the development and application of EM policy models. Models do not forecast but rather provide an insight into how economies can develop. Internalising environmental costs will affect an economy's income; thus, it is best achieved with macroeconomic analyses.

3.3 Environmental-Macroeconomics Framework Analyses

This section presents a literature review of EM analyses with two sub-categories, namely, conceptual/theoretical analyses and applied policy analyses. As Hanley et al. (1999) stipulated, the need for EM analyses stems from the fact that the economy and the natural environment are linked to each other in the following two ways: (1) environmental capital (KN) acts as a source of inputs and (2) KN acts as a sink for economy's waste. This close inter-relationship between the economy and the environment suggests that the environment cannot serve both as a sink and a source simultaneously.

Conceptual/Theoretical Analyses

The conceptual/theoretical analyses are centred on tools of inter-temporal dynamic analyses, such as optimal control theory, difference and differential equations, and dynamic programming, for example, see Dasgupta et al. (1994) and Munasinghe (2001). The main difficulty with this literature is that they deal predominantly with specific exhaustible or depletable resources and not KN in an aggregate sense. That is, they do not treat KN as analogous to manufactured capital stock. Daly (1991) identified this weakness as an empty box in macroeconomic analysis. Daly's (1996) argument was aimed towards the development of EM, where natural capital has replaced human capital as the limiting factor over time (see Figure 3.1).

Thus, policies should be geared towards maximising natural capital's present productivity and increasing its future supply. This implies that measurement of income should include investment in natural capital, therefore, maintaining the natural capital as priority. To maintain the natural capital, there must be continued investment. This is because the value of investment will fall over time. And there must be some form of allowance that takes the depreciation of the natural capital into consideration.

For this allowance to be fully captured in income measurement, there must be a price as well as a volume of exchange attached to the natural capital (Natural Capital Committee, 2013). Often, this is not a simple task. Let's first consider the volume of exchange. The volume of exchange can be accounted for by looking at the interaction between different economic models, that is, micro, macro, and environmental. Firms and households (micro) operate within the aggregated (macro) economy. An aggregated economy operates within the natural ecosystem and is considered a sub-system as per Figure 3.1. The sub-system depends on the natural ecosystem for both its sink and source functions. EM would focus on the volume of exchanges that cross the boundary between the sub-system and the natural ecosystem. Thus, when one compares EM with macroeconomics, the focus is on the volume of

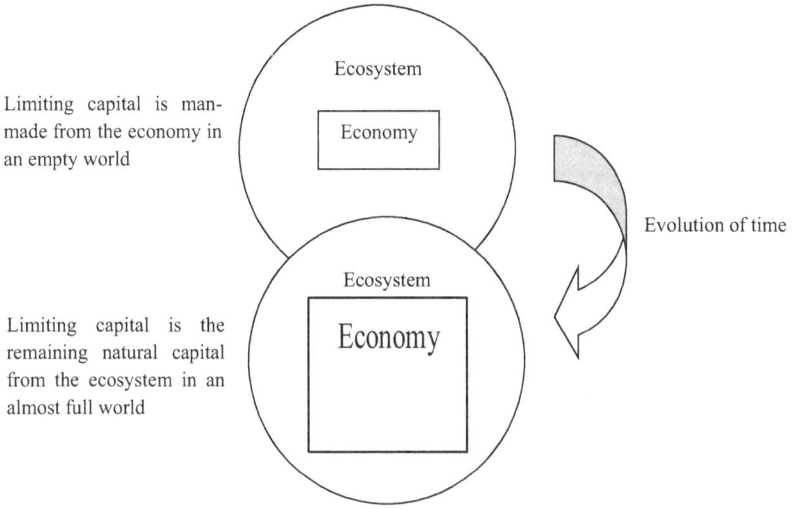

Figure 3.1 From Human Capital to Natural Capital.

Source: Adapted from Daly (1996).

transactions rather than relative prices (Daly, 1996). When it comes to prices, it is about internalising the external environmental costs to arrive at prices that fully reflect a socially optimal marginal cost. The natural ecosystem refers to the environment that living organisms interact and live in. It encompasses the air, soil, sunlight, and water. These are public goods without any property rights assigned. Consuming one more unit does not reduce the amount available for consumption (non-rivalry) and does not exclude (non-excludability) another individual from consuming. There are two challenges here. Firstly, it is not easy to arrive at a mutually agreeable price as there is obviously a market failure. Secondly, the range of the natural ecosystem means that one price for all will not accurately reflect the socially optimal marginal cost. The challenge is compounded as there are different measurement methods for each of the natural ecosystems. In the case of water, there are at least 80 assessment tools measuring water security (Octavianti and Staddon, 2021) as well as error assessments to ensure an effective water management policy (Foster et al., 2020).

Stiglitz et al. (2009) argued that placing a monetary value on the natural environment is often difficult and separate sets of physical indicators will be needed to monitor the state of the environment. Measurement and valuation of the environment have always been the central challenge when affording recognition to the natural ecosystem. This is especially true when it comes to irreversible and or discontinuous alterations to the environment. Methods of valuation are questioned as there is neither an agreeable way nor a universal approach. In the interim, the search and use of proxies take precedence. For ease of convenience, the natural ecosystem can be generically referred to as KN. One way to internalise environmental costs is made through the AD-AS model (Thampapillai, 1993). This model encourages the development of "environment-saving technologies" by including environment in the production function. This was further evident in Thampapillai and Hanf (2000) where a reduction in KN reliance required technological improvements in utilising the environment as a capital. Such an effect was more pronounced when KN was incorporated into the production function. Thus, when the sustainability and non-substitutability of KN are recognised, all rents owing to the entire stock of KN need to be set aside as a depreciation allowance. The value accorded for depreciation was found to overstate the performance of an economy when KN is aggregated (Thampapillai et al., 2005). This finding can be seen as a response to omitting KN from the production function in contemporary economics, where technology can be used to persistently offset the scarcity of KN (Thampapillai, 2008).

However, investing in environmental technologies does add to AD expenditures and potentially expand an economy's capacity. Moreover, policy decisions should be based on income domains that do not exceed the productive capacity dictated by KN (Thampapillai, 2008). This was illustrated with respect to Australia (Thampapillai, 2007) and Sweden (Thampapillai et al., 1998) – economies that have reasonable compliance to environmental standards but with the policy domain significantly misplaced. The original policy domain, as opposed to the policy domain dictated by KN, would have only considered labour and capital as the standard inputs to output production (Solow, 1956) and that both labour and capital could be easily substituted (Todaro and Smith, 2002). Such a policy domain renders a false economic equilibrium as production takes place with nature in the backdrop. If an economy driving towards economic growth continues to embrace the original policy domain, policies will continue to be incorrectly implemented. Although fiscal intervention can minimise the impacts from an incorrect income domain, such as prevent worsening unemployment and related financial problems (Tan and Thampapillai, 2011), a change in fundamental perceptions to embrace KN is vital.

There has been a noticeable change in perception as the continued neglect of the role of nature in the production for economic growth is progressively being overcome. This is evident by more eco-friendly or "green" buildings, more initiatives towards sustainable living, eco-tourism, and a greater awareness towards environmentally friendly consumption goods and services. Indeed, economic growth generates environmental pressure, but environmental improvements have also been reached in agriculture, industrial production, energy production, household energy use, food supply, and waste removal. Environmental stewardship should not solely focus on the supply side but should also entail a shift to the demand side with equal responsibility on the demand side. This will be a lengthy transition as there may be incomplete information on the benefits and costs of environmentally friendly consumption (Welsch, 2009) and there will be continual evaluation of consumption levels relative to other people's consumption and their own past consumptions. EM serves to understand the interaction between consumers, the economy, and the environment to direct economies towards sustainability. The question points to the level of sustainability that can be attained. Therefore, policies should focus on restoring and maintaining KN to allow for future consumption.

Policy Intervention

Economies have the capacity to adjust to different conditions via different policy tools. The OECD (2012) quotes, "without new policies, progress in reducing environmental pressures will continue to be overwhelmed by the sheer scale of growth". A mix of policies is needed because the different environmental issues are complex and closely linked. Thus, policies must be carefully designed to account for cross-cutting environmental functions and their wider economic and social implications (OECD, 2012). To keep an economy near its full employment potential, monetary policy can be used as it aims to preserve the value of money over time. For example, a person with no debt and no savings will feel little or no impact from interest rate changes. And "automatic stabilisers" of fiscal policy will take more taxes from population that is doing well (assuming income rises relatively quickly) and transfer it to others that are not doing as well in the form of welfare payments. There is a similarity between the effects of the two policies. A person with no debt and savings will be indifferent to interest rate changes, just as a person with low income will be indifferent to tax rate changes. Taxes have a dark side (death of politics) with socially regressive effects. The 1993 SNA describes taxes as unrequited because government provides nothing in return to the individual unit making the payment (United Nations, 1993). Thus, there must be compensation in the form of reduced income tax or added social security; the latter benefit is something that, arguably, would elicit appreciation from the poorer segments of the population. The poor tend to benefit less from tax reductions because they do not have significant incomes to be taxed. A direct subsidy offered to the poor is usually better than a tax reduction. However, if the economy faces a problem of a different nature, for example, excessive environmental degradation caused by market failure, an integration of environmental taxes, or "green" tax reform (Gago and Labandeira, 2000) would be a much more efficient response.

The 2008 SNA defined an environmental tax as one whose tax base is a physical unit that has a proven specific negative impact on the environment (United Nations, 2008). There are four types of environmental taxes: energy, pollution, resource, and transport. Hecht (2005) defined environmental taxes as "green taxes" intended to discourage the use of polluting products by raising their prices. The revenue from taxes can cut budget deficits while meeting environmental objectives. However, "green taxes" may be detrimental to economic growth (Myles, 2000) which makes the tax structure more critical than the tax level. The optimal environmental tax would internalise the externality and would restore the efficiency of the market mechanism (Sandmo, 2003).

Environmental taxes can also refer to those revenues dedicated to environmental expenditures. Such expenditures are defensive as they are aimed at preventing pollution and managing natural resources. But environmental taxes alone cannot be accountable for the maintenance of the environment. Effectiveness of the policy would also have to depend on the holistic nature of the wider economic society. The revenue from "green taxes" can be recycled to allow other forms of taxes, for example, income tax, to be reduced towards a "green income". This was evident in the case of Sweden (Sterner, 1994), where a 1991 tax reform changed the tax mix. Direct taxes on individuals and firms were reduced, without incurring additional public deficit, when a value-added tax on energy consumption and environmental taxes on carbon dioxide (CO_2) and sulphur dioxide (SO_2) emissions were introduced. Similarly, Collier (2010) advocated a carbon tax because it allows taxation on other economic activity to be reduced and would be better than a heavily compromised emissions trading scheme (Garnaut, 2008).

There can also be tax relief and other "green" investment incentives for businesses and consumers alike. These can help prioritise "green" jobs over other jobs that are less "green". Although "grand-fathering" may be required for businesses that may be disadvantaged by these introductions in the early stages of implementation, this is not a feasible option it does not help to improve the existing debt position of an economy. Nonetheless, these initiatives have a double dividend with positive effects on employment and the environment. Double dividend refers to taxes levied on goods causing environmental damage, which have the twin benefits of reducing the environmental damage and raising revenue (Goulder, 1995). And Kolstad (2000) had suggested that such taxes could reduce pollution and also reduce the distortions associated with existing taxes. Thus, "green taxes" can shift the economy towards a green equilibrium, especially in periods of economic crisis or public debt. But this may not be the case, as income might still play a crucial role (Schumacher, 2009). Although there are obstacles to environmental fiscal reforms, these obstacles can be overcome (Ekins and Speck, 2000) as the environmental benefits may not be economically harmful. The overriding concern from a policy viewpoint is whether double dividend from environmental taxes can raise revenue without limiting economic growth (Myles, 2000) which was highlighted by Sandmo (2003) that even though taxes raised revenues, it was inconclusive regarding their contribution to economic growth.

Daly (2007) suggested raising the price of natural capital through a public policy of taxation. In line with macroeconomic objectives, taxing income should be avoided because income and employment are importantly crucial, being the key components of an economy. Taxes should be applied increasingly to pollution because it is what an economy can do without. Daly (1996) proposed that labour and income should be taxed less, and resource throughput taxed more. This is in line with Sedjo's (2010) response to Nordhaus (2010), which stated that taxes should be imposed according to emissions instead of at the source. This provides an incentive to develop technologies that better utilise fossil fuels and, at the same time, control the release of emissions into the environment (Sedjo, 2010). The regressive effects of taxes can be offset by spending the tax revenues progressively with emphasis on spending on industries that need it the most, an action that might help soften the regressive tax effects as well as satisfy the distributive concerns while raising public revenue. Emerging economies can reinvest tax revenues towards sewerage treatment systems, cooling and heating systems, energy supply systems, and commodity development (Tan and Thampapillai, 2011). There are no doubts about what taxes can achieve – after all, taxes have been used in most economies for centuries.

According to the OECD report on Taxation, Innovation and the Environment (October 2010), OECD governments are increasingly using environmentally related taxes because they are typically one of the most effective policy tools available (OECD, 2010). Green growth policies can stimulate economic growth (and create jobs) while preventing environmental degradation, biodiversity loss, and unsustainable natural resource use. Environmental policy tools should strive to ensure environmental improvement is not delayed and at the same time, stimulate innovation and development of clean technologies for the future. It is important that the government takes the lead in such innovations as market forces alone are inadequate to provide the right signals as there is no price attached to environmental degradation.

To minimise the tax commitment, environmentally related taxation provides an opportunity for innovation to stimulate development and diffusion of new technologies and practices. A study conducted by the OECD found that the higher the tax rate, the more significant the incentives for innovation. Thus, innovation can be encouraged by increasing or decreasing the level of taxes. This would be assuring for innovating practices when additional taxes are reinvested within the confines of fiscal balance (Thampapillai et al., 2010) for an economy to recoup its resilience following a period of adjustment. It was also found that when used with environmental policy instruments to protect environmental quality and public good provisions, taxes can complement each other (OECD, 2010). See earlier studies by Bovenberg and Goulder (1996) and Parry and Bento (2000) in which the findings are less favourable when such interactions are ignored. However, for such complements to occur, pollution must be adequately priced via taxation. Optimal policies (OECD, 2012) should (i) address the oversupply of environmental damage in society, (ii) place a significance on taxing environmentally harmful activities to address the environmental damage; and (iii) such market-based instruments can also generate much-needed fiscal revenues. For instance, the emissions tax and the tradable permit system[1] must be reviewed as they do not consider the accumulation of pollution loads but rather only the marginal loads. The emissions trading scheme seems to be accepted as carbon pricing seems inevitable, and reporting is likely to become a standard feature of any company's reporting (Harris and Brander, 2011). Thus, solutions to environmental problems require a review of the paradigm, that is, a fundamental transformation of the way individuals live their daily lives.

Consider the following scenario to illustrate the two points cited above: A pollutant-emitting plant is located not far from a vineyard. The pollutant discharges waste into the water catchment that the vineyard uses. A moderate approach would encourage the plant to relocate through the enticement of a tax concession or rebate for the first production year, followed by a progressive tax structure from the second year onwards. The plant can choose to pass on the tax savings as lower product pricing to the end consumer. Lower taxes can also encourage product innovation, which can stimulate greater investment to increase AD in the short run and an economy's capacity in the long run. Alternatively, the plant can choose to reinvest the tax money in initiatives that would contribute to maintaining the environment. With the departure of the plant, the clean water catchment would be more conducive to winemaking. The environment can be maintained and provides an opportunity for the plant to explore green innovative methods of production in another location. Assume now that the plant in question is old. A more complicated approach would be to increase taxes as opposed to tax concessions. This would either push the plant to be efficient in its methods of production or completely force it out of production.

It has been suggested that taxes serve as a bridging mechanism between doing nothing and preparing for a time when the economy is required to reach certain emission reduction targets (Parkinson, 2010). To be sure, taxes are not simply bridging mechanisms. Instead, they are an immediate response to slowing the rate at which natural resources are being utilised in an economy. Natural resources are being utilised faster than they are being replaced. This is illustrated by developed economies operating at close to or beyond their capacities. In addition, environmentally related taxes can help maintain the degraded environment by reinvestment of the tax revenues. The tax revenues can be reinvested through a portfolio of KN investments. In the interest of climate, economic development, and energy security, effective policy will be critical to shift investment towards green growth (ClimateWorks Foundation and European Climate Foundation, 2010). This would mean that policy choices must be coupled with appropriate financial support. The literature review on

1 On 24 January 2011, Daphne Wysham, a fellow at the Washington-based institute for Policy Studies and founder of the Sustainable Energy and Economy Network, commented that carbon trading is a "recipe for corruption" (Win, 2011). This is not untrue for one trades to gain, not to lose. Two days later, on 26 January 2011, it was reported that Europe's physical carbon trading market suffered an attack from hackers, which crippled leading exchanges. The future of such trading market has been thrown into doubt (Stafford, 2011).

policy intervention suggests that such reinvestment in KN can be financed by taxes. However, there are certainly other forms of intervention, such as lifestyle changes through income and wages policies, and be complemented with fiscal intervention.

3.4 Conclusion

This chapter focused on the literature review of EM. Environmental accounting failed to formally account for KN in National Income Accounting, thus setting the basis for the conceptual/theoretical analyses on EM with due recognition being given to KN. National accounts are based on the principle that they cover market activities whilst external effects are activities that are by definition excluded from market transactions. The discussion on applied policy analyses showed how the internalisation of KN had been used – albeit recommendations for further enhancements. An elementary EM framework introduced by Tan and Thampapillai (2011) hinges from the consumption perspective with a KN proxy and associated costing from the literature. To operationalise this framework, a simple time-series illustration using the Chinese economy is discussed (a priori published work). The results from this illustration show differing paths of economic progression and clearly highlight the path taken (without KN) as opposed to that should have been taken (with KN). Notably, there are known limitations (and these will be addressed in Chapter 4); but an elementary framework to accommodate KN has been established.

Although Stiglitz et al. (2009) deemed that climate change (due to increases in atmospheric concentrations of greenhouse gases) is uniquely a global issue that cannot be measured across national boundaries, the valuation of the environment as a capital should not be deemed impossible. For effective policy interventions, the elements of climate science, economics, and regulation must be considered. The state of development of economies plays a part in determining what would be an appropriate level of policy intervention. Developed economies have liquidated most of their natural wealth in the developing process. Their national incomes are now derived mainly from secondary and tertiary production. On the contrary, developing economies would predominantly depend on primary production. Exchanges are made through the sale of assets, as opposed to value-added services. Economies at their development stage will make no attempt to distinguish between renewable and non-renewable assets. Natural resources are being utilised faster than they are being replaced. This is illustrated by developed economies operating at close to or beyond their capacities (evidence will be presented in later chapters of this book). Therefore, the discussion on whether it was income from revenue or income from the sale of assets (or an allowance for depletion) would not have been a priority for developing economies. Recommendations for the development of a robust advanced macroeconomic modelling need to be considered in order for sustainable policies to be formulated. Chapter 4 will provide recommendations for the proposed EM framework and a presentation of a worked model.

References

Alfsen, K. H., Greaker, M. (2007), "From natural resources and environmental accounting to construction of indicators for sustainable development", *Ecological Economics*, 61(4), pp. 600–610.

Amin, S. (1992), "Can environmental problems be subject to economic calculations?", *World Development*, 20(4), pp. 523–530.

Bagheri, A., Babaeian, F. (2020), "Assessing water security of Rafsanjan Plain, Iran – Adopting the SEEA framework of water accounting", *Ecological Indicators*, 111, 105959.

Banerjee, O., Cicowiez, M., Vargas, R., Horridge, M. (2019), "The SEEA-based integrated economic-environmental modelling framework: An illustration with Guatemala's forest and fuelwood sector", *Environmental and Resource Economics*, 72, pp. 539–558.

Bartelmus, P. (2007), "SEEA-2003: Accounting for sustainable development?", *Ecological Economics*, 61(4), pp. 613–616.

Bartelmus, P. (2014), "Environmental–economic accounting: progress and digression in the SEEA revisions", *Review of Income and Wealth*, 60(4), pp. 887–904.

Booth, D. E. (2004), *Hooked on Growth: Economic Addictions and the Environment*, Rowman and Littlefield, Lanham, MD.

Bovenberg, A. L., Goulder, L. H. (1996), "Optimal equilibrium taxation in the presence of other taxes: General-equilibrium analyses", *The American Economic Review*, 86(4), pp. 985–1000.

Brekke, J. A. (1997), "Hicksian income from resource extraction in an open economy", *Land Economics*, 73(4), pp. 516–527.

Cannon, T. (1994), "Vulnerability analysis and the explanation of 'natural' disasters", in A. Varley (ed), *Disasters, Development and Environment*, John Wiley & Sons, The United Kingdom, pp. 13–30.

Carsons, R. T. (2007), *The Stated Preference Approach to Environmental Valuation – Volume III: Benefit-Cost Analysis and Natural Resource Damage Assessment*, Ashgate Publishing Company, Routledge, London, United Kingdom.

ClimateWorks Foundation and European Climate Foundation (2010), From Climate Finance to Financing Green Growth, Briefing Paper, 23 November 2010, Project Catalyst, The United States of America.

Collier, P. (2010), *The Plundered Planet*, Oxford University Press, Oxford, The United Kingdom.

Cropper, M. L., Oates, W. E. (1992), "Environmental Economics: A Survey", *Journal of Economic Literature*, 30(2), pp. 675–740.

Daly, H. E. (1991), "Towards an Environmental Macroeconomics", *Land Economics*, 67(2), pp. 255–259

Daly, H. E. (1993), "Sustainable growth: An impossible theorem", in Daly, H. E., Townsend, K. N. (eds), *Valuing the Earth: Economics, Ecology, Ethics*, Cambridge: MIT Press, pp. 267–273.

Daly, H. E. (1996), *Beyond Growth*, Beacon Press, Boston, United States of America.

Daly, H. E. (2007), *Ecological Economics and Sustainable Development, Selected Essays of Herman Daly*, Edward Elgar Northampton, Massachusetts, United States of America.

Dasgupta, P., Kristöm, B., Mäler, K-G. (1994), "Current Issues in Resource Accounting", Report 105, Umeå, Department of Forest Economics, Swedish University of Agricultural Sciences, Sweden.

Dietz, S., Neumayer, E. (2007), "Weak and strong sustainability in the SEEA: Concepts and measurement", *Ecological Economics*, 61(4), pp. 617–626.

Dixon, J. A., Scura, L. F., Carpenter, R. A., Sherman, P. B. (1997), *Economic Analysis of Environmental Impacts*, Earthscan Publications Ltd, London, The United Kingdom.

Edens, B., Graveland, C. (2014), "Experimental valuation of Dutch water resources according to SNA and SEEA", *Water Resources and Economics*, 7, pp. 66–81.

Edens, B., Maes, J., Hein, L., Obst, C., Siikamaki, J., Schenau, S., Javorsek, M., Chow, J., Chan, J. Y., Steurer, A., Alfieri, A. (2022), "Establishing the SEEA Ecosystem Accounting as a global standard", *Ecosystem Services*, 54, 101413.

Eigenraam, M., Obst, C. (2018), "Extending the production boundary of the System of National Accounts (SNA) to classify and account for ecosystem services", *Ecosystem Health and Sustainability*, 4(11), pp. 247–260.

Ekins, P., Speck, S. (2000), "Proposals of environmental fiscal reforms and the obstacles to their implementation", *Journal of Environmental Policy & Planning*, 2, pp. 93–114.

El Serafy, S. (1981), "Absorptive capacity, the demand for revenue, and the supply of petroleum", *Journal of Energy & Development*, 7, p. 73.

El Serafy, S. (1991), "The environment as capital", in R. Costanza (ed.), Ecological Economics: The Science and Management of Sustainability, Columbia University Press, New York, pp. 168–171.

El Serafy, S. (2002), "The 'El Serafy' method for estimating income from extraction and its importance for economic analysis", A Synoptic Paper.

Foster, T., Mieno, T., Brozović, N. (2020), "Satellite-based monitoring of irrigation water use: Assessing measurement errors and their implications for agricultural water management policy", *Water Resources Research*, 56(11), e2020WR028378.

Gago, A., Labandeira, X. (2000), "Towards a green tax reform model", *Journal of Environmental Policy & Planning*, 2, pp. 25–37.

Garnaut, R. (2008), The Garnaut Climate Change Review, 2008. "Final Report", September 2008, Cambridge University Press, The United Kingdom.

Goulder, L. H. (1995), "Environmental taxation and the double dividend: A reader's guide", *International Tax and Public Finance*, 2, pp. 155–182.

Gundimeda, H., Sukhdev, P., Sinha, R. K., Sanyal, S. (2007), "Natural resource accounting for Indian states—illustrating the case of forest resources", *Ecological Economics*, 61(4), pp. 635–649.

Hanley, N., Moffatt, I., Faichney, R., Wilson, M. (1999), "Measuring sustainability: A time series of alternative indicators for Scotland", *Ecological Economics*, 28(1), pp. 55–73.

Harris, L., Brander, M. (2011), "Technical Paper, Carbon reporting in Directors' Reports", January 2011, econometrica, The United Kingdom.

Harris, M., Fraser, I. (2002), "Natural resource accounting in theory and practice: A critical assessment", *The Australian Journal of Agricultural and Resource Economics*, 46(2), pp. 139–192.

Hecht, J. E. (2005), *National Environment Accounting – Bridging the Gap between Ecology and Economy*, Resources for the Future, Washington DC, United States of America.

Heston, A. (1994), "A brief review of some problems in using national accounts data in level of output comparisons and growth studies", *Journal of Development Economics*, 44(1), pp. 29–52.

Hicks, J. (1946), *Value and Capital – 2nd Edition*, Oxford University Press, Oxford, United States of America.

Holub, H. W., Tappeiner, G., Tappeiner, U. (1999), "Some remarks on the System of Integrated Environmental and Economic Accounting of the United Nations", *Ecological Economics*, 29(3), pp. 329–336.

Ison, S., Peake. S., Wall, S. (2002), *Environmental Issues and Policies*, Prentice Hall, London, The United Kingdom.

Janice, W. (1990), *Natural Resource Accounting: An Overview from a New Zealand Perspective with Special Reference to the Norwegian Experience.* Lincoln University & University of Canterbury, Centre for Resource Management, Christchurch, New Zealand.

Kolstad, C. D. (2000), *Environmental Economics*, Oxford University Press, New York, United States of America.

Knetsch, J. L. (1994), "Environmental valuation: Some problems of wrong questions and misleading answers", *Environmental Values*, 3, pp. 351–368.

Lone, O., Nyborg, K., Aaheim, A. (1993), "Natural resource accounting: The Norwegian experience", In Approaches to Environmental Accounting: Proceedings of the IARIW Conference on Environmental Accounting, Baden (near Vienna), Austria, 27–29 May 1991, pp. 446–457, Physica-Verlag HD.

Moulton, B. R. (2004), "The system of national accounts for the new economy: What should change?", *Review of Income and Wealth*, 50(2), pp. 261–278.

Muller, N. Z., Mendelsohn, R., Nordhaus, W. (2011), "Environmental accounting for pollution in the United States economy", *American Economic Review*, 101, pp. 1649–1675.

Munasinghe, M. (2001), *Macroeconomics and the Environmental*, Edward Elgar Publications, London, The United Kingdom.

Myles, G. D. (2000), "Taxation and economic growth", *Fiscal Studies*, 21(1), pp. 141–168.

Natural Capital Committee (2013), The State of Natural Capital: Towards a framework for measurement and valuation, UK Government, UK.

Nordhaus, W. D. (2010), "Carbon taxes to move toward fiscal sustainability", *The Economists' Voice*, September 2010, Berkeley Electronic Press.

Nunes, P. A. L. D., can den Bergh, J. C. J. M. (2001), "Economic valuation of biodiversity: Sense or nonsense?", *Ecological Economics*, 39, pp. 203–222.

Octavianti, T., Staddon, C. (2021), "A review of 80 assessment tools measuring water security", *Wiley Interdisciplinary Reviews: Water*, 8(3), e1516.

OECD (2010), *Multilingual Summaries (October 2010), Taxation, Innovation and the Environment, Green Growth Strategy.*

OECD (2012), *OECD Environmental Outlook to 2050: The Consequences of Inaction (March 2012).*

Parkinson, G. (2010), "Climate spectator: Playing carbon games", Business Spectator Commentary, Australia, 18 Oct 2010.

Parry, I. W. H., Bento, A. M. (2000), "Tax deductions, environmental policy, and the 'double dividend' hypothesis", *Journal of Environmental Economics and Management*, 39, pp. 67–96.

Repetto, R. (1992), "Accounting for environmental assets", *Scientific American*, 266(6), pp. 94–101.

Repetto, R., Magrath, W., Wells, M., Beer, C., Rossini, F. (1989), *Wasting Assets: Natural Resources in the National Income Accounts*, World Resource Institute, Washington, DC.

Sandmo, A. (2003), "Environmental Taxation and Revenue for Development", Discussion Paper No. 2003/86, United Nations University – World Institute for Development Economics Research.

Schumacher, I. (2009), "The dynamics of environmentalism and the environment", *Ecological Economics*, 68(11), pp. 2842–2849.

Sedjo, R. A. (2010), "Comment on Nordhaus: Tax carbon, not fossil fuels", *The Economists' Voice*, October 2010, Berkeley Electronic Press.

Sève, J. (2002), "A Discussion Paper on Environmental and Natural Resources Accounting and Potential Applications in African Countries", ENCAP IV, Subtask 5c, Environmental Policy and Institutional Strengthening Indefinite Quantity Contract (EPIQ), March 2002.

Sinden, J. A. (1994), "A review of environmental valuation in Australia", *Review of Marketing and Agricultural Economics*, 62(3), pp. 337–368.

Smith, R. (2007), "Development of the SEEA 2003 and its implementation", *Ecological Economics*, 61(4), pp. 592–599.

Solow, R. M. (1956), "A Contribution to the theory of economic growth", *Quarterly Journal of Economics*, 70(1) pp. 65–94.

Solow, R. M. (1974a), "The economics of resources or the resources of economics", *American Economic Review*, 64(2), May, pp. 1–14.

Solow, R. M. (1974b), "Intergenerational equity and exhaustible resources", *The Review of Economic Studies*, 41, pp. 29–45.

Solow, R. M. (2005), "Sustainability: An economist's perspective." Chapter 26 in *Economics of the Environment.* 5th ed. Edited by Robert N. Stavins. W.W. Norton & Company, New York, United States of America.

Stafford, P. (2011), "Confusion over spot carbon trading restart", *Financial Times*, 26 January 2011.

Statistics Netherlands (2009), *Progress towards sustainability development in Netherlands*, Sustainability Monitor for the Netherlands.

Statistics New Zealand (2002), *Natural Resource Accounts for New Zealand – Overview Document*, New Zealand.

Stavins, R. N. (2007), "Environmental Economics", NBER Working Paper Series, Paper No. 13574.

Sterner, T. (1994), "Environmental tax reform: The Swedish experience", *European Environment*, 4, pp. 20–25.

Stiglitz, J. E., Sen, A., Fitoussi, J-P. (2009), Report by the Commission on the Measurement of Economic Performance and Social Progress, France.

Tan, S., Thampapillai, D. J. (2011), "Assessment of fiscal intervention measures in China: Perspectives from environmental macroeconomics", in Kreise, L., Sirisom, J., Ashiabor, H., Milne, J. E. (eds), *Critical Issues in Environmental Taxation, Volume IX, Environmental Taxation in China and Asia-Pacific – Achieving Environmental Sustainability through Fiscal Policy*, Edward Elgar, United Kingdom, pp. 55–65.

Thampapillai, D. J. (1993), "Environmental macroeconomics: Some conceptual considerations", Sweden.

Thampapillai, D. J. (2002), *Environmental Economics – Concepts, Methods and Policies*, Oxford University Press, South Melbourne, Australia.

Thampapillai, D. J. (2007), "The scarcity of KN and economic growth: A comparative study of Australia and the US", *The Singapore Economic Review*, 52(2), pp. 251–263.

Thampapillai, D. J. (2008), "Environmental capacity constraints in macroeconomic policy analysis", *International Journal of Environment, Workplace and Employment*, 4(1), pp. 1–14.

Thampapillai, D. J., Hanf, C-H. (2000), "The internalization of environmental capital stocks into an aggregated Cobb-Douglas function", *Economic Analysis & Policy*, 30(2), pp. 209–215.

Thampapillai, D. J., Maleka, P. T., Milimo, J. T. (1992), "Quantification of the trade-offs in Zambia between environment, employment, income and food-security", World Employment Programme Research, Working Paper [Case Study].

Thampapillai, D. J., Thangavelu, S. M., Quah, E., Padaya, P. M. (2005), "The internalization of environmental capital in Keynesian model of income determination: Revised approaches to public policy", in Ashiabor, H., Deketelaere, K., Kreiser, L., Milne, J. (eds), *Critical Issues in Environmental Taxation – International and Comparative Perspectives: Volume II*, Richmond Law & Tax Ltd, New York, pp. 85-95.

Thampapillai, D. J., Wanden, S., Larsson, M., Uhlin, H-E (1998), "The environment in macroeconomic analyses – comparisons between Sweden and the US", *Australasian Journal of Regional Studies*, 4(2), pp. 349–362.

Thampapillai, D. J., Wu, X., Tan, S. (2010), "Fiscal balance: Environmental taxes and investments" *Journal of Natural Resources Policy Research*, 2(2), pp. 137–147.

Todaro, M. P., Smith, S. C. (2002), *Economic Development – 8th Edition*, Addison Wesley, London, The United Kingdom.

United Nations (1993), System of National Accounts, United Nations, New York, The United States of America.

United Nations (2008), System of National Accounts, United Nations, New York, The United States of America.

Vanoli, A. (2005), *A History of National Accounting*, IOS Press, The Netherlands.

Welsch, H. (2009), "Implications of happiness research for environmental economics", *Ecological Economics*, 68(11), pp. 2735–2742.

Win, T. L. (2011), "World ponders alternatives to troubled carbon market", *AlertNet*, 24 January 2011.

Young, M. D. (1993), "Natural resource accounting: Some Australian experiences and observations", in Approaches to Environmental Accounting: Proceedings of the IARIW Conference on Environmental Accounting, Baden (near Vienna), Austria, 27–29 May 1991, pp. 111–125, Physica-Verlag HD.

Zhong, S., Geng, Y., Liu, W., Gao, C., Chen, W. (2016), "A bibliometric review on natural resource accounting during 1995–2014", *Journal of Cleaner Production*, 139, pp. 122–132.

4 Measuring Environmental Capital and Evidence from Select Organisation of Economic Co-operation and Development (OECD) Economies

4.1 Introduction

This chapter provides the basis for establishing the role of environmental capital (KN) in economic growth and begins with a discussion of the concept of factoring KN into the factor utilisation model. The measurement and accounting of KN in gross domestic product (GDP) has (remains in development) yet to be fully reconciled. Although mainstream economics has started to recognise KN, there remains no consensual approach for the measurement of KN. Such complexity does not suggest that the measurement of KN, critical to the development of sustainable macroeconomic policies, is impossible. To improve the elementary framework (introduced in Chapter 3), the valuation of KN must first be ascertained. Unavoidably, however, there will be assumptions and limitations to consider.

The utility of KN is operationalised on a select group of OECD economies, which has attained the developed economy status to highlight the service that KN offers as economies grow over a time period. Subject to availability of time-series data, this demonstration addresses some of the flaws of the two-factor model and also serves to underline the ease with which KN can be internalised into a model. An association will be made between utilisation of KN and increase in GDP, and the corresponding employment outcome. This implies that a relationship between capacity of an economy and the level of employment exists and is reinforced with consideration for KN.

An economy which functions as a subsystem to the ecosystem (as highlighted in Chapter 3's literature review) is evidence that KN is utilised as a natural resource towards economic growth. Therefore, an approach arising from the production (as opposed to consumption by Tan and Thampapillai, 2011) perspective would offer a more robust model compared to what had been established in the earlier chapter. Traditionally, the economic performance of an economy has been measured with reference to a commonly used two-factor Cobb–Douglas (C-D) factor utilisation function, which is given by income (Y) = f (KM, L) where KM is physical capital and L is labour. In this chapter, a three-factor utilisation model will be introduced to accommodate KN, that is, Y = g (KM, L, KN) as shown in Thampapillai (2012).

DOI: 10.4324/9781003002550-4

As Daly (1997) argued and in support of a similar view offered earlier by Nordhaus and Tobin (1972), outcomes would differ if natural resources were included in the economics of production. To illustrate this view, Daly (1997) used a simple example of baking a cake without the ingredients. To bake a larger cake, the cook needs only to stir it faster in a larger bowl and bake it in a larger oven. The bowl and oven are the capital, and the cook is the labour. However, without the ingredients (natural resources), there will be no cake. Thus, one way to appreciate the function of KN is through the inclusion of KN in the factor income model.

The next two sections offer a conceptual basis for measuring KN and a methodological framework for measuring KN [these were published in Tan (2016)]. Updated empirical evidence of KN utilisation for eight selected Organisation for Economic Co-operation and Development (OECD) economies (Australia, Canada, Germany, Japan, Korea, New Zealand, United Kingdom, and the USA) from 1990 to 2021 is then presented. The chapter concludes with a brief discussion relating KN utilisation to income gaps (economic capacity) and employment.

4.2 Conceptual Basis for Measuring Environmental Capital

The literature explains the distribution of national income between two factors, namely, KM and L. A widely used model is the C-D factor utilisation function which describes the relationship between income and the inputs KM and L. Assuming that this function displays constant returns to scale ($\theta + \lambda = 1$) [Hartwick (1978, 1991, 1997), Solow (1986), and Nordhaus (1992)], the C-D function takes the following form:

$$Y = \alpha\, KM^{\theta}\, L^{\lambda} \tag{4.1}$$

where α is the total factor productivity coefficient, θ is the share of income to capital, and λ is the share of income to labour. This is based on the assumption that the factors are paid their respective marginal products. The coefficients θ and λ of the assumed functional forms can be estimated using point estimate data on the premise that equation (4.1) is valid. Income statements in national accounts contain an identity that allows for this estimation. This identity is:

$$Y \equiv OS + CE \tag{4.2}$$

where OS is the operating surplus, which is the sum of the payments to KM and CE is the compensation to the employees, which is the sum of the payments to L. Therefore, it follows that:

$$\theta = \left[\frac{OS}{Y}\right] \tag{4.3}$$

$$\lambda = \left[\frac{CE}{Y}\right] \tag{4.4}$$

The contention in environmental-macroeconomics (EM) analyses is that income, Y, is not purely attributed to KM and L. KN must also be accounted for because it plays an important role in the formation of Y, similar to the above cake-making example from Daly. This relationship suggests that the contributions of KM and L in the standard factor utilisation function are overstated. In terms of this premise, there is a need to revise the C-D factor utilisation function to the three-factor utilisation function as follows:

$$Y = \alpha \, KM^{\theta'} \, L^{\lambda'} \, KN^{\phi} \tag{4.5}$$

where α is the total factor productivity coefficient, θ' is the share of Y to KM, λ' is the share of Y to L, and ϕ is the corresponding share of Y that accrues to KN. When KN is considered as a third factor, the same level of income would then be attributed three ways to KM, L, and KN. As a result, income in the three-factor income model will fall below that of the two-factor income model (Thampapillai, 2012). The following discussion on the conceptual basis for measuring KN draws on Thampapillai (2012) and Thampapillai and Sinden (2012).

Figure 4.1 displays both the two-factor and three-factor income models. The income definition in the two-factor model does not make any allowance for the depreciation of KN (D_{KN}). However, the definition in the three-factor model makes an allowance for D_{KN}. With this consideration for D_{KN}, the three-factor income model will fall below that of the two-factor income model as indicated in Figure 4.1. There are two horizontal scales in Figure 4.1: the first is KM, which is the accumulated stock of manufactured capital; the second is K, which is a composite measure that comprises the amount of KM accumulated and the amount of KN utilised. Thampapillai and Sinden (2012) assumed that KM and KN can be measured with the same numerical scale and, hence, can be aggregated.

The role of KN in determining Y can be explained by comparing Y = f (KM, L) with Y = g (KM, L, KN). In the two-factor model, the amount of KM that is required for Y_t is KM_t. However, the same level of Y_t in the three-factor model is explained by K_t, which is larger than KM_t. This observation suggests that KN_t can be estimated as the difference (K_t – KM_t). The utilisation of KN represents the depreciation in the level of existing KN stock. When Y_t is explained by the three-factor model, the following two observations can be made:

i KM_t is responsible for a lower value of Y_t' (known as sustainable Y) and not Y_t, in other words, $Y_t' < Y_t$. Hence, there is an over-estimation of the income ($Y_t - Y_t'$)
ii At the level of Y_t, more of the aggregated capital K_t (greater than KM_t) is required to maintain this level of income

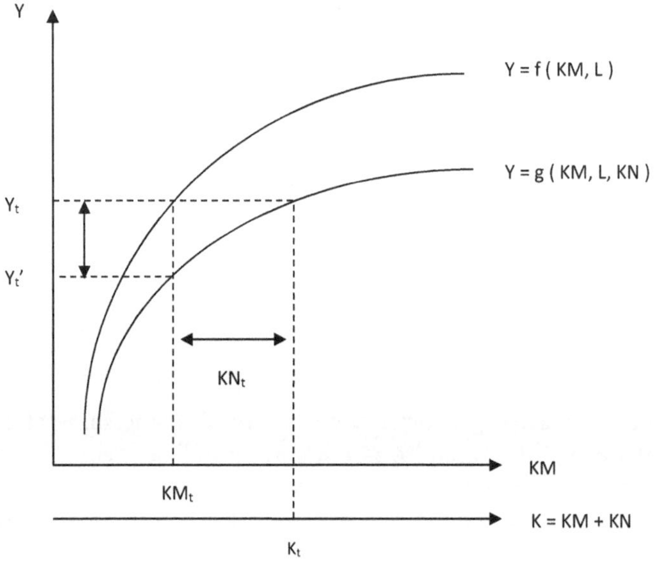

Figure 4.1 Conceptual Basis for Measuring Environmental Capital.

Source: This is reproduced from Figure 13-2 of Thampapillai and Sinden (2012).

To achieve a given rate of economic growth, the amount of KN used towards production will increase. However, there are two challenges associated with this: (i) ensure that KN increment is constant and (ii) use KN saving technology process. To recognise D_{KN}, the income Y must be adjusted to the sustainable income, Y', by adjusting for the depreciation of the KN stock. In other words, Y' = Y – D_{KN}. Suppose that D_{KN} is a proportion of Y, as follows:

$$\phi = \left[\frac{D_{KN}}{Y}\right] \tag{4.6}$$

Thampapillai and Sinden (2012) assume that ϕ can be regarded as the share of Y that accrues to KN. Hence, it follows that a sustainable income, Y', would be adjusted accordingly by a factor of (1 – ϕ) as follows:

$$Y' = \alpha' \, KM^{\theta'} \, L^{\lambda'} \, KN^{\phi} \tag{4.7}$$

where α' = (1 – ϕ) α. The time-series point estimate is assumed valid in each year of the time series. The analysis of point estimates captures productivity changes for each year of the time series. Therefore, any change in multi-factor productivity (MFP) is made through α and α' as point estimates for each year. Now that both Y and Y' are ascertained, an expression for KN can be obtained by dividing Y by Y' as follows:

$$KN=KM^{\frac{\theta-\theta'}{\phi}}\,L^{\frac{\lambda-\lambda'}{\phi}} \tag{4.8}$$

4.3 Methodological Framework for Measuring Environmental Capital

The following methodological framework details the steps taken to estimate KN:

i The OECD database was selected because it has a full set of national income accounts with data dating to 1980. The economies selected for this study are Australia, Canada, Germany, Japan, Korea, New Zealand, the United Kingdom, and the USA. The variables selected from 1990 to 2021 are the following: Final Consumption Expenditure (C), Final Consumption Expenditure of Government (G), Gross Capital Formation (GCF), Net Balance of Goods and Services, National Income Expenditure Approach (Y), Compensation of Employees (CE), Gross Operating Surplus (OS), Net Taxes (T), Income Approach to National Accounts (IANA), GDP Deflator, and Employment (L). All monetary estimates are in the appropriate national currency at current prices.

   KM and L in expression KN equation (4.8) are represented by OECD variables GCF for KM, and CE and OS for L.

ii The GDP deflator was used to convert the current value estimates to constant values. Note that the base year is 2015. To smooth any cyclical variations and minimise business cycle contaminations, the Hodrick–Prescott (HP) filter was applied to time-series variables C, GCF (I), S (GDP – C – G), CE, and OS with the first and last three observations of the data points excluded as per Baxter and King (1999).

iii The perpetual inventory method was used to estimate the capital stock (KM). The approach of perpetual inventory is used for the calculation of fixed assets when direct information is difficult to obtain (Eurostat, 1995). GCF is the Investment (I) and the logarithm of GCF is computed to express the values in a more natural way. The size of the capital at the initial period of the time series can be determined and estimated by the coefficient ω, which is defined as the ideal rate of increase for KM per annum. The initial size of the capital stock is denoted as $KM_{t=1}$ for the first year and is estimated from the GCF value. This value is defined as follows:

$$KM_{t=1} = GCF_{t=1}/(\delta + \omega) \tag{4.10}$$

where δ is the rate at which capital stock depreciates over 30 years, which is assumed to be $(1/30) = 0.0333$. The size of the capital stock for subsequent years can now be estimated by:

$$KM_{t+1} = KM_t + GCF_{t+1} - (\delta^* KM_t) \qquad (4.11)$$

iv The labour (L) is estimated to be the level of total labour force employed. This is obtained directly from the OECD database.

v The value of θ is estimated to be (OS/Y) as in equation (4.3) and λ is (CE/Y) as shown in equation (4.4).

vi The variable ϕ is estimated to be (D_{KN}/Y) as per equation (4.6). The value of D_{KN} is restricted to the cost of carbon dioxide (CO_2) abatement and the greenhouse gases (GHG) data are obtained from the World Development Indicators (WDI) (World Bank, 2023) from 1990. The GHG used in the calculations are CO_2, methane (CH_4), nitrous oxide (N_2O), and other GHG [which includes hydrofluorocarbons (HFC), perfluorinated compounds (PFC), sulphur hexaflourinated compounds (PFC), and sulphur hexafluoride (SF_6)]. All gases are converted to tons of CO_2 equivalent at a cost of USD100/tonne (2015 constant prices). The literature has proposed for a cost of USD100/tonne of CO_2 emissions which is the rate Intergovernmental Panel on Climate Change (IPCC) believes is needed to limit warming to 1.5°C. See Nordhaus (2017), Karstad (2012), Hope (2011), Ackerman et al. (2009), and Stern (2007).

vii With the introduction of ϕ (the share of income to KN), θ and λ must be revised to capture changes in the constituent of income. If the assumption that a constant return to scale holds, then $\theta' + \lambda' + \phi = 1$. Hence, θ and λ must be revised to θ' and λ'. This revision necessary because the original variables are overstated from the inclusion of the income share from KN. Thampapillai (2012) estimated KN by apportioning KN from KM and L. This method has limitations because it does not account for changes in ϕ, which is the share of income to KN, as a factor of income. In this study, θ' and λ' were estimated using shadow pricing. The shadow price is the price of the factor of production when the market is perfect, for example, when full employment is observed. Thus, the coefficients θ' and λ' can be defined as follows:

$$\theta' = (1-\phi)\left(\frac{P_{KM}}{P_L + P_{KM}}\right) \qquad (4.12)$$

$$\lambda' = (1-\phi)\left(\frac{P_L}{P_L + P_{KM}}\right) \qquad (4.13)$$

where P_{KM} is the shadow price of KM, which is estimated to be (OS/KM) and P_{Lt} is the shadow price of CE, which is estimated to be the capital equivalent price of L. The method adopted in Thampapillai (2012) is to convert CE to explain the context of unemployment. This conversion is performed by dividing CE by the labour force to estimate a wage rate that would support full employment. The revised value of CE, namely, CE_{St} is then the product of the employment and the shadow wage rate, which is $(L_t{}^*W_{St})$. Then λ' is (CE_{St}/Y). P_{Lt} is estimated to be (CE_{St}/KM_t), which is a KM equivalent price.

viii From equation (4.8), KN can be calculated by substituting all parameters that are described from steps iii to vii. Note that these parameters are point estimates and not estimation of long-run steady state.

4.4 Empirical Evidence of Environmental Capital from Select OECD Economies 1990 to 2021

Based on the definition of KN given equation (4.8), the utilisation of KN was empirically measured for eight selected OECD economies. The selected economies are Australia, Canada, Germany, Japan, Korea, New Zealand, the United Kingdom, and the USA. The values for KN are presented in Table 4.1 and are displayed in Figure 4.2.

Based on the values from Table 4.1, Japan and Korea displayed declines in KN utilisation in the year 1998 which followed the 1997 Asian Financial Crisis (AFC) with declines commencing from the year 1997. Most economies (Australia, Canada, Japan, Korea, New Zealand, the United Kingdom, and the USA) showed a significant decline of KN utilisation in the year 2009 which followed the 2007–2008 financial crisis or the Global Financial Crisis (GFC) though Australia, Canada, and the USA were already showing declines from the year 2008. Germany was the only economy that did not show a significant decline of KN utilisation; instead, it showed the greatest KN utilisation for the year 2009. All economies (barring Australia) had pronounced decline of KN utilisation in the year 2020 which followed the COVID-19 pandemic in the year 2019 though Japan and Korea were already experiencing declines in 2019.

The historical display of KN utilisation in Figure 4.2 enables the economies to be classified into two groups, as follows:

i Group One – Upward trending KN utilisation
The economies that belong to this group are Australia, Canada, Germany, and New Zealand. These economies display an increase in the use of KN.

ii Group Two – Downward trending KN utilisation
The economies that belong to this group are Japan, Korea, the United Kingdom, and the USA. These economies display a decrease in the use of KN.

Note that KN utilisation is plotted on the vertical axis with time on the horizontal axis.

Table 4.1 KN Utilisation (in Year 2015 Constant National Currency) for Eight OECD Economies from 1990 to 2021

	1990	*1991*	*1992*	*1993*	*1994*
AUS	128546080	87733208	62514283	65717101	105382103
CAN	80634733	20049784	12128185	12166417	18922244
GER	1673178647	5882480154	1718345670	681069574	698035382
JAP	1915721335233	2273017882574	1865438291872	1129724978277	698737525109
KOR	67230085685	51415760587	53497746012	37903303550	56066719340
NZL	21641601	22520275	9168324	7153031	15860375
GBR	50305099	13310324	4959711	4238766	7201792
USA	4317657051	2356353036	1488539607	2103864734	2835649056
	2000	*2001*	*2002*	*2003*	*2004*
AUS	185205658	177776831	243383270	176016175	449259412
CAN	127679892	63379043	60183821	89024764	90454264
GER	42331554141	30335853440	21981736625	8317976208	7570228191
JAP	5479901674	4195320204	3376393085	5867285448	19389709899
KOR	26539848041	33381414994	49170195749	34474415597	31800202721
NZL	43555285	62121960	54889999	74668476	80917981
GBR	56450713	70359151	49099709	53547060	59566769
USA	6560819665	4123167483	2025957237	1778541822	2418413811
	2011	*2012*	*2013*	*2014*	*2015*
AUS	353642061	286086965	141763529	201282778	178036109
CAN	79989124	75581019	94502472	95854788	108861802
GER	202710431296	369101742126	341698901999	515771175356	900309379362
JAP	87910803334	67068623307	65511232297	76644694506	61159027258
KOR	33836524112	36854663284	36101160974	20407739417	19712516297
NZL	45263108	28419450	76188379	87892365	66366860
GBR	114409	230822	236310	872096	2157688
USA	118787129	188352449	365467979	903843469	1655180357

The general observation from Figure 4.2 is that declining KN utilisation from 1990 to 2021 appeared to be a prelude to exogenous shocks (Japan and Korea in the 1997 AFC and COVID-19 pandemic; Australia, Canada, and the USA in the GFC). Similarly, it can also be argued that declining KN utilisation is a result of crises which is evident from all economies studied. And during other periods, KN utilisation rises; thus, the utilisation of KN is required for economic growth.

4.5 Environmental Capital (KN) Utilisation, Gross Domestic Product (GDP) Income and Employment

The utilisation of KN in an economy will affect the level of income that is generated. This relationship can be demonstrated with the three-factor income model by looking at the gap between the equilibrium income and full employment income. An income gap exists between the income level at full

1995	*1996*	*1997*	*1998*	*1999*
87376006	61596157	82460024	100067111	196948555
23893747	32029171	49364472	56978448	105121929
1404367280	1467344679	1172722257	1981500337	5841132411
710056628453	357238088830	218896342533	43633286779	10380172459
83608850875	96441228178	81031844896	2665871525	3925922971
22908840	23984686	16585588	31277928	79258618
10565538	17517236	31767072	47327259	41753696
3350931546	3533648008	4521593246	5321153881	5848959748

2005	*2006*	*2007*	*2008*	*2009*	*2010*
335411488	565066900	583972880	271827298	226633058	270123856
169219712	165810661	253649900	161630829	23074882	43733892
1964281424	1726244478	4884173322	19987454497	137741496943	191165764069
47215731060	85934136871	169357212693	158325256598	45346986779	59707601893
24170828917	26723237916	31875587901	33192329155	21337681898	25254963607
152995775	130409694	96595162	162316845	47327716	49132011
47153775	22178261	19508840	9999414	419315	365588
3135896038	4154274449	4264904182	1823831320	103684330	96231891

2016	*2017*	*2018*	*2019*	*2020*	*2021*
222724851	287587485	268187728	296561810	389251311	1405655908
115564379	203188964	335436913	333309692	250830	17788656
408434605024	971725292192	4085121204725	6875830129185	6397642527017	8781893493798
71950987074	98060779538	95265529177	63695102412	28089604843	20511859781
16805550237	15896667299	12222523329	7840837289	4230562164	4839460098
81069559	116177277	81433036	124558420	25617366	47192170
3408422	5788379	8617698	8926528	1482583	854754
2071451855	2999586594	4647993295	5049848327	39396077	624110678

employment and the current level of income. Hence, income gap is defined as the difference between income (Y_f) that is generated when total labour force (L_f) is employed and income (Y_t) that is generated when labour is at the current level of employment (L_t). Note that $L_t < L_f$.

The income gap for the two-factor income model is estimated to be ($Y_f - Y_t$) and the income gap for the three-factor income model is ($Y'_f - Y'_t$). Both gaps can be estimated for all the years by making substitutions for α, θ, λ, α', θ', λ', and ϕ from point estimate data. This gap measures the capacity that is available in an economy and is measured for both of the factor income models. The effect of KN on the income model is apparent because the gap is generally smaller in the three-factor income model relative to the two-factor income model. Such a phenomenon where the income gap in the two-factor income model is overstated can be explained by the concept of income efficiency. For example, an economy is considered efficient when the income gap is rising with a low level of KN utilisation.

Group One – Upward Trending KN Utilisation Economies

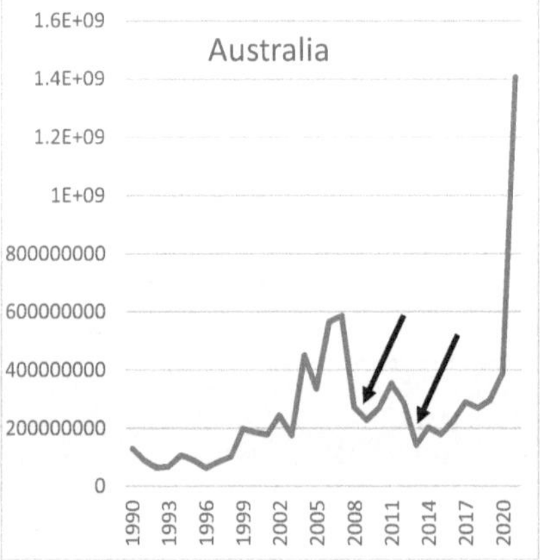

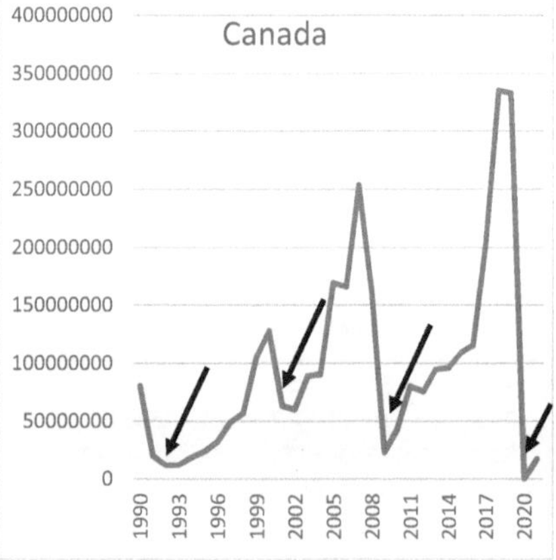

Two significant dips observed in KN utilisation for Australia happened after the GFC, and flood in end 2010 and early 2011.

The dips observed in KN utilisation for Canada are attributed to the 1990 oil shock, dot-com bust in 2000, GFC, and COVID-19.

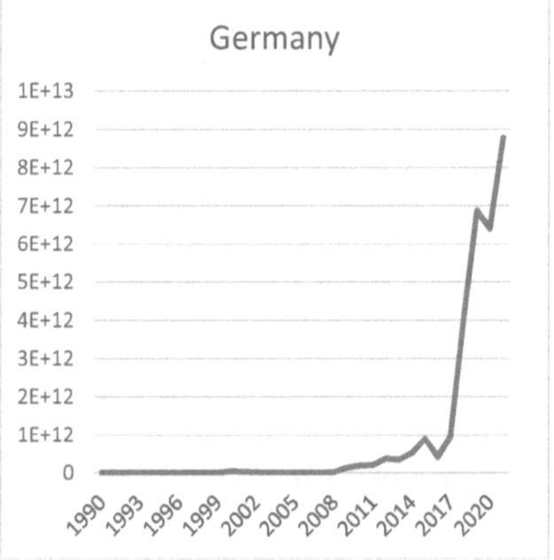

During the observed period, Germany did not display significant declines of KN

The dips observed in KN utilisation for New Zealand are attributed to the 1990 oil shock, GFC, and COVID-19. The dip between 1999-

Figure 4.2 KN Utilisation for Eight OECD Economies from 1990 to 2021.

utilisation; instead it showed increase in KN utilisation.	2000 was a result of the New Zealand Dollar (NZD) depreciating against USD in a bid by the Reserve Bank of New Zealand (RBNZ) to slow economic activity and prevent imported inflation.
Group Two – Downward Trending KN Utilisation Economies	
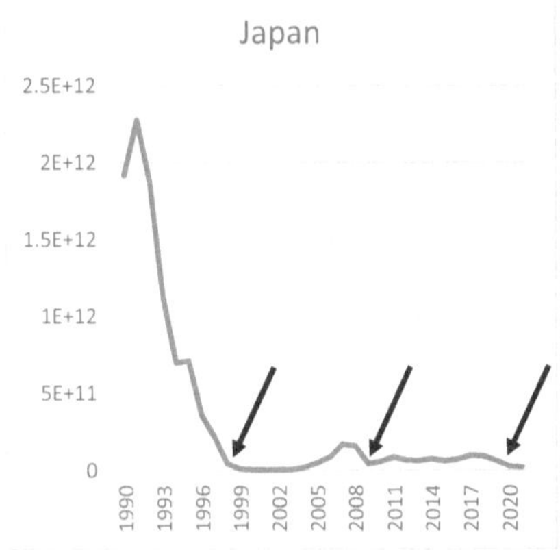	
The decline of Japan's KN utilisation can be observed in 1998 which followed the AFC with declines commencing from 1997, GFC, and COVID-19.	The dips in Korea's KN utilisation are attributed to the 1990 oil shock, AFC, GFC, and COVID-19.

Figure 4.2 (continued)

An appropriate measure to exemplify the presence of KN across both models would be:

$$[Y_f - Y_t] - [Y'_f - Y'_t]$$

If this value is positive (>Ø), then it is evident that in the presence of KN, the income domain has been reduced. Furthermore, if this value is positive and the trend is an increasing one, then it appears that the capacity constraint is becoming more stringent over time. The results are presented in Table 4.2 as well as in Figure 4.3 which shows the time-series trends of the economies' income gaps.

Figure 4.3 shows the trends of the economies' income gaps (on the vertical axis) against time (horizontal axis). The economies are grouped in the same category (as in Figure 4.2) to allow a comparison with the trends of KN utilisation and the income gaps of the economies.

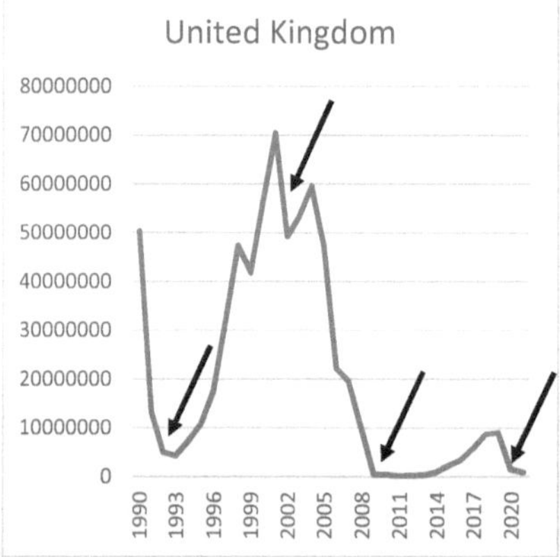

The dips observed in KN utilisation for United Kingdom are attributed to the 1990 oil shock, dot-com bust in 2000, GFC, and COVID-19. Its withdrawal from the European Exchange Rate Mechanism (ERM) delinking Pound from the Deutschemark in 1992 (Bonefeld and Burnham, 1996) coincided with a trough of KN utilisation in 1993.

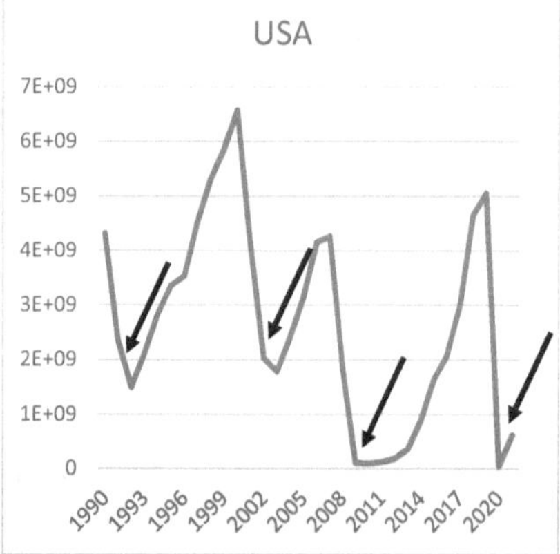

The dips observed in KN utilisation for the USA are attributed to the 1990 oil shock, dot-com bust in 2000, GFC, and COVID-19.

Figure 4.2 (continued)

For the economies in Group One (Australia, Germany, and New Zealand) which display upward trending KN utilisation, the income gaps displayed in Figure 4.3 have decreasing trends. These trends suggest that an increase in KN utilisation reduces the income domain. Canada is displaying a peak at the end of observed period which can be explained by the COVID-19 pandemic.

The economies in Group Two (Japan, Korea, and the USA) which display downward trending KN utilisation are displaying income gaps with an increasing trend. Such trends appear to suggest that the capacity constraint becomes more stringent over time when there is a decrease in the utilisation of KN. Thus, Japan, Korea, and the USA are considered efficient economies as their income gaps rise with a low level of KN utilisation. Based on Figure 4.3, the United Kingdom is considered a less efficient economy as its income gap is falling with a low level of KN utilisation.

Comparing the KN utilisation and the income trends in Figures 4.2 and 4.3, it is possible to reach a conclusion about the efficiency of an economy. An economy can be considered efficient when the income gap is rising with a low level of KN utilisation. For ease of comparison, the focus is on select Group One (with an increasing usage of KN) and select Group Two (with a decreasing usage of KN) economies.

Table 4.2 Gap $[Y_f - Y_t] - [Y'_f - Y'_t]$ for Group One and Group Two OECD Economies from 1990 to 2021

Group One	*1990*	*1991*	*1992*	*1993*	*1994*	*1995*	*1996*	*1997*	*1998*	*1999*
AUS $(Y_f - Y_t) - (Y'_f - Y'_t)$	4.82E + 09	5.81E + 09	6.58E + 09	5.06E + 09	3.79E + 09	4.3E + 09	5.05E + 09	4.27E + 09	4.19E + 09	2.93E + 09
CAN $(Y_f - Y_t) - (Y'_f - Y'_t)$	2.88E + 09	4.47E + 09	5.33E + 09	5.1E + 09	4.37E + 09	3.77E + 09	4.07E + 09	3.94E + 09	3.43E + 09	2.94E + 09
GER $(Y_f - Y_t) - (Y'_f - Y'_t)$	1.82E + 09	1.54E + 08	1.32E + 09	2.57E + 09	2.49E + 09	1.60E + 09	1.66E + 09	1.80E + 09	1.18E + 09	2.35E + 08
NZL $(Y_f - Y_t) - (Y'_f - Y'_t)$	9.77E + 08	9.75E + 08	1.38E + 09	1.4E + 09	1.1E + 09	9.6E + 08	9.26E + 08	1.09E + 09	8.11E + 08	5.68E + 08

Group Two	*1990*	*1991*	*1992*	*1993*	*1994*	*1995*	*1996*	*1997*	*1998*	*1999*
JAP $(Y_f - Y_t) - (Y'_f - Y'_t)$	−7.1E + 10	−7.8E + 10	−8.2E + 10	−7.5E + 10	−5.8E + 10	−6E + 10	−2E + 10	1.36E + 10	1.32E + 11	2.77E + 11
KOR $(Y_f - Y_t) - (Y'_f - Y'_t)$	4.06E + 11	4.86E + 11	5.58E + 11	7.28E + 11	6.49E + 11	5.59E + 11	5.85E + 11	8.05E + 11	2.57E + 12	2.67E + 12
GBR $(Y_f - Y_t) - (Y'_f - Y'_t)$	3.45E + 09	5.11E + 09	5.98E + 09	6.07E + 09	5.28E + 09	4.61E + 09	4.29E + 09	3.39E + 09	2.91E + 09	2.72E + 09
USA $(Y_f - Y_t) - (Y'_f - Y'_t)$	1.33E + 10	2.03E + 10	2.59E + 10	2.34E + 10	1.97E + 10	1.76E + 10	1.76E + 10	1.62E + 10	1.41E + 10	1.28E + 10

Group One	*2000*	*2001*	*2002*	*2003*	*2004*	*2005*	*2006*	*2007*	*2008*	*2009*	*2010*
AUS $(Y_f - Y_t) - (Y'_f - Y'_t)$	3.34E + 09	3.71E + 09	2.83E + 09	2.57E + 09	1.39E + 09	1.68E + 09	1.16E + 09	1.12E + 09	2.19E + 09	2.62E + 09	2.22E + 09
CAN $(Y_f - Y_t) - (Y'_f - Y'_t)$	2.51E + 09	2.92E + 09	3.32E + 09	3.76E + 09	3.36E + 09	3.01E + 09	3.04E + 09	3.04E + 09	2.92E + 09	5.05E + 09	4.55E + 09
GER $(Y_f - Y_t) - (Y'_f - Y'_t)$	−7.58E + 08	-6.36E + 08	−4.49E + 08	1.03E + 08	1.84E + 08	1.14E + 09	1.29E + 09	4.91E + 08	−2.32E + 08	-6.77E + 08	-7.59E + 08
NZL $(Y_f - Y_t) - (Y'_f - Y'_t)$	7.05E + 08	6.36E + 08	6.63E + 08	5.94E + 08	5.52E + 08	4.05E + 08	4.28E + 08	4.71E + 08	3.48E + 08	5.77E + 08	5.63E + 08

(*Continued*)

Table 4.2 (Continued)

Group Two											
JAP $(Y_f - Y_t) - (Y'_f - Y'_t)$	3.58E + 11	3.78E + 11	4.22E + 11	3.63E + 11	2.28E + 11	1.45E + 11	8.87E + 10	4.42E + 10	4.26E + 10	1.2E + 11	1.08E + 11
KOR $(Y_f - Y_t) - (Y'_f - Y'_t)$	1.61E + 12	1.46E + 12	1.15E + 12	1.32E + 12	1.44E + 12	1.47E + 12	1.37E + 12	1.30E + 12	1.30E + 12	1.61E + 12	1.76E + 12
GBR $(Y_f - Y_t) - (Y'_f - Y'_t)$	2.42E + 09	2.25E + 09	2.31E + 09	2.24E + 09	2.08E + 09	2.15E + 09	2.57E + 09	2.49E + 09	2.72E + 09	4.23E + 09	4.54E + 09
USA $(Y_f - Y_t) - (Y'_f - Y'_t)$	1.19E + 10	1.67E + 10	2.31E + 10	2.5E + 10	2.21E + 10	1.95E + 10	1.65E + 10	1.7E + 10	2.5E + 10	5.62E + 10	6.16E + 10
Group One	*2011*	*2012*	*2013*	*2014*	*2015*	*2016*	*2017*	*2018*	*2019*	*2020*	*2021*
AUS $(Y_f - Y_t) - (Y'_f - Y'_t)$	2.4E + 09	2.85E + 09	3.22E + 09	2.69E + 09	2.75E + 09	2.15E + 09	2.05E + 09	2.09E + 09	3.02E + 09	2.27E + 09	1.13E + 09
CAN $(Y_f - Y_t) - (Y'_f - Y'_t)$	4.16E + 09	4.09E + 09	3.91E + 09	3.97E + 09	3.91E + 09	3.82E + 09	3.25E + 09	2.75E + 09	2.57E + 09	1.43E + 10	5.6E + 09
GER $(Y_f - Y_t) - (Y'_f - Y'_t)$	−7.04E + 08	−7.59E + 08	−7.86E + 08	−7.07E + 08	−6.80E + 08	−7.35E + 08	−6.58E + 08	−3.77E + 08	−2.22E + 08	−2.01E + 08	−1.23E + 08
NZL $(Y_f - Y_t) - (Y'_f - Y'_t)$	5.66E + 08	7.3E + 08	4.8E + 08	4.52E + 08	5.03E + 08	4.93E + 08	4.75E + 08	5.95E + 08	5.29E + 08	5.83E + 08	4.4E + 08
Group Two											
JAP $(Y_f - Y_t) - (Y'_f - Y'_t)$	8.84E + 10	1.17E + 11	1.19E + 11	9.76E + 10	1.07E + 11	9.2E + 10	6.66E + 10	6.31E + 10	6.62E + 10	1.03E + 11	1.18E + 11
KOR $(Y_f - Y_t) - (Y'_f - Y'_t)$	1.65E + 12	1.58E + 12	1.54E + 12	1.79E + 12	1.96E + 12	2.07E + 12	2.13E + 12	2.31E + 12	2.28E + 12	2.39E + 12	2.05E + 12
GBR $(Y_f - Y_t) - (Y'_f - Y'_t)$	4.67E + 09	4.65E + 09	4.27E + 09	2.95E + 09	2.35E + 09	2.01E + 09	1.7E + 09	1.52E + 09	1.4E + 09	1.69E + 09	1.69E + 09
USA $(Y_f - Y_t) - (Y'_f - Y'_t)$	5.29E + 10	4.34E + 10	3.8E + 10	2.78E + 10	2.12E + 10	1.84E + 10	1.5E + 10	1.26E + 10	1.12E + 10	4.64E + 10	2.17E + 10

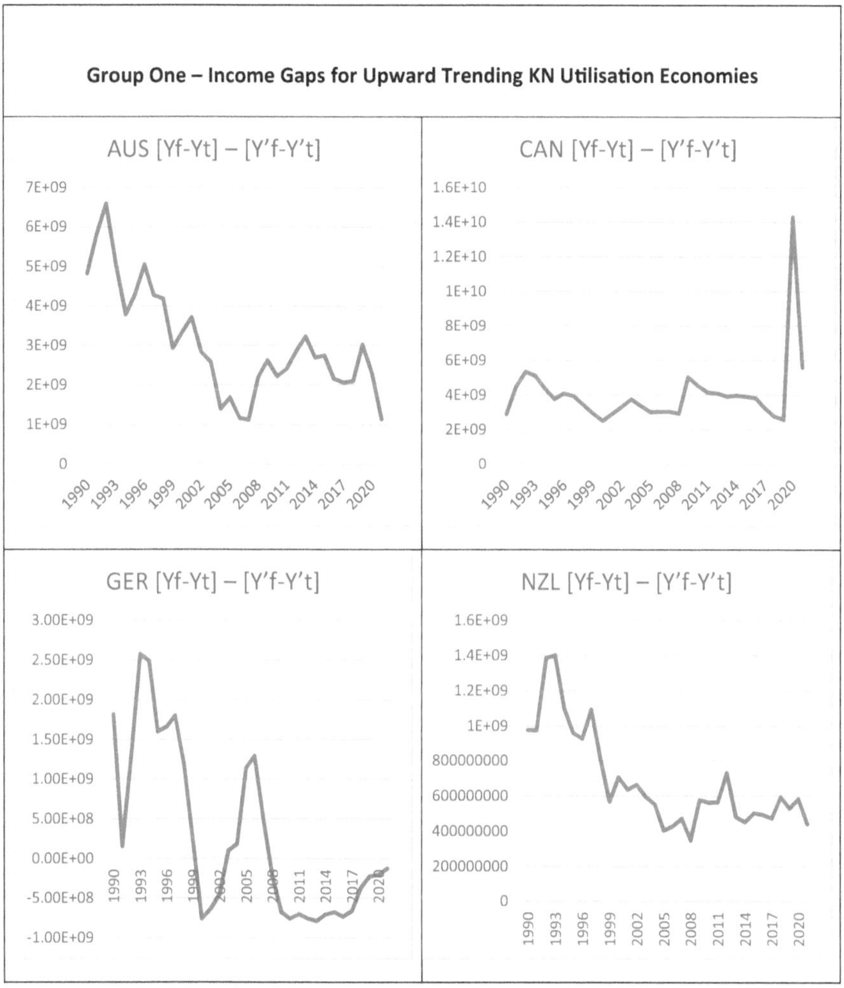

Figure 4.3 Income Gaps of the OECD Economies from 1990 to 2021.

4.6 Group Two – Income Gaps for Downward Trending KN Ulisaon Economies

Australia and New Zealand in Group One display an increase in KN utilisation. It is observed that the corresponding income gaps display a decreasing trend. Japan and Korea in Group Two show a decrease in KN utilisation. These economies can be classified as efficient since the income gap is rising with a corresponding low level of KN utilization. The corresponding income gaps for the two economies in Group Two display an upward trend. Unemployment levels across the same time period are decreasing for Australia and New

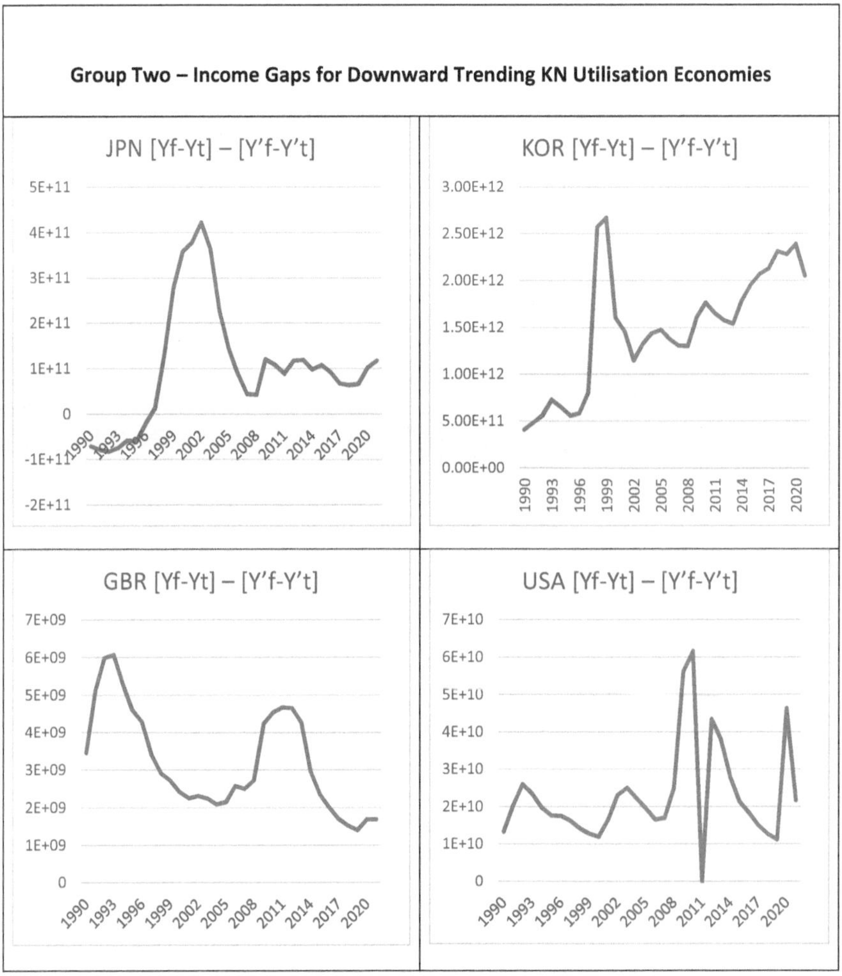

Figure 4.3 (continued)

Zealand (Group One economies) (see Figure 4.4). On the other hand, Japan and Korea (Group Two economies) display an increasing trend in the level of unemployment (see Figure 4.5).

The above discussion is summarised in Table 4.3. The utilisation of KN increases when the income gap and unemployment are decreased and vice-versa where the utilisation of KN is decreased when income gap and unemployment are increased.

Note that λ and λ' are the share of income to labour in both the two- and three-factor income models. And ϕ is the share of income to KN in the three-factor income model. The calculated values are shown in Table 4.4 for Group One and Two economies. The years 2009 and 2021 are chosen as they

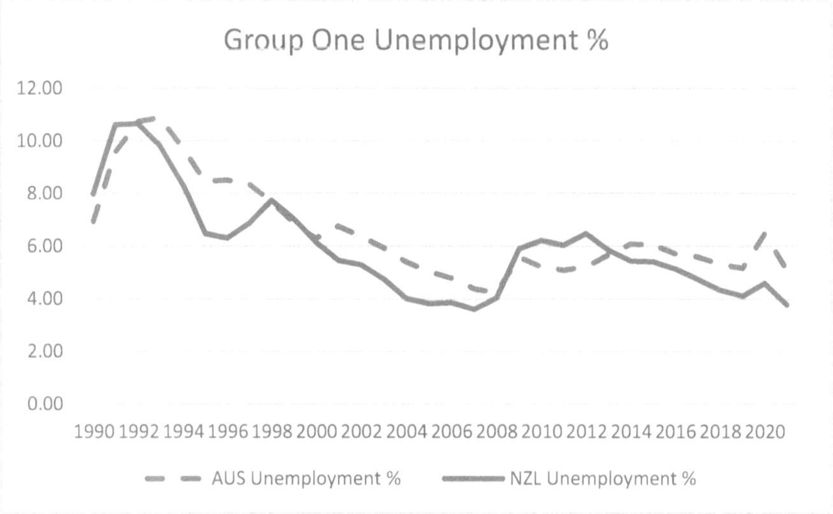

Figure 4.4 Unemployment Levels for Australia and New Zealand.

precede the GFC and COVID-19 pandemic; and it would be fitting to determine how economies restart after crises.

From Table 4.4, λ and λ' are in the range of 0.45 to 0.64, respectively. If the share of income to labour is higher than the other coefficients, that is the share of income to KM (θ and θ') and the share of income to KN (ϕ), then the economy relies more on L than on the other factor/s. Although the reliance on labour is more prominent in Group One increasing KN utilisation economies, the share of income to labour is falling as Australia and New Zealand relies more on capital stock KM as its share of income with rising θ and θ'. For Group Two economies with decreasing KN utilisation, Japan and Korea's share of income to labour remains high with lower dependence on capital stock as its share of income. Therefore, labour productivity, wage policy, and initiatives towards increasing the economy's capacity are key determinants to ensuring that employment levels are maintained. And these policies are especially critical as economies recover from crises, such as, the GFC and COVID-19 pandemic.

The range for ϕ in the sample of economies lies between 0.03 and 0.07. This range suggests that the share of income to KN is low relative to L. Note that the low estimated value (0.03) of ϕ is for Japan for both years of 2009 and 2021. Australia has the relatively higher estimated value (0.07 and 0.04) of ϕ for 2009 and 2021. Japan is environmentally efficient, with a rising level of income but high unemployment. Australia is not environmentally efficient because KN utilisation is rising with falling level of income and low unemployment. This is likely to result in capacity constraints for Australia and can potentially lead to rising prices. Although Japan is less likely to face capacity

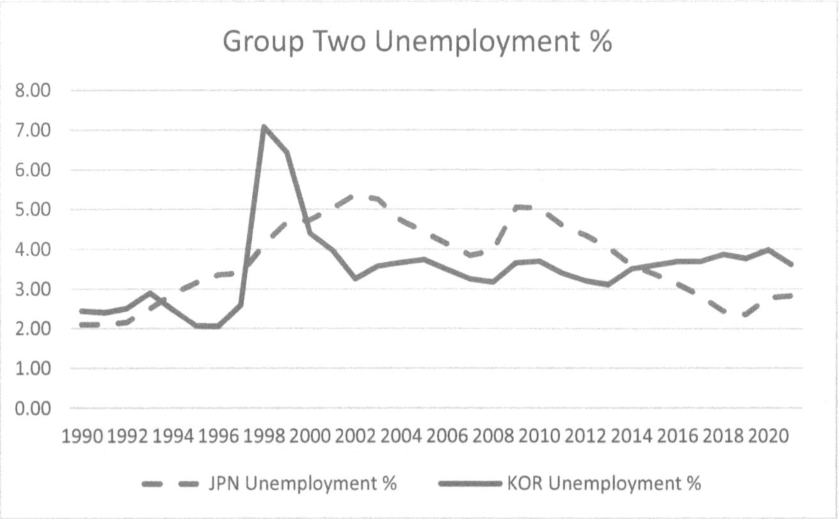

Figure 4.5 Unemployment Levels for Japan and Korea.

Table 4.3 Trends of KN Utilisation, Income Gap, and Unemployment for Group One and Two Economies

Group	*KN utilisation*	*Income gap*	*Unemployment*
One (AUS and NZL)	Increasing	Decreasing	Decreasing
Two (JPN and KOR)	Decreasing	Increasing	Increasing

Table 4.4 Share of Income to Labour (λ and λ') in Both the Two- and Three-Factor Income Model

	λ_{2009}	λ_{2021}	λ'_{2009}	λ'_{2021}	θ_{2009}	θ_{2021}	θ'_{2009}	θ'_{2021}	ϕ_{2009}	ϕ_{2021}
Group One (increasing KN utilisation)										
AUS	0.64	0.50	0.58	0.47	0.36	0.50	0.35	0.48	0.07	0.04
NZL	0.50	0.49	0.45	0.46	0.50	0.51	0.49	0.50	0.06	0.04
Group Two (decreasing KN utilisation)										
JPN	0.54	0.57	0.51	0.55	0.46	0.43	0.46	0.42	0.03	0.03
KOR	0.48	0.53	0.45	0.50	0.52	0.47	0.50	0.45	0.05	0.05

constraints, its high level of unemployment (close to one million in absolute numbers compared to Australia) suggests that targeted labour fiscal policies would prioritise over monetary policies aimed at prices.

The capacity of an economy and the level of employment will be discussed in Chapters 5 and 6.

4.7 Conclusion

This chapter introduced the three-factor income model, which includes KN as a consideration for economic growth. Issues pertaining to economic growth are of interest because they concern a nation's wealth and its people. Traditionally, such an expected growth path does not consider KN. If KN was considered in this growth model, the plausibility of a variation in the path of the economy cannot be ruled out. Economic progress is based on the propensity to save, capital accumulation, population growth rate, and the expected growth path that an economy would take. Policy decisions are made depending on where an economy is expected to be in the future. Unfortunately, these same policy decisions tend to be made without consideration to KN. There will be changes in income from the internalisation of KN. In Chapter 5, the Swan–Solow growth model will be used to show how KN affects Y and how KN will alter the steady state from k^{*} (in the standard macroeconomic model) to k^{**} (in the EM model).

Chapters 5 and 6 will focus on long-run and short-run analyses as these discussions form the basis for policy formulation.

References

Ackerman, F., Stanton, E. A., DeCanio, S. J., Goodstein, E., Howarth, R. B., Norgaard, R. B., Norman, C. S., Sheeran, K. A. (2009), "The economics of 350: The benefits and costs of climate stabilization", *Economics for Equity and the Environment Network.*

Baxter, M., King, R. G. (1999), "Measuring business cycles: Approximate band-pass filters for economic time series", *Review of Economics and Statistics*, 81(4), pp. 575–593.

Bonefeld, W., Burnham, P. (1996), "1990–1992: Britain and the politics of the European exchange rate mechanism", *Capital and Class*, 20(3), pp. 5–38.

Daly, H. E. (1997), "Georgescu-Roegen versus Solow/Stiglitz – Forum", *Ecological Economics*, 22, pp. 261–266.

Eurostat(1995), *European System of Accounts*, Eurostat, Germany, ISBN: 92-827-7954-8.

Hartwick, J. M. (1978), "Investing returns from depleting renewable stocks and intergenerational equity", *Economics Letters*, 1(1), pp. 85–88.

Hartwick, J. M. (1991), "Degradation of environmental capital and national accounting procedures", *European Economic Review*, 35(2–3), pp. 642–649.

Hartwick, J. M. (1997), "Paying down the environmental debt", *Land Economics*, 73(4), pp. 508–515.

Hope, C. W. (2011), "The Social Cost of CO2 from the PAGE09 Model", Economics, Discussion Paper 2011-39.

Karstad, P. I. (2012), "The Price on Carbon should Increase", *Statoil Innovate Blog*, 24 April 2012.

Nordhaus, W. D., Tobin, J. (1972), *Economic Growth, National Bureau of Economic Research*, Columbia University Press, New York, United States of America.

Nordhaus, W. D. (1992), "Lethal Model II: The limits to growth revisited," *Brooking Papers on Economic Activity*, 1992(2), pp. 1–59.

Nordhaus, W. D. (2017), "Revisiting the social cost of carbon", *Proceedings of the National Academy of Sciences*, 114(7), pp. 1518–1523.

Solow, R. M. (1986), "On the intergenerational allocation of natural resources", *The Scandinavian Journal of Economics*, 88(1), pp. 141–149.

Stern, N. H. (2007), *The Economics of Climate Change: The Stern Review*, Cambridge University Press, Cambridge, The United Kingdom.

Tan, S. (2016), "Framework for valuing the utilisation of the environment", *International Journal of Social Economics*, 43(6), pp. 619–642.

Tan, S., Thampapillai, D. J. (2011), "Assessment of fiscal intervention measures in China: Perspectives from environmental macroeconomics", in Kreise, L., Sirisom, J., Ashiabor, H., Milne, J. E. (eds), *Critical Issues in Environmental Taxation, Volume IX, Environmental Taxation in China and Asia-Pacific – Achieving Environmental Sustainability through Fiscal Policy*, Edward Elgar, United Kingdom, pp. 55–65.

Thampapillai, D. J. (2012), "Macroeconomics versus Environmental-Macroeconomics", *Australian Journal of Agricultural and Resource Economics*, 55, pp. 1–16.

Thampapillai, D. J., Sinden, J. (2012), *Environmental-Macroeconomics, Environmental Economics: Concepts, Methods and Policies*, Oxford University Press, Australia.

World Bank (2023), World Development Indicators, On-Line Edition.

5 Steady States of the Standard and Environmental-Macroeconomics Models

5.1 Introduction

Issues pertaining to economic growth are of interest because they concern an economy's wealth and its people. Traditionally, such an expected growth path does not consider environmental capital (KN). If KN was considered in a growth model, the plausibility of a variation in the path of the economy cannot be ruled out. Economic progress hinges on the propensity to save, capital accumulation, population growth rate, and the expected growth path that an economy would take. Corresponding policy decisions are made subject to where an economy is expected to be in the future – with no consideration to KN.

In this chapter, the Swan–Solow growth model will be used to show how KN affects income and how KN will alter the steady state from k^* (in the standard macroeconomic model) to k^{**} [in the environmental-macroeconomics (EM) model]. An economy's capacity is considered in terms of the steady-state equilibrium (SSE) as explained in the early neoclassical work of Solow (1956) and Swan (1956). The choice of the neoclassical growth model is favoured for reasons of illustrative convenience especially in terms of the analytics of point estimate. Furthermore, it is also noteworthy that the endogenous formulation (Romer, 1986) is based on the neoclassical Swan–Solow (1956) framework.

The focus of this chapter is on the long-term analysis of both standard macroeconomic model and the EM model. The standard macroeconomic model is based on the Cobb–Douglas (C-D) factor utilisation function. And the EM model is based on a three-factor utilisation function, the third factor being KN. The steady states will be operationalised for the same group of selected Organisation for Economic Co-operation and Development (OECD) economies (which KN was empirically measured for). The long-run analysis of the model discussed will be made with respect to the steady-state ratios of the OECD economies. Based on the discussion, an economy can either operate with excess capacity available, at beyond capacity, or at steady state. The capacity available in an economy can be determined by how an economy's long-term macroeconomic goals (output, employment, and inflation) are

DOI: 10.4324/9781003002550-5

addressed, such as, which goal(s) (if any) have priority or whether all the goals have equal precedence.

This chapter is structured with the next section on a discussion on SSE, followed by an empirical illustration of SSE on the selected OECD economies studied in Chapter 4. A comparison of SSE between k^* (in the standard macroeconomic model) and k^{**} (in the EM model) will ensue. The chapter concludes with how the availability of capacity in an economy can be determined by long-term macroeconomic goals.

5.2 Steady-State Equilibrium (SSE)

The SSE in the Swan–Solow framework is the amount of capital accumulated that is just sufficient to meet the needs of capital (KM) depreciation and the entry of new workers. Capital accumulation is assumed to emerge directly from savings. In other words, savings (S) is equal to investment (I), S = I. Furthermore, the pertinent variables in the framework are described in per worker terms. These variables are as follows:

i Capital per worker $k = \left[\frac{KM}{L}\right]$ (5.1)

ii Savings per worker $s = \left[\frac{S}{L}\right]$ (5.2)

iii Output per worker $y = \left[\frac{Y}{L}\right]$ (5.3)

The two-factor [Y = f (KM, L)] C-D model is used to explain the relationship between k and y; and between k and s. That is,

$$y = \alpha k^{\theta} \tag{5.4}$$

$$s = \alpha \rho k^{6} \tag{5.5}$$

where α is the total factor productivity (TFP) and ρ is the savings rate per worker.

The SSE can be derived in terms of a point estimate as:

$$\left[\frac{KM}{L}\right]^{*} = \left[\frac{\rho\alpha}{\delta + \eta}\right]^{\frac{1}{1-\theta}} \tag{5.6}$$

This scenario is illustrated in Figure 5.1.

In Figure 5.1, the curve labelled y = f (k) shows how the output per worker (y = Y/L) increases when the capital per worker (k = KM/L) is increased.

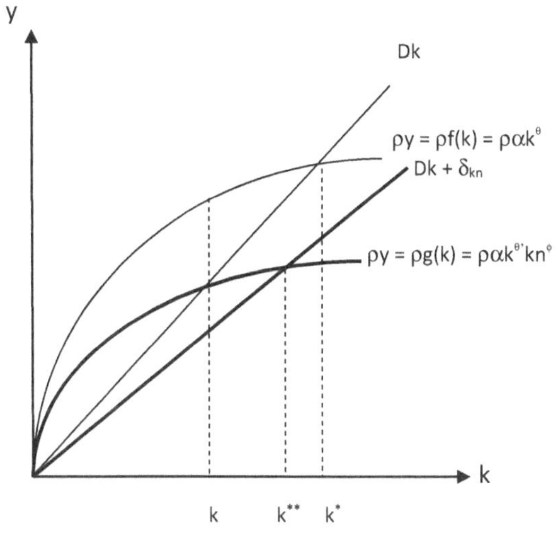

Figure 5.1 Steady-State Equilibrium of Two-Factor C-D Model (k^*) and Three-Factor Model (k^{**}).

When y = f (k) is multiplied by the savings ratio (ρ), the curve $\rho\alpha k^{\theta}$ is the result. The straight line from the origin describes the amount of KM stock replacement that is required for the depreciation of existing KM. It corresponds to the equation Dk, where (D = δ + η), δ is the rate of KM depreciation, and η is the rate of entry of new workers. The point of intersection between the straight-line Dk and the curve describing savings $\rho\alpha k^{\theta}$ is the SSE, k^*. The SSE is defined by the quantity of KM per worker as shown in equation (5.3). The derivation of the SSE is presented in Appendix 5.1 of this chapter. Comparing k^* and k, k is the current level of KM per worker.

When the three-factor [Y = g (KM, L, KN)] model is used, there will be one more variable in addition to the three variables (5.1, 5.2, 5.3) discussed earlier. The result is the KN per worker, kn = (KN/L). Because KN is measured on the same scale as KM (assumed), it can be costed and depreciated in the same way as KM. In this revised model, the curve (**bold**) $\rho\alpha k^{\theta'}kn^{\phi}$ is the result when y = g (k) is multiplied by the savings ratio (ρ). Please refer to Figure 5.1. With a new variable kn, there is a new parameter ϕ which is the share of income that accrues to KN. The straight line (**bold**) from the origin corresponds to the equation Dk + δ_{kn}, where δ_{kn} is the depreciation of KN. The SSE is the point of intersection between the straight line Dk + δ_{kn} and the curve $\rho\alpha k^{\theta'}kn^{\phi}$. The SSE is defined by the quantity for KM per worker:

$$\left[\frac{KM}{L}\right]^{**} = \left[\frac{\rho\alpha\gamma^{\phi}}{D + \gamma\delta_{KN}}\right]^{\frac{1}{1-\theta'-\phi}} \qquad (5.7)$$

The derivation of the revised SSE is presented in Appendix 5.2 of this chapter.

It is apparent from Figure 5.1 that there are changes to the SSE. In the two-factor C-D model, the current level of k and the SSE is (k, k^*). Comparing this model with the three-factor model, the respective levels are (k, k^{**}). SSE is reached earlier in the three-factor model relative to the two-factor model because allowance has been made for KN. It is now fitting to compare the observed trend of k with the SSE. Let's consider three possible scenarios. For scenario A, the economy's observed level of capital accumulation is lower than that required for the SSE $(k < k^*)$, that is $(k^* / k) > 1$. The economy is experiencing savings surplus and is under-utilising its available resources. There is capacity available in the economy. In scenario B, the economy's observed level of capital accumulation exceeds the SSE $(k > k^*)$ and $(k^*/k) < 1$. In this context, the economy is experiencing a savings deficit and is over-utilising its available resources. The economy may be over-capitalised and have a possibility of rising inflation. In scenario C, the economy is at the SSE $(k = k^*)$ and $(k^*/k) = 1$.

Please see Table 5.1 for the definition of these contexts.

For an illustration of the SSE for both the two-factor and three-factor model, the following data were used:

- i ρ is estimated as the savings rate per worker
- ii α is the TFP
- iii δ is the rate of depreciation of KM
- iv η is the entry of new workers into the workforce (or the annual growth of labour)
- v γ is KN as a factor of KM
- vi δ_{KN} is the depreciation of KN which is estimated using a method outlined in Thampapillai and Hanf (2000). Here P_{KN} is defined as $(\phi Y/KN)$. Recall from Chapter 4 that ϕ is the share of Y that accrues to KN. Then δ_{KN} is $(P_{KN} - i_{KN})$ and is based on the premise that the price of any capital is the sum of the interest rate and the depreciation. As in Thampapillai and Hanf (2000), the interest rate was assumed to be the same as that of KM.

Next, the following steps were used to estimate the SSE values of capital accumulation prevailing at k^* and k^{**}:

Table 5.1 Three Different Scenarios for the Economy

Scenarios	*Accumulated capital stock relative to SSE in both two-factor (k*) and three-factor models (k**)*	*State of the economy*
A	$(k^*/k) > 1/(k^{**}/k) > 1$	Excess Capacity
B	$(k^*/k) < 1/(k^{**}/k) < 1$	Beyond Capacity
C	$(k^*/k) = 1/(k^{**}/k) = 1$	Steady State

i From the Swan–Solow model, k is estimated as KM per worker employed, that is (KM/L)

ii Equation (4.10) is used to estimate the initial size of the capital stock for the first year. Equation (4.11) is used to estimate the size of the capital stock for subsequent years. The C-D factor utilisation function, which displays constant returns, is a valid descriptor of the distribution of Y between KM and L, in other words $Y = \alpha KM^{\theta}L^{\lambda}$. Hence, the TFP is

$$\alpha = [Y/(KM^{\theta}L^{\lambda})] \tag{5.8}$$

iii Based on the Swan–Solow model of economic growth and using information gathered from the steps above, the estimated steady-state value of KM per worker $[KM/L]^*$ or k^* is defined as (see Appendix 5.1 for workings):

$$\left[\frac{KM}{L}\right]^* = \left[\frac{\rho\alpha}{\delta+\eta}\right]^{\frac{1}{1-\theta}} \tag{5.9}$$

where δ, the rate of depreciation of KM is 1/30 because KM is assumed to have a lifespan of 30 years. The variable η is the entry of new workers into the workforce (or the annual growth of labour). The savings rate (ρ) per worker and the national savings (S) are defined as S = GDP – C – G and ρ = (S/GDP). Here, α is as shown in equation (5.1).

iv With the measurement for KN derived in Chapter 4, a steady state for the three-factor utilisation function can be obtained. The steady-state k^{**} is the following (see Appendix 5.2 for workings):

$$\left[\frac{KM}{L}\right]^{**} = \left[\frac{\rho\alpha\gamma^{\phi}}{D+\gamma\delta_{KN}}\right]^{\frac{1}{1-\theta'-\phi}} \tag{5.10}$$

The new parameters in equation (5.10) are the following: ϕ is the share of Y that accrues to KN; D is a constant, that is (δ + η); γ = KN/KM, where KN is a factor of KM; and δ_{KN} is the depreciation of KN.

In summary, the steady states for the C-D factor utilisation function (k^*) and the three-factor utilisation function (k^{**}) and the estimation of KN are reproduced in Table 5.2.

The standard macroeconomic model will be based on the C-D factor utilisation function with k^* as the steady state. The EM model will be based on the three-factor (KN internalised) utilisation function with k^{**} as the steady state. Economic models are meaningful only if they are applied. Both the standard macroeconomic model and the EM model (based on the three-factor utilisation function) are now established with their SSE. The next section will

Table 5.2 Steady States k*, k**, and Environmental Capital

	Estimation of variables
Two-factor (k*)	$\left[\frac{KM}{L}\right]^{*} = \left[\frac{\rho\alpha}{\delta+\eta}\right]^{\frac{1}{1-\theta}}$
Three-factor (k)**	$\left[\frac{KM}{L}\right]^{**} = \left[\frac{\rho\alpha\gamma^{\phi}}{D+\gamma\delta_{KN}}\right]^{\frac{1}{1-\theta'-\phi}}$
KN	$KN = KM^{\frac{\theta-\theta'}{\phi}} L^{\frac{\lambda-\lambda'}{\phi}}$

operationalise both models via time-series empirical results on selected OECD economies.

5.3 Empirical Illustration of Steady-State Equilibrium

The standard macroeconomic model and the EM model were operationalised for eight selected OECD economies. The economies are Australia, Canada, Germany, Japan, Korea, New Zealand, the United Kingdom, and the USA. The OECD database was used because it had a complete set of national income accounts (expenditure and income accounts) from 1990 to 2021.

The following approach is used to analyse the data. The year 1990 is the initial period and 2021 is the terminal period which gives a time-series of 32 years. The observed period includes several crises, such as, the 1990 oil shock, 1997 Asian Financial Crisis (AFC), dot-com bust in 2000, 2007–2008 financial crisis or the Global Financial Crisis (GFC), and COVID-19 which made varying contextual impacts to the OECD economies studied. The years 2009 and 2021 were followed immediately and respectively from a financial crisis (the GFC) and a pandemic (COVID-19). Using 2009 and 2021 as the years for comparison is appropriate because both were years that immediately followed an exogenous shock. Thus, 2009 is used as the base year for comparison and 2021 is used as the current state of the economy. The current state of the economy in 2021 will dictate its subsequent trajectory into the future and offer an expectation of how economies would react.

The selected economies are classified according to the state of affairs in both the initial and terminal periods. From Table 5.1, there are three possible scenarios: Scenario A, in which there is excess capacity, with $(k^*/k) > 1$; scenario B, in which the economy is operating beyond capacity, with $(k^*/k) < 1$; and scenario C, in which the economy is operating at its steady state, with $(k^*/k) = 1$. A comparison is made to each economy for 2009 as well as 2021 with respect to the scenario that it is in. This comparison is conducted for both steady-state ratios of the standard model (k^*/k) and the EM model (k^{**}/k).

Empirical Results

The empirical results of the standard macroeconomic (k^*/k) model and the EM (k^{**}/k) model are presented in Tables 5.3 and 5.5. The observation is made depending on whether an economy is operating with excess capacity (k^*/k) > 1 or beyond capacity (k^*/k) < 1. The significance being in determining if the steady state of an economy has changed or stayed the same post an exogenous shock. This comparison is made for the time periods of 2009 and 2021. Table 5.3 shows the steady-state ratios of the economies based on the standard model (k^*/k).

Based on Table 5.3, the selected economies can be categorised into four broad groups in Table 5.4.

Economies in Group One and Group Two remained in the same capacity state over both time periods; after both crises, Group One economies appear to be operating at beyond capacity while the result for those in Group Two being excess capacity. None of the economies falls into Group Three. Based

Table 5.3 Standard Macroeconomic Steady-State Ratio (k^*/k) of Economies in 2009 and 2021

Economies/Year (Grouped based on capacity)	*2009*		*2021*	
	(k^*/k) > 1 (Excess Capacity)	(k^*/k) < 1 (Beyond Capacity)	(k^*/k) > 1 (Excess Capacity)	(k^*/k) < 1 (Beyond Capacity)
Australia		✓	✓	
Japan		✓		✓
New Zealand		✓		✓
United Kingdom		✓		✓
USA		✓		✓
Canada	✓		✓	
Germany	✓		✓	
Korea	✓		✓	

Table 5.4 Categorising Economies Based on the Steady-State Ratio (k^*/k) of Economies in 2009 and 2021 for the Standard Macroeconomic Model

Group	*2009*	*2021*	*Economies*
One	(k^*/k) < 1 (Beyond Capacity)	(k^*/k) < 1 (Beyond Capacity)	Japan, New Zealand, United Kingdom, USA
Two	(k^*/k) > 1 (Excess Capacity)	(k^*/k) > 1 (Excess Capacity)	Canada, Germany, Korea
Three	(k^*/k) > 1 (Excess Capacity)	(k^*/k) < 1 (Beyond Capacity)	N.A.
Four	(k^*/k) < 1 (Beyond Capacity)	(k^*/k) > 1 (Excess Capacity)	Australia

on the standard macroeconomic model, it can be argued that Australia is the only economy that had changes in their economic capacity as a result of an exogenous shock. Australia operated beyond capacity after the GFC and had excess capacity post-COVID-19.

When KN is internalised in the standard macroeconomic model, the model is revised to the EM model. Table 5.5 shows the steady-state ratios of the economies based on the EM model.

Based on Table 5.5, the selected economies can also be categorised into four broad groups in Table 5.6.

Economies in Group One and Group Two remained in the same capacity state over both time periods: after both crises Group One economies (Japan, New Zealand, United Kingdom, and the USA) appear to be operating at beyond capacity while the result for Group Two with only one economy (Korea) being one of excess capacity. Australia, Canada, and Germany in Group Four moved from operating with beyond capacity to excess capacity and, based on the EM model, were the only economies with economic changes

Table 5.5 Environmental-Macroeconomics Steady-State Ratio (k^{**}/k) of Economies in 2009 and 2021

Economies/Year (Grouped based on capacity)	*2009*		*2021*	
	$(k^{**}/k) > 1$ (Excess Capacity)	$(k^{**}/k) < 1$ (Beyond Capacity)	$(k^{**}/k) > 1$ (Excess Capacity)	$(k^{**}/k) < 1$ (Beyond Capacity)
Australia		✓	✓	
Canada		✓	✓	
Germany		✓	✓	
Japan		✓		✓
New Zealand		✓		✓
United Kingdom		✓		✓
USA		✓		✓
Korea	✓		✓	

Table 5.6 Categorising Economies Based on the Steady-State Ratio (k^{**}/k) of Economies in 2009 and 2021 for the Environmental-Macroeconomics Model

Group	*2009*	*2021*	*Economies*
One	$(k^{**}/k) < 1$ (Beyond Capacity)	$(k^{**}/k) < 1$ (Beyond Capacity)	Japan, New Zealand, United Kingdom, USA
Two	$(k^{**}/k) > 1$ (Excess Capacity)	$(k^{**}/k) > 1$ (Excess Capacity)	Korea
Three	$(k^{**}/k) > 1$ (Excess Capacity)	$(k^{**}/k) < 1$ (Beyond Capacity)	N.A.
Four	$(k^{**}/k) < 1$ (Beyond Capacity)	$(k^{**}/k) > 1$ (Excess Capacity)	Australia, Canada, Germany

in capacity where they operated beyond capacity after the GFC and had excess capacity post COVID-19.

There appears to be a degree of consistency for five of the economies studied where Group One economies (Japan, New Zealand, United Kingdom, and the USA) and Group Four (Australia) remained the same across both the standard macroeconomic and the EM models. However, the grouping of the economies changed for Group Two when the EM model was used as opposed to the standard macroeconomic model (Tables 5.4 and 5.6). Whilst Korea remained in Group Two across both models, Canada and Germany moved from Group Two in the standard macroeconomic model to Group Four in the EM model. The inconsistency of such observations between the two models suggests the plausibility of policy domains being incorrectly identified should the standard macroeconomic model be employed.

The above discussion was based on the steady state of the economy in 2009 and 2021. For a better appreciation of the differences when the EM model is applied, the following sub-section shows the presentation of the economies from the time period 2009 to 2021. In the steady state, k^* (of the standard macroeconomic model) will always be greater than k^{**} (of the EM model). This scenario causes two different steady states when comparing the standard macroeconomic model and the EM model.

5.4 Standard Macroeconomic Model versus Environmental-Macroeconomics Model

The selected OECD economies are graphed using the steady-state ratios of $[(k^*/k), (k^{**}/k)]$. Please refer to Table 5.1 for a description of what each of the ratios represents. The ratios are obtained for all of the selected OECD economies over the time period of 1990 to 2021. Both ratios $[(k^*/k), (k^{**}/k)]$ are graphed on the same X-Y plot, with the steady-state ratio on the vertical axis and time on the horizontal axis. This strategy allows for a comparison between the two ratios across the two different models. The following shows the economies grouped according to the trends displayed.

All of the selected OECD economies shown in Figure 5.2 show that the ratio of (k^{**}/k) in the EM model will always reach a steady state earlier than the ratio of (k^*/k) in the standard macroeconomic model. The line of (k^{**}/k) is always below that of (k^*/k) which shows that the capacity of an economy can be overstated if KN is not taken into consideration. Although this observation has been reviewed for the past 31 years, it does present to the policymaker either one of two possible paths that an economy could have taken at the time of policymaking, viz: the path that was (k^*/k) versus the path that should have been (k^{**}/k).

The long-run analysis of the model discussed in this section has been made with respect to the steady-state ratios of the selected OECD economies. Based on the discussion, an economy can either operate with excess capacity available, at beyond capacity, or at steady state. The capacity available in an economy can

Group One – Upward Linear Trends with Spare Capacity

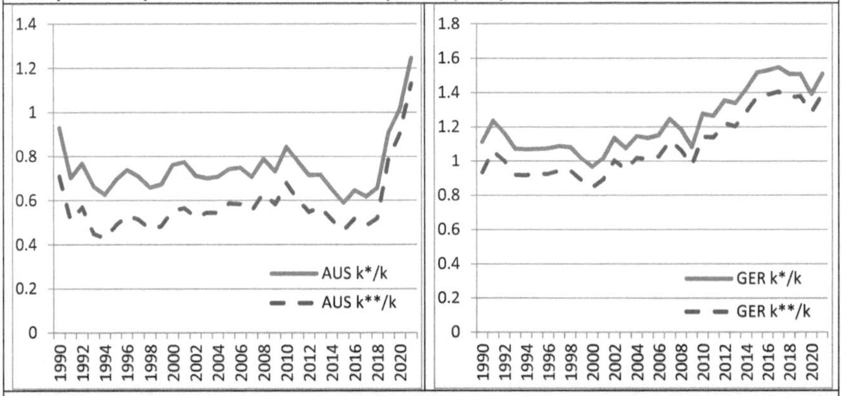

Australia and Germany are two economies that are displaying upward linear trends with capacity to spare (the ratio is more than one). During the observed period, the Australian economy is operating beyond capacity (the ratio is less than one) but building up capacity as it trends towards spare capacity; whereas the German economy starts with spare capacity and continue to build more capacity.

Germany tended towards steady state (a ratio value of one) in the EM model till 2009 and build more capacity for rest of period. However, the Australian economy remains at beyond capacity (at a ratio of less than one) in the EM model for most of the observed period.

These economies demonstrate a convergence of both standard macroeconomic model and EM model during the oil shock (1990) and COVID-19 for Australia (2020), and the GFC (2009) and COVID-19 (2020) for Germany.

Group Two - Upward Linear Trends Beyond Capacity

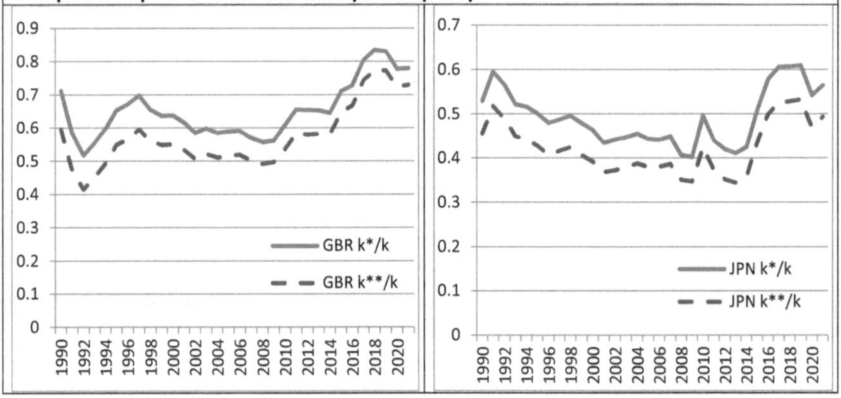

Figure 5.2 Grouping of Economies Based on the Steady-State Ratios of (k^*/k) and (k^{**}/k).

Both the United Kingdom (GBR) and Japanese economies are operating beyond capacity (a ratio of less than one). The GBR economy is scaling closer towards steady state (a ratio value of one) relative to the Japanese economy which continued to linger at beyond capacity at start and end of observed period.

There is an observed convergence of both GBR graphs till end of observed period with snapshot convergence at start (1990 oil shock) and end (2020 COVID-19) of period. The Japanese graphs appear to only converge during the 1990 oil shock, GFC (2010), and subsequent recessions through to 2015.

Group Three – Cyclical Trends with Spare Capacity

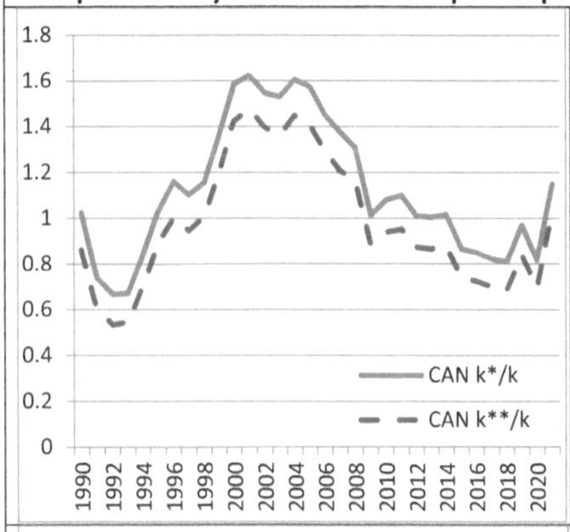

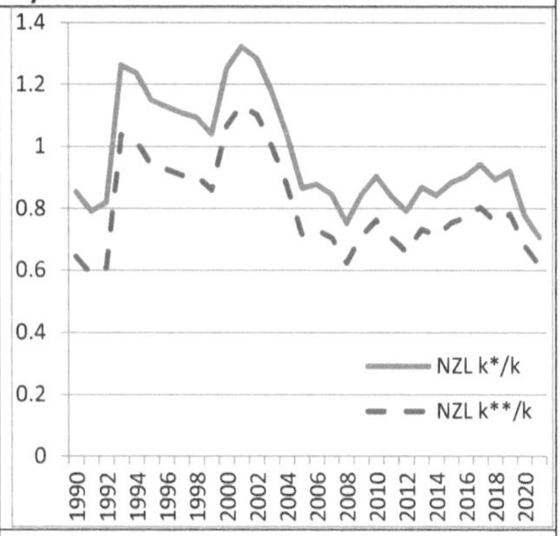

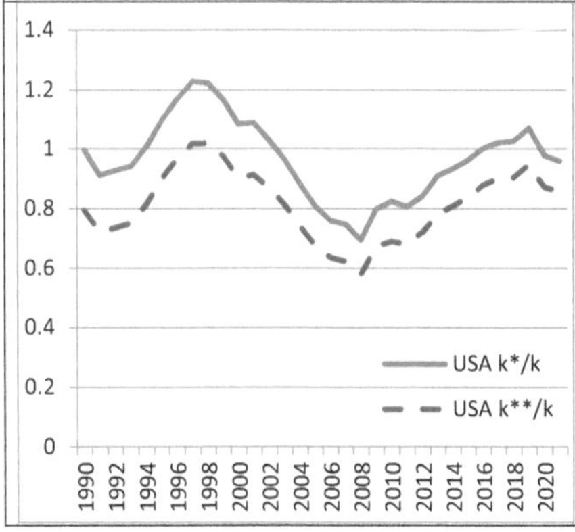

The three economies of Canada, New Zealand and the US displayed similar cyclical trends where the standard model operated with spare capacity (a ratio of greater than one) between 1990 to 2009 (2002 for the US and 2005 for New Zealand) before tapering from steady state (a ratio value of one). All but Canada finished the observed period beyond capacity (a ratio of less than one).

The EM model is closely mapped to the standard macroeconomic model for Canada and New Zealand with observed convergence during the 1990 oil shock, GFC, and COVID-19 (2020).

Figure 5.2 (continued)

be determined by how an economy's long-term macroeconomic goals (inflation, employment, and per capita GDP) are addressed such as which goal(s) (if any) have priority or whether all the goals have equal precedence. The next section will revisit some of the key points that relate to long-run macroeconomic goals.

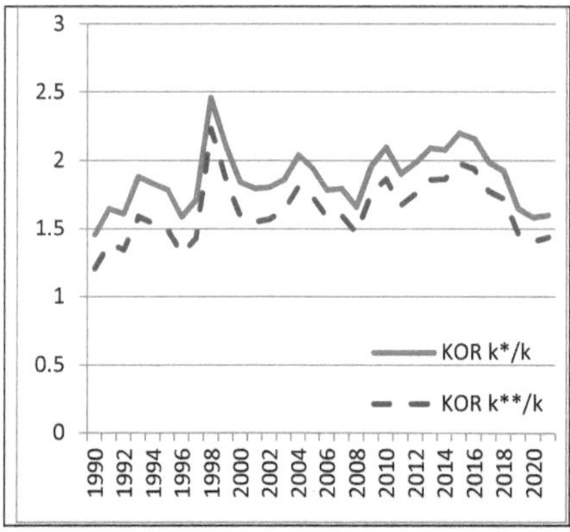

The Korean economy is the sole operator with spare capacity (a ratio of greater than one) and is the highest observed ratio value amongst all eight OECD economies throughout the observed period.

The EM model is very closely mapped to its standard macroeconomic model with strong convergence during 1997 AFC, dot-com bust in 2000, GFC, and COVID-19 (2020).

Figure 5.2 (continued)

5.5 Long-Run Macroeconomic Goals of Gross Domestic Product (GDP), Employment, and Inflation

As demonstrated by the empirical results presentation, macroeconomic goals ought to be properly reviewed and adjusted according to the immediate priorities of an economy. This task is especially critical if there is a chance that policy ranges are not correctly identified. This chapter will conclude with a re-examination of the long-run macroeconomic goals of output, employment, and inflation, which was first discussed in Chapter 1.

Before discussing each of the long-run macroeconomic goals, it is important to differentiate the different time periods in macroeconomics. Please refer to Figure 5.3.

In the long run, an economy is focused on steady economic growth. In the short run, there will be cycles of booms and busts which over the long run are, however, expected to smooth over and result in steady economic growth. Reducing such volatility in the economy will instil confidence and will reduce uncertainty for investors and citizens alike. Effective surveillance and timely analysis of macroeconomic trends ensure that policies are shaped towards macroeconomic stability. Macroeconomic stability lies at the core of economic policy formulation in all economies. The macroeconomic trends that the policymakers are concerned with include the GDP, unemployment, inflation, budget deficits, and the balance of payments. For the purpose of this analysis, the focus will be on inflation, employment, and per capita GDP.

Inflation refers to the overall increase in the prices of goods and services in an economy and can be attributed to an increase in the quantity of money. Economists' definition of full employment could include a reference to existence of unemployment in terms of frictional and structural categories. This level of unemployment is an economy's natural rate of unemployment. Per capita GDP is the level of growth determined by the amount of goods and

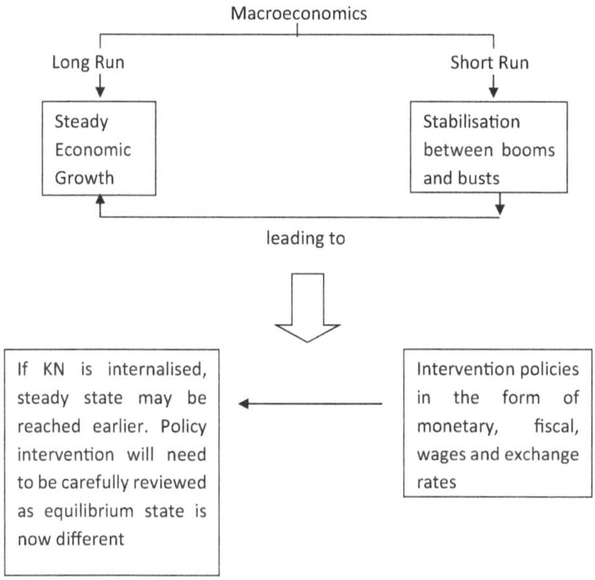

Figure 5.3 Long Run and Short Run of Macroeconomics.

services produced divided by the population of an economy. A higher level of GDP growth can translate to a higher level of living standard for the citizens. From the long-run analysis, the macroeconomic goals of inflation, employment, and per capita GDP can suffice to move an economy to steady state. However, by taking KN into consideration, a different steady state will arise. Hence, there should be an allowance for KN when considering sustainable development.

In the long run, an economy is expected to exhibit steady economic growth. The factor utilisation functions discussed in Chapter 4 are the compelling forces that drive this observation. The economics of growth or growth economics are of interest to policymakers. In an ideal situation, equilibrium in the long run would tend towards or be at a steady state. Economic growth would be exogenously determined, with capital accumulation becoming less significant, and technological progress becoming more dominant as a factor for economic growth. Technological progress is often measured by the Solow residual or the TFP. TFP is enhanced as new capital becomes more valuable than old capital. This is because new capital is based on new technology improving over time. Therefore, it can be argued that technological progress and other external factors may be the main sources of economic growth in the long run by being add-ons to steady-state changes, which invariably will affect macroeconomic goals in the long run.

According to Holt (2005), natural capital is based on a dynamic relation between a physical and a biotic environment (which can be unpredictable).

The Bruntland Report proposed a change in the exploitation process of resources that would be consistent with future as well as present needs. Hence, there should be moderation of the increase in economic growth. It is crucial to measure the effects of economic activities that are sustainable and resilient with the ecosystems and natural resources. Because of the level of uncertainty, it may be difficult to know the effects of economic growth on the resilience of the environment and natural resources (Holt, 2005).

The challenges for policymakers with respect to macroeconomic goals are as follows. First, is inflation set within acceptable levels for policies to be effective? Second, can greater employment be achieved without significantly impacting inflation? Third, how much is an economy allowed to grow? To sustain natural resources, reduce environmental degradation, and protect a fragile ecosystem for future generations, a steady state should consider KN in addition to the three macroeconomic goals. Sustainability is incorporated by focusing on the macroeconomic and policy outcomes, and on the uncertainties in an economy.

5.6 Conclusion

The aim of this chapter is to present a steady-state analysis of the standard macroeconomic model and the EM model. It has been demonstrated that the policy ranges can be incorrectly identified. In addition, the capacity of an economy can be overstated without appropriate consideration for KN. However, should KN be taken into consideration, there are two possible paths that an economy could take at the time of policymaking, namely, the path of the EM model and the path of the standard macroeconomic model. The operationalisation of the standard macroeconomic model and EM model is made on selected OECD economies to illustrate the difference in steady-state ratios between two identified time periods. That is, this illustration highlights if developed economies are operating at close to or beyond their capacities post an exogenous shock. In the long run, macroeconomic stability is central to economic policy formulation in all economies. Policy formulation must consider the capacity of an economy with respect to the long-run macroeconomic goals of maintaining inflation within an agreed band and ensuring low unemployment and a smooth GDP growth.

Chapter 6 will evaluate these macroeconomic goals with respect to the steady-state ratios of the selected OECD economies for both the standard macroeconomic model and the EM model.

References

Holt, R. P. F. (2005), "Post-Keynesian economics and sustainable development", *International Journal of Environment, Workplace and Employment*, 1(2), pp. 174–186.

Romer, P. M. (1986), "Increasing returns and long-run growth", *Journal of Political Economy*, 94(5), pp. 1002–1037.

Solow, R. M. (1956), "A contribution to the theory of economic growth", *Quarterly Journal of Economics*, 70(1), pp. 65–94.

Swan, T. W. (1956), "Economic Growth and Capital Accumulation", Economic Record, November, pp. 334–361.

Thampapillai, D. J., Hanf, C-H. (2000), "The internalization of environmental capital stocks into an aggregated cobb-douglas function", *Economic Analysis & Policy*, 30(2), pp. 209–215.

Appendix 5.1

C-D Production Function and Steady-State Values

The C-D function is one that displays constant returns to scale. In other words

$$Y = \alpha KM^{\theta} L^{1-\theta} \tag{5A.1}$$

Income, Y, is divided by L to express the equation in terms of the output per worker (Y/L) as a function of the capital per worker (KM/L):

$$y = \frac{Y}{L} = \alpha \frac{KM^{\theta} L^{1-\theta}}{L} = \alpha \left(\frac{KM}{L} \right)^{\theta} \tag{5A.2}$$

$$y = \alpha k^{\theta} \text{ where } k = \frac{KM}{L} \tag{5A.3}$$

The savings per worker is explained by multiplying (5A.3) by the savings ratio (ρ):

$$\rho y = \rho \alpha k^{\theta} \tag{5A.4}$$

Assume that there is a need for new workers and that depreciated capital must be replaced. The rate of entry of new workers is η, and the rate of depreciation is δ. The savings per worker is then defined as

$$\rho y = (\delta + \eta) k \tag{5A.5}$$

To solve for k^*, equate (5A.4) and (5A.5), as follows:

$$(\delta + \eta) k = \rho \alpha k^{\theta} \tag{5A.6}$$

Rearranging (5A.6),

$$k^{1-\theta} = \frac{\rho \alpha}{(\delta + \eta)} \tag{5A.7}$$

The steady-state value of k is

$$k^* = \left[\frac{\rho\alpha}{\delta + \eta}\right]^{\frac{1}{1-\theta}} \quad (5A.8)$$

Appendix 5.2
Revised C-D Production Function and Steady-State Values

The revised C-D function is one that displays constant returns to scale. In other words

$$Y. = \alpha k^{\theta'} L^{\lambda'} KN^{\phi} \quad (5A.9)$$

Income, Y, is divided by L to express the equation in terms of the output per worker (Y/L) as a function of the capital per worker (KM/L):

$$y = \frac{Y.}{L} = \alpha \frac{K^{\theta'} L^{\lambda'} KN}{L} = \alpha k^{\theta'} L^{\lambda'-1} KN^{\phi} \quad (5A.10)$$

For the index of L,

$$\theta' + \lambda' + \phi = 1, \lambda' = 1 - \theta' - \phi, \lambda' - 1 = -\theta' - \phi, \lambda' - 1 = -(\theta' + \phi)$$

Equation (5A.10) can be expressed as

$$y = \alpha k^{\theta'} L^{-(\theta'+\phi)} KN^{\phi} \quad (5A.11)$$

Rearranging (5A.11),

$$y = \frac{\alpha k^{\theta'} KN^{\phi}}{L^{\theta'+\phi}} = \frac{\alpha k^{\theta'} KN^{\phi}}{L^{\theta'} L^{\phi}} = \alpha \left(\frac{K}{L}\right)^{\theta'} \left(\frac{KN}{L}\right)^{\phi} \quad (5A.12)$$

$$y = \alpha k^{\theta'} kn^{\phi} \quad \text{where} \quad k = \frac{K}{L}, kn = \frac{KN}{L} \quad (5A.13)$$

The savings per worker is explained by multiplying (5A.13) by the savings ratio (ρ):

$$\rho y = \rho \alpha k^{\theta'} kn^{\phi} \quad (5A.14)$$

As shown in Appendix 5.1, the SSE k** can be defined by equating (5A.14) with the rate of entry of new workers η, the rate of capital depreciation δ, and the rate of environmental capital depreciation δkn:

$$\rho\alpha k^{\theta'} kn^{\phi} = (\delta + \eta)k + \delta_{kn} \tag{5A.15}$$

Because KN is costed and depreciated in the same way as KM, it can be expressed as a function of KM. In other words

$$kn = \gamma k \tag{5A.16}$$

Substituting (5A.16) into (5A.15)

$$\rho\alpha k^{\theta'} (\gamma k)^{\phi} = Dk + \delta(\gamma k) \tag{5A.17}$$

where D = δ + η
Rearranging (5A.17),

$$\frac{k}{k^{\theta'+\phi}} = k^{1-\theta'-\phi} = \frac{\rho\alpha\gamma^{\phi}}{D + \delta\gamma} \tag{5A.18}$$

The steady-state value of k is

$$k^{**} = \left[\frac{\rho\alpha\gamma^{\phi}}{D + \gamma\delta_{KN}}\right]^{\frac{1}{1-\theta'-\phi}} \tag{5A.19}$$

6 Macroeconomic Goals and Steady States, Short-Run Policy Analysis

A Methodology

6.1 Introduction

Steady-state analysis gauges an economy's future performance. As an economy continues to be in a state of flux (with no comparative guidance), a desired long-run state would guide short-run equilibrium macroeconomic goals of output, employment, and inflation, and in turn, sustainability with respect to steady-state equilibrium (SSE). The long run comprises of many short runs; snapshots in the short run allow for policy formulation that would stabilise an economy in the long run. This chapter presents the methodology for analysing how macroeconomic goals are affected by the SSE.

The objective is to provide a basis for evaluating the relationship between SSE and the macroeconomic goals (policy variables of output, employment, and inflation); and of the fact that SSE can explain or account for such goals. Therefore, the independent variable is SSE and the dependent variables are the macroeconomic goals. This relationship will be tested with both the standard macroeconomic model and the environmental-macroeconomic (EM) model to determine if the relationship differs depending on which model is used. An explanatory relationship will be formalised between the macroeconomic goals and the SSE for the eight selected OECD economies.

Panel regression will be used as an approach to explore relationships between the independent and dependent variables. For economies that cannot be explained using panel regression, linear regression will be used to explain such relationships. Snapshots for years 2009 and 2021 of the economies for both the standard macroeconomic and EM models will be compared for consistency of the findings. These findings will form the core of policy formulation to stabilise an economy in the long run.

The next section will offer a discussion on short-run macroeconomic goals and economies' SSE, followed by a panel regression to determine relationships (if any) between SSE (independent variable) and macroeconomic goals (dependent variables). The subsequent section is snapshots of years 2009 and 2021 for the OECD economies for both standard macroeconomic and EM models. On the basis of the ascertained relationships, this chapter concludes

DOI: 10.4324/9781003002550-6

with findings from the snapshots between macroeconomic goals and capacity of an economy.

6.2 Short-Run Macroeconomic Goals and Economies' Steady-State Equilibrium

In the Swan–Solow framework, which is discussed in Chapter 5, the SSE is the amount of capital (KM) accumulated that is just sufficient to meet the needs of depreciation and the entry of new workers. Hence, SSE is defined by the quantity of KM per worker. Economic growth is endogenously attributed to the accumulation of an economy's physical capital in the short run. An economy's capital accumulation is determined by its savings rate as well as by the rate of KM depreciation. The savings rate is the proportion of income that is used towards greater KM investment in the current period as opposed to deferring the proportion of this income for future consumption. Although increased expenditure towards productivity (for example, increased spending on education and training) can lead to a higher growth of output per labour, these considerations do not necessarily translate to a sustained growth of output per labour.

In the short run, macroeconomic goals are concerned with pricing and employment, that is short-run economics. To attain the desired levels of macroeconomic goals, an economy will either use up capacity or free up capacity. An economy must trade-off between the short-run macroeconomic goals to arrive at a steady state or to approach a steady state. A steady state can demand levels of inflation and employment that may not adhere to initial expectations. The short-run macroeconomic goals of inflation and employment levels will, in turn, shape the long-run macroeconomic goal of GDP growth. Most economies would prefer a stable GDP growth because this type of growth provides stability, injects confidence for investors, and ensures that employment levels are sustained.

The distinction between short run, long run, and the very long run is addressed by point estimate analysis – which makes steady state a moving target for each time period as opposed to the steady state being a target for policymakers in the very long run. Therefore, the gap between the relative position of the economy and the steady state will vary for each time period. In this framework, steady state occurs when the savings rate is equal to the rate of replacement of manufactured KM. Figure 6.1 shows the capacity of an economy relative to its SSE for both the standard macroeconomic (Y^*) and EM (Y^{**}) models.

The variables k^* and k^{**} are the SSE for the standard macroeconomic and the EM models, respectively, and k is the current level of KM per worker. Figure 6.1 illustrates the level of excess capacity in an economy, namely, $(k^* - k)$ for the standard macroeconomic model and $(k^{**} - k)$ for the EM model. Note that if $[(k > k^*), (k > k^{**})]$, then the capacity in terms of capital per worker is exceeded.

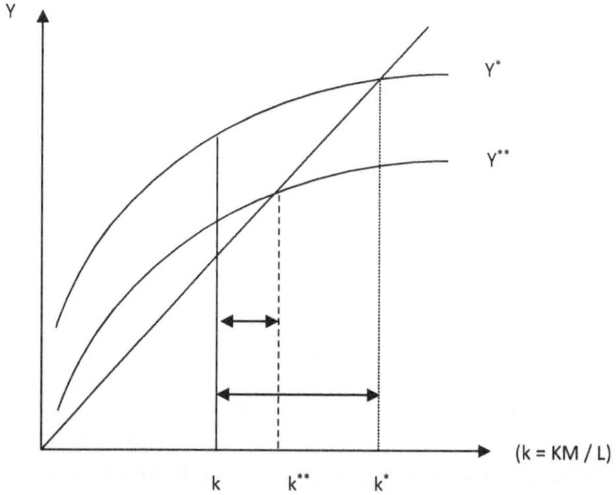

Figure 6.1 Capacity of an Economy Relative to Steady-State Equilibrium (SSE).

Each of the variables of the macroeconomic goals, namely, inflation (π), employment (N), and per capita GDP will be formalised by regression analysis as a function of an economy's capacity. Regression analysis is used to help understand how the value of the dependent variable changes when the independent variables are varied. Specific to this analysis, the dependent variables are the variables of the macroeconomic goals π, N, and per capita GDP. The independent variable is the economy's steady-state ratios [(k^*/k), (k^{**}/k)]. (Please refer to Table 5.1 for the definitions of the steady-state ratios.) Depending on which macroeconomic goal is the dependent variable, the other two macroeconomic goals will be assumed to be constant. For example, if π is the macroeconomic goal, then the other two macroeconomic goals of N and per capita GDP will be assumed to be constant. This scenario leaves a single variable, the economy's capacity, as the determining variable that influences π. The analysis is now simplified to a single variable relationship, for which each macroeconomic goal will be directly affected by the steady-state ratio of an economy.

For a selected economy, the following table illustrates the respective dependent (row, Y) variables with respect to the independent (column, X) variables.

From Table 6.1, each variable of the macroeconomic goals will be directly determined by an economy's steady-state ratio. Note that the steady-state ratio [(k^*/k), (k^{**}/k)] differs depending on whether it is the standard macroeconomic model or the EM model.

The economy's steady state is calculated via a ratio (see Table 5.1), and the values for each variable of the macroeconomic goals are computed via the

Table 6.1 Macroeconomic Variables with respect to an Economy's Steady-State Ratios

	Inflation, π	*Employment, N*	*Per capita GDP*	*Steady-state ratios [(k*/k), (k**/k)]*
Inflation, π		Constant	Constant	Variable
Employment, N	Constant		Constant	Variable
Per Capita GDP	Constant	Constant		Variable

Table 6.2 Measurement Ratios for Each Macroeconomic Variable and Steady State

Inflation, π	*Employment, N*	*Per capita GDP*	*Steady-state ratios [(k*/k), (k**/k)]*
$\left[\frac{Deflator_t}{Deflator_{(t-1)}}\right]$	$\left[\frac{\text{Employment}_t}{\text{Employment}_{(t-1)}}\right]$	$\left[\frac{\text{GDPpercapita}_t}{\text{GDPpercapita}_{(t-1)}}\right]$	Standard Model $\left[\frac{k^*}{k}\right]$ Environmental Model $\left[\frac{k^{**}}{k}\right]$

ratio of the current year's (t) value to past year's (t – 1) value. This computation ensures consistency in the calculation of all variables and ensures that the values are positive for the operation of Ln. Because the present year values are weighted against the prior year's values, a ratio of greater than one represents an increase in the value of the variable and a ratio of less than one represents a decrease in the value of the variable. Logs of the ratios are taken (or ln) to scale the ratios to their natural forms. Thus, for each of the variables, the computation is as follows (Table 6.2).

In the OECD iLibrary, inflation is proxied by the GDP Deflator; employment is Total Employment; and the per capita GDP is the GDP divided by the total population. The general equations are reduced to a single variable equation for which each of the macroeconomic goals will be directly determined by the economy's steady-state ratio. For the years 2009 and 2021, the reduced equation that relates an economy's steady-state ratio to each of the macroeconomic goals is given in Table 6.3.

6.3 Panel Regression for Select OECD Economies

The eight selected OECD economies are Australia, Canada, Germany, Japan, Korea, New Zealand, the United Kingdom, and the USA and the studied time period is from 1990 to 2021. The data are multi-dimensional because there are multiple phenomena observed over multiple time periods for each of the economies. When such a phenomenon is observed, it is best to use panel data

Table 6.3 Simplified Equations of Macroeconomic Variables and Steady-State Ratios

t = 2009, 2021	*Standard model*	*EM model*
Inflation, π	$\text{Ln } P = a + \text{Ln } (k^*/k)$ where $a = \text{Ln } N + \text{Ln } GDP$	$\text{Ln } \pi = a' + \text{Ln } (k^{**}/k)$ where $a' = \text{Ln } N + \text{Ln } GDP$
Employment, N	$\text{Ln } L = b + \text{Ln } (k^*/k)$ where $b = \text{Ln } \pi + \text{Ln } GDP$	$\text{Ln } L = b' + \text{Ln } (k^{**}/k)$ where $b' = \text{Ln } \pi + \text{Ln } GDP$
Per capita GDP	$\text{Ln } GDP = c + \text{Ln } (k^*/k)$ where $c = \text{Ln } \pi + \text{Ln } N$	$\text{Ln } GDP = c' + \text{Ln } (k^{**}/k)$ where $c' = \text{Ln } \pi + \text{Ln } N$

and to run a panel regression. Because panel data displays both cross-sectional and time-series dimensions, it is a more complex application compared to the simple cross-sectional or time-series data sets.

It is typically recognised that panel data possess several advantages. One advantage is that it allows for a larger number of data points, which is beneficial because there is no need to go very far back into historical data points. This reduces measurement errors that can arise from a lack of data because the time interval will be restricted to the parameters of the analysis. Another advantage is that panel data can capture unobserved heterogeneity (variances) of the variables. This property helps to reduce the possible biases of the model. A third advantage is that issues of under-estimation (Auffhammer and Carson, 2008) can be addressed by running panel regression. This property can result in revealing dynamics that is difficult to detect with cross-sectional data (Doughtery, 2011).

The following details the steps that are taken for panel regression for the selected OECD economies as well as the accompanying findings:

Steps

- i The ratios for the variables of macroeconomic goals (π, N, per capita GDP) and an economy's steady-state ratios [(k^*/k), (k^{**}/k)], as shown in Table 6.2, were calculated for all of the eight selected OECD economies for the observed years from 1990 to 2021
- ii The OECD economies were then grouped geographically into four groups. The groups are ASIA (Japan and Korea), AMERICAS (Canada and the USA), EUROPE (Germany and the United Kingdom), and PACIFIC (Australia and New Zealand)
- iii Each group was subjected to a panel regression application to determine a general equation for each of the macroeconomic goals. Based on a 20% level of significance, stepwise regression was applied to filter the independent non-significant variables, in a continuing process until all variables in the equations were significant. When panel regression was unable to arrive at a convincing conclusion, linear regression was used and followed a similar stepwise approach until all variables in the equations were significant

Findings

The AMERICAS and PACIFIC had two macroeconomic variables of employment (N) and per capita GDP that were well explained by the panel regression results. The other two groups of ASIA and EUROPE had one macroeconomic variable each that were explained by the panel regression results, ASIA (per capita GDP) and EUROPE (inflation, π). The equations generated for each of the macroeconomic variables are applied for each of the economies in the specific group.

Panel regression did not generate an equation for inflation in the PACIFIC group and linear regression was performed for each of the two economies, Australia and New Zealand. One drawback is that there could be an underestimation with using regression results. However, this is the ideal way for deriving a relationship between the macroeconomic variable inflation and steady state (as panel regression did not achieve a desired outcome). The equation for Australia was significant but that of New Zealand's was not as significant. Although the *p*-value (0.271) of lny1 (k^{**}/k) is higher than 20%, the equation generated from regression is used as the *p*-value is significantly lower relative to the result from panel regression.

And even though employment equations generated for Australia and New Zealand by panel regression failed to satisfy the 20% level of significance with *p*-values of lny (k^*/k) (0.232) and lny1 (k^{**}/k) (0.289), panel is used as the *p*-value is significantly lower relative to the result from linear regression. Similarly, Korea's employment and steady-state (lny) equation could not be generated by both panel (0.456) and linear (0.559) regressions as *p*-values of lny (k^*/k) were significantly higher than 20%.

Panel regression failed to produce significant results for EUROPE group and linear regression analysis was undertaken but the regression results remain insignificant. The per capita GDP equations generated for Germany will be rejected with *p*-values of lny (k^*/k) (0.444) and lny1 (k^{**}/k) (0.392) that are significantly higher than 20%. Equations generated for the United Kingdom will also be rejected where the *p*-values of lny (k^*/k) (0.615) and lny1 (k^{**}/k) (0.534) are significantly higher than 20%.

The main objective of this analysis is to observe the trends between each macroeconomic variable with respect to the economy's steady-state ratio as well as the different outcomes when the same analysis is made for the standard macroeconomic model and the EM model. There are macroeconomic equations which could not be generated by both panel and linear regressions and will be rejected. Please refer to Appendix 6.1 for all the STATA regression outputs.

Results

The results of the regressions are presented in Appendix 6.2. Table A6.1 shows the general regression equations, and Table A6.2 the general panel regression equations. The equations in Tables A6.1 and A6.2 can be simplified into a direct causal relationship between the macroeconomic variables and the steady-state ratio of the economy for the years 2009 and 2021. This is attained by making the macroeconomic variable/s on the right-hand side of the equation constant. That is, variables are substituted with 2009 and 2021 values. The resulting equations (in *italics*) which relate the macroeconomic variables to the steady-state ratios of an economy are presented in Tables A6.3 to A6.6 in Appendix 6.2.

6.4 Snapshots (2009 and 2021) of Standard Macroeconomic Model versus Environmental-Macroeconomic (EM) Model

The equations for the three macroeconomic variables of each economy are plotted to obtain an explanatory relationship with respect to the steady-state ratios of the economy for the years 2009 and 2021. However, 2009 was an immediate year after an exogenous shock, the 2008 Global Financial Crisis (GFC), and 2021 was an immediate year after another shock, the COVID-19 pandemic. However, the consistency of the results for both time periods seems to offer some evidence to how macroeconomic variables of economies would respond to exogenous shocks. There is a possibility though that this analysis could have been skewed as a result of these exogenous shocks. Note that the year 2021 is the latest complete set of required data at the time of the study.

The graphs for each of the economies are presented in Appendix 6.3. There are three economies (Australia, Japan, and Korea) with macroeconomic variables that display a significant disparity in the explanatory relationship when the standard macroeconomic model and the EM model are applied. They are Australia's inflation, Japan's GDP growth, and Korea's inflation. The plot for macroeconomic variable inflation and the steady-state ratio in Australia pivots when the standard macroeconomic model and the EM model are applied (refer to Figures 6.2 and 6.3). Japan's macroeconomic variable GDP growth and steady-state ratio converges between the standard macroeconomic model and the EM model (refer to Figures 6.4 and 6.5). And the macroeconomic variable inflation and the steady-state ratio in Korea shows a significant pivot for the standard macroeconomic model and the EM model (refer to Figures 6.6 and 6.7). Although these observations are consistent for years 2009 and 2021, the gap for Korea's inflation and steady-state ratio plot appears to be significantly large.

Although these are only three illustrations in this exercise, these are strong basis that incorrect policy domains are being identified when the standard macroeconomic model is employed with no consideration for KN. These graphs are presented in Figures 6.2 to 6.7.

- AUS $Ln(\pi)_{2009} = 0.034 + 0.032ln(k^{*}/k)$; $Ln(\pi)_{2009} = 0.037 + 0.022ln(k^{**}/k)$

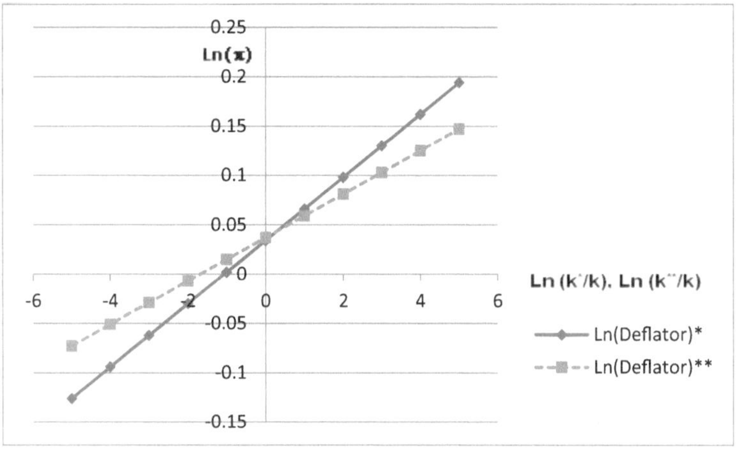

Figure 6.2 Australia's Inflation and Steady-State Ratio in 2009.

- AUS $Ln(\pi)_{2021} = 0.034 + 0.032ln(k^{*}/k)$; $Ln(\pi)_{2021} = 0.037 + 0.022ln(k^{**}/k)$

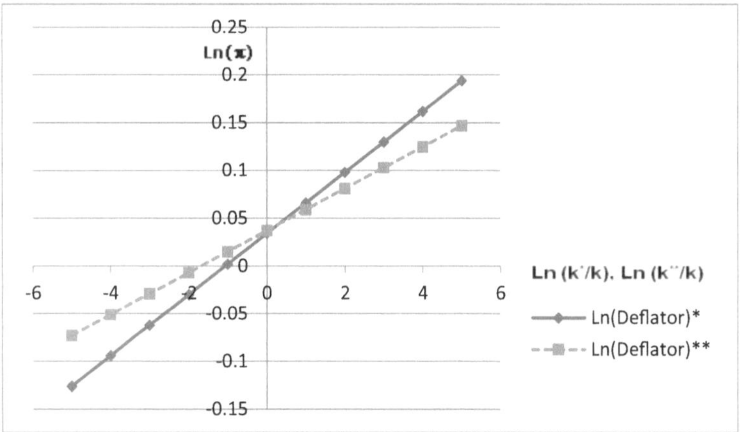

Figure 6.3 Australia's Inflation and Steady-State Ratio in 2021.

- JAP $Ln(GDP)_{2009} = 0.012 + 0.015ln(k^{*}/k)$; $Ln(GDP)_{2009} = 0.016 + 0.013ln(k^{**}/k)$

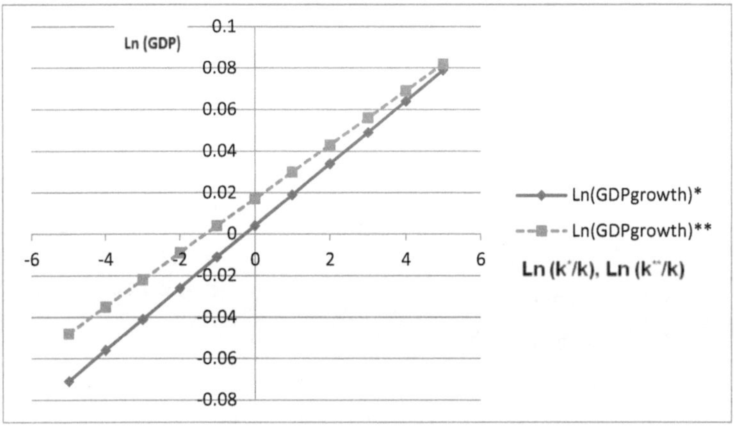

Figure 6.4 Japan's GDP Growth and Steady-State Ratio in 2009.

- JAP $Ln(GDP)_{2021} = 0.004 + 0.015ln(k^{*}/k)$; $Ln(GDP)_{2021} = 0.017 + 0.013ln(k^{**}/k)$

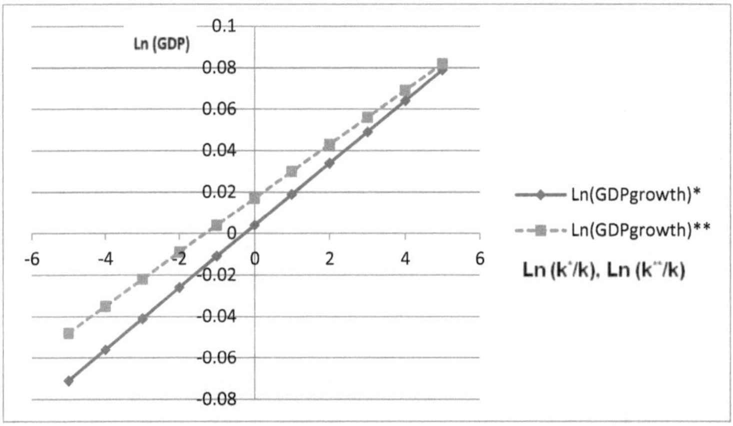

Figure 6.5 Japan's GDP Growth and Steady-State Ratio in 2021.

- KOR $Ln(\pi)_{2009} = 0.036 - 0.019ln(k^{*}/k)$; $Ln(\pi)_{2009} = 0.032 - 0.056ln(k^{**}/k)$

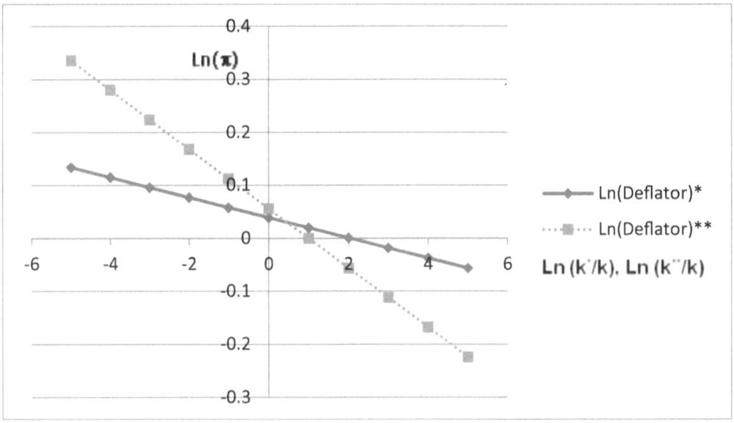

Figure 6.6 Korea's Inflation and Steady-State Ratio in 2009.

- KOR $Ln(\pi)_{2021} = 0.039 - 0.019ln(k^{*}/k)$; $Ln(\pi)_{2021} = 0.056 - 0.056ln(k^{**}/k)$

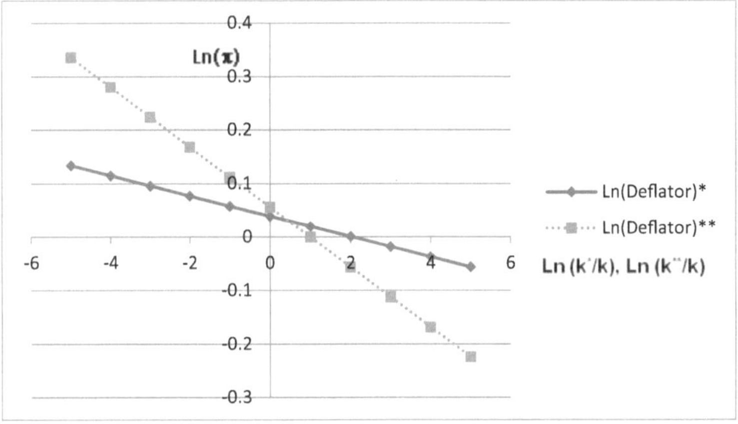

Figure 6.7 Korea's Inflation and Steady-State Ratio in 2021.

Of interest are the two economies of Australia and Korea in this discussion (refer to Tables 5.4 and 5.6). Australia progressed from beyond capacity to excess capacity across both time periods and for both standard macroeconomic and EM models. Korea remains in excess capacity across both time periods and for both standard macroeconomic and EM models. And these appear to contradict the plots from Figures 6.2, 6.3, 6.6, and 6.7 where both Australia's and Korea's inflation pivots between the standard macroeconomic model and the EM model.

Table 6.4 Nature of the Relationship of Macroeconomic Variables with $[(k^*/k), (k^{**}/k)]$

Economies	*π: f [ln (k*/k), ln (k**/k)]*	*N: f [ln (k*/k), ln (k**/k)]*	*Per capita GDP: f [ln (k*/k), ln (k**/k)]*
Group A: Excess Capacity, $(k^*/k) > 1$			
Canada	Positive Relationship	Positive Relationship (Panel)	Positive Relationship (Panel)
Germany	Negative Relationship (Panel)	Positive Relationship	N.A.
Group A: Beyond Capacity, $(k^{**}/k) < 1$			
Canada	Positive Relationship	Positive Relationship	Positive Relationship
Germany	Negative Relationship	Positive Relationship	N.A.
Group B: Beyond Capacity, (k^*/k) or $(k^{**}/k) < 1$			
Japan	Positive Relationship	Positive Relationship	Positive Relationship (Panel)
New Zealand	Negative Relationship	Positive Relationship (Panel)	Positive Relationship (Panel)
United Kingdom	Negative Relationship (Panel)	Positive Relationship	N.A.
USA	Negative Relationship	Positive Relationship (Panel)	Positive Relationship (Panel)

Table 6.4 summarises the relationship between the macroeconomic variables and the steady-state ratios of the respective economies.

6.5 Findings and Analysis of Snapshots (2009 and 2021) between Macroeconomic Goals and the Capacity of an Economy

There are four main findings from the graphical representation and the results are in Table 6.4.

i The status of the selected economies with respect to the SSE changes when KN is internalised. In other words, an economy moves from below the SSE to beyond the SSE. This is illustrated in Figure 6.8. An economy is at k with a steady-state ratio at (k^*/k) in the standard model. When KN is internalised in the EM model, an economy's steady-state ratio shifts leftwards to (k^{**}/k), at which a lower level of income Y^{**} is observed. Here,

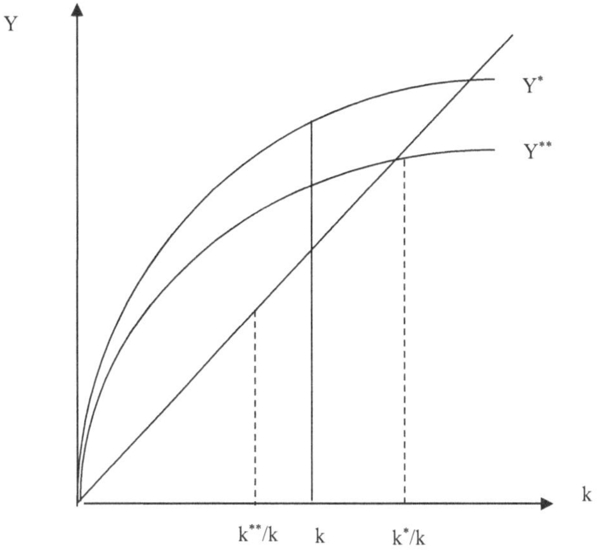

Figure 6.8 Economy Moving from Below the Steady-State Equilibrium to Beyond the Steady-State Equilibrium when Environmental Capital Is Internalised.

(k^{**}/k) is reached sooner in the EM model compared to the standard macroeconomic model.

This relationship is true for the economies in Group A (Canada and Germany); these economies move from excess capacity to beyond capacity when KN is internalised in the EM model (refer to Tables 5.4 and 5.6). The fact that there are two different states of capacity in two different models suggests a policy error for the selected economies in Group A. The capacity of the economies is exacerbated by the standard macroeconomic model. This was earlier emphasised in Section 5.3 of Chapter 5 where the inconsistency between the two models suggests the plausibility of policy domains being incorrectly identified should the standard macroeconomic model be employed.

ii Economies that are beyond the SSE have the extent of exceedance of capital per labour (KM/L) increased, when KN is internalised in the EM model, with plausibility of the exceedance having an impact on the steady-state ratio of an economy. This is illustrated in Figure 6.9, in which the steady-state ratio of the EM model is significantly below that of the standard macroeconomic model.

This relationship is evident in the economies in Group B (Japan, New Zealand, the United Kingdom, and the USA), for which an increase in the extent of exceedance is observed when KN is internalised in the EM model (refer to Tables 5.4 and 5.6).

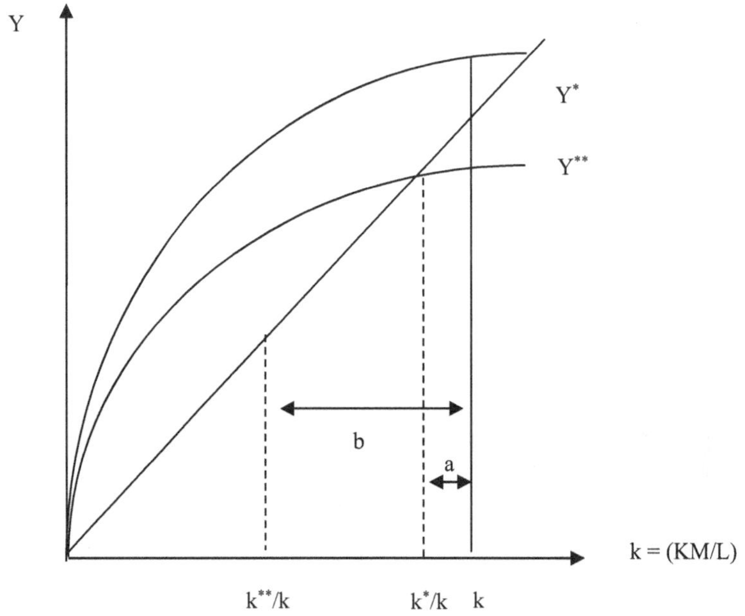

Figure 6.9 Economies Operating Beyond the Steady-State Equilibrium with Significant Exceedance Observed.

iii The nature of the relationship between the macroeconomic variables and steady-state ratios [(k^*/k), (k^{**}/k)] is the same across both the standard macroeconomic model and the EM model.

In other words, the positive or negative relationship demonstrated by π, N, and per capita GDP with respect to (k^*/k) and (k^{**}/k) remain unchanged be it the standard macroeconomic model or the EM model.

iv The functional forms derived do not display similarity in terms of the groupings based on whether an economy is operating within or beyond capacity. In accordance with expectations, the similarities are in terms of the panel groupings based on the geographic considerations discussed earlier.

There are two economies, namely, Canada and Japan for which all of the variables that describe the macroeconomic goals show a positive relationship. Whilst Canada moves from excess capacity to beyond capacity when KN is internalised, Japan remained operating at beyond capacity when KN is internalised.

For the rest of the economies, all of the macroeconomic variables do not show a consistent positive or negative relationship. Germany and the United Kingdom show a negative for inflation and positive for employment; New Zealand and the USA have a negative for inflation and positives for employment and GDP growth. The EM model is not the source of this discrepancy. Hence, there could be other factors that result from institutional, social, or political constraints.

While most of the economies are operating at beyond capacity (including Australia), Korea is the only one which operates with excess capacity in both the standard and EM models.

6.6 Conclusion

Panel regression was used to provide an explanatory relationship between the macroeconomic goals and the steady-state ratios for the economies of Australia, Canada, New Zealand, and the USA. However, there are some economies for which panel regression failed to provide a conclusive finding between the macroeconomic goals and the steady-state ratios. A linear regression was used (instead of panel regression) to explain the relationships for the economies of Japan and Korea. And neither panel nor linear regression could ascertain a relationship between macroeconomic goal of GDP growth and the steady-state ratios for Germany and the United Kingdom.

Based on the observation that there exist two different steady states in two different models, namely, the standard macroeconomic and the EM models, the type of regression used to determine such relationships between macroeconomic goals and the steady-state ratios appears to be inconsequential. This observation plainly suggests the existence of a policy error for the selected economies exhibiting such phenomenon. In addition, the strength of the relationships was different across the two different models for selected macroeconomic variables. These results are sufficient grounds to argue that the policy ranges presented to policymakers for policymaking were incorrect based on the standard macroeconomic model. Instead, the EM model should be used so that flawed policy decisions can be avoided.

The next and final chapter will conclude this study by presenting the policy implications of the results and a discussion of directions for future research.

References

Auffhammer, M., Carson, T. C. (2008), "Forecasting the path of China's CO_2 emissions using province-level information", *Journal of Environmental Economics and Management*, 55 (3), pp. 229–247.

Doughtery, C. (2011), *Introduction to Econometrics – Fourth Edition*, Oxford University Press, The United Kingdom, Chapter 14.

Appendix 6.1 Regression Output

JPN Regression Deflator and Steady-State Ratios

```
. reg lndeflatorratio lny lnemploymentratio , r

Linear regression                               Number of obs     =         31
                                                F(2, 28)          =       7.16
                                                Prob > F          =     0.0031
                                                R-squared         =     0.3215
                                                Root MSE          =      .0104
```

lndeflatorratio	Coef.	Robust Std. Err.	t	P>|t|	[95% Conf.	Interval]
lny	.0371459	.0164045	2.26	0.031	.0035428	.070749
lnemploymentratio	.366938	.2476934	1.48	0.150	-.140439	.874315
_cons	.0244797	.0121585	2.01	0.054	-.0004259	.0493854

```
. reg lndeflatorratio lny1 lnemploymentratio , r

Linear regression                               Number of obs     =         31
                                                F(2, 28)          =       7.26
                                                Prob > F          =     0.0029
                                                R-squared         =     0.3218
                                                Root MSE          =     .01039
```

lndeflatorratio	Coef.	Robust Std. Err.	t	P>|t|	[95% Conf.	Interval]
lny1	.0350021	.0156553	2.24	0.034	.0029336	.0670705
lnemploymentratio	.3602331	.2503523	1.44	0.161	-.1525905	.8730566
_cons	.0283943	.0140084	2.03	0.052	-.0003006	.0570892

KOR Regression Deflator and Steady-State Ratios

```
. reg lndeflatorratio lny lnemploymentratio lngdpgrowthratio , r

Linear regression                               Number of obs     =         31
                                                F(3, 27)          =      26.44
                                                Prob > F          =     0.0000
                                                R-squared         =     0.5005
                                                Root MSE          =     .01829
```

lndeflatorratio	Coef.	Robust Std. Err.	t	P>|t|	[95% Conf.	Interval]
lny	-.0187684	.0143123	-1.31	0.201	-.0481348	.010598
lnemploymentratio	-.1819332	.1090601	-1.67	0.107	-.4057062	.0418397
lngdpgrowthratio	.9541381	.1255264	7.60	0.000	.6965792	1.211697
_cons	.0035165	.0104303	0.34	0.739	-.0178847	.0249178

```
. reg lndeflatorratio lny1 lnemploymentratio lngdpgrowthratio , r

Linear regression                               Number of obs     =         31
                                                F(3, 27)          =      24.16
                                                Prob > F          =     0.0000
                                                R-squared         =     0.5299
                                                Root MSE          =     .01774
```

lndeflatorratio	Coef.	Robust Std. Err.	t	P>|t|	[95% Conf.	Interval]
lny1	-.0564881	.0328357	-1.72	0.097	-.1238615	.0108853
lnemploymentratio	-.3193169	.1444427	-2.21	0.036	-.615689	-.0229449
lngdpgrowthratio	.8443232	.1443123	5.85	0.000	.5482188	1.140428
_cons	.0268335	.0209121	1.28	0.210	-.0160745	.0697415

JPN Regression Employment and Steady-State Ratios

```
. reg lnemploymentratio lny lndeflatorratio lngdpgrowthratio , r

Linear regression                               Number of obs     =         31
                                                F(3, 27)          =      10.43
                                                Prob > F          =     0.0001
                                                R-squared         =     0.4039
                                                Root MSE          =     .00678
```

lnemploymentra~o	Coef.	Robust Std. Err.	t	P>|t|	[95% Conf.	Interval]
lny	.025418	.0096975	2.62	0.014	.0055204	.0453157
lndeflatorratio	.1647041	.097373	1.69	0.102	-.0350887	.3644969
lngdpgrowthratio	.1737603	.0543035	3.20	0.004	.0623388	.2851818
_cons	.0192582	.0068797	2.80	0.009	.0051422	.0333743

```
. reg lnemploymentratio lny1 lndeflatorratio lngdpgrowthratio , r

Linear regression                               Number of obs     =         31
                                                F(3, 27)          =      10.54
                                                Prob > F          =     0.0001
                                                R-squared         =     0.4115
                                                Root MSE          =     .00674
```

lnemploymentra~o	Coef.	Robust Std. Err.	t	P>|t|	[95% Conf.	Interval]
lny1	.0246145	.0091673	2.69	0.012	.0058047	.0434243
lndeflatorratio	.1589956	.0973061	1.63	0.114	-.0406601	.3586513
lngdpgrowthratio	.1757835	.055688	3.16	0.004	.0615212	.2900458
_cons	.0224879	.0079026	2.85	0.008	.0062732	.0387027

KOR Panel and Regression Employment and Steady-State Ratios

Note that the *p*-value of lny from panel (0.456) and linear (0.559) regressions are significantly higher than 20%, the equation generated for employment, Korea will be rejected.

```
. xtreg lnemploymentratio lny lngdpgrowthratio , r

Random-effects GLS regression                   Number of obs      =        62
Group variable: country                         Number of groups   =         2

R-sq:                                           Obs per group:
     within  = 0.0771                                         min =        31
     between = 1.0000                                         avg =      31.0
     overall = 0.2185                                         max =        31

                                                Wald chi2(1)       =         .
corr(u_i, X)   = 0 (assumed)                    Prob > chi2        =         .

                                (Std. Err. adjusted for 2 clusters in country)
```

lnemploymentra~o	Coef.	Robust Std. Err.	z	P>|z|	[95% Conf.	Interval]
lny	.0023537	.00316	0.74	0.456	-.0038398	.0085471
lngdpgrowthratio	.23627	.0738421	3.20	0.001	.0915422	.3809979
_cons	.0021811	.0018092	1.21	0.228	-.0013648	.005727
sigma_u	0					
sigma_e	.01337033					
rho	0	(fraction of variance due to u_i)				

```
. reg lnemploymentratio lny lngdpgrowthratio , r

Linear regression                               Number of obs      =        31
                                                F(2, 28)           =      6.33
                                                Prob > F           =    0.0054
                                                R-squared          =    0.0900
                                                Root MSE           =    .01725
```

lnemploymentra~o	Coef.	Robust Std. Err.	t	P>|t|	[95% Conf.	Interval]
lny	-.0086014	.0145482	-0.59	0.559	-.0384021	.0211993
lngdpgrowthratio	.2714	.088759	3.06	0.005	.0895854	.4532146
_cons	.0071989	.0086089	0.84	0.410	-.0104356	.0248333

```
. reg lnemploymentratio lny1 lndeflatorratio lngdpgrowthratio , r

Linear regression                               Number of obs     =         31
                                                F(3, 27)          =       3.14
                                                Prob > F          =     0.0415
                                                R-squared         =     0.2976
                                                Root MSE          =     .01544

------------------------------------------------------------------------------
                 |               Robust
lnemploymentra~o |      Coef.   Std. Err.      t    P>|t|     [95% Conf. Interval]
-----------------+------------------------------------------------------------
            lny1 |  -.0670403   .0492861    -1.36   0.185    -.1681672    .0340865
 lndeflatorratio |  -.2418451   .1769154    -1.37   0.183    -.6048455    .1211554
lngdpgrowthratio |   .3451481   .1661389     2.08   0.047     .0042593    .6860369
           _cons |   .0393295   .0275156     1.43   0.164    -.0171279    .0957868
------------------------------------------------------------------------------
```

JPN KOR Panel GDP Growth and Steady-State Ratios

```
. xtreg lngdpgrowthratio lny lnemploymentratio lndeflatorratio , r

Random-effects GLS regression                   Number of obs     =         62
Group variable: country                         Number of groups  =          2

R-sq:                                           Obs per group:
     within  = 0.3169                                         min =         31
     between = 1.0000                                         avg =       31.0
     overall = 0.6816                                         max =         31

                                                Wald chi2(1)      =          .
corr(u_i, X)   = 0 (assumed)                    Prob > chi2       =          .

                                 (Std. Err. adjusted for 2 clusters in country)
-------------------------------------------------------------------------------
                  |               Robust
 lngdpgrowthratio |      Coef.   Std. Err.      z    P>|z|     [95% Conf. Interval]
------------------+------------------------------------------------------------
              lny |   .0145183   .0027757     5.23   0.000      .009078    .0199585
lnemploymentratio |   .2396171   .0065868    36.38   0.000     .2267072    .2525271
  lndeflatorratio |   .4087395    .167816     2.44   0.015     .0798261    .7376529
            _cons |   .0168181    .002144     7.84   0.000     .0126159    .0210203
------------------+------------------------------------------------------------
          sigma_u |          0
          sigma_e |  .01387492
              rho |          0   (fraction of variance due to u_i)
-------------------------------------------------------------------------------

. xtreg lngdpgrowthratio lny1 lnemploymentratio lndeflatorratio , r

Random-effects GLS regression                   Number of obs     =         62
Group variable: country                         Number of groups  =          2

R-sq:                                           Obs per group:
     within  = 0.2818                                         min =         31
     between = 1.0000                                         avg =       31.0
     overall = 0.6637                                         max =         31

                                                Wald chi2(1)      =          .
corr(u_i, X)   = 0 (assumed)                    Prob > chi2       =          .

                                 (Std. Err. adjusted for 2 clusters in country)
-------------------------------------------------------------------------------
                  |               Robust
 lngdpgrowthratio |      Coef.   Std. Err.      z    P>|z|     [95% Conf. Interval]
------------------+------------------------------------------------------------
             lny1 |   .0126547   .0030144     4.20   0.000     .0067466    .0185628
lnemploymentratio |   .2667685   .0014773   180.58   0.000     .2638731     .269664
  lndeflatorratio |   .4314632   .1715822     2.51   0.012     .0951682    .7677582
            _cons |   .0176808   .0023581     7.50   0.000      .013059    .0223025
------------------+------------------------------------------------------------
          sigma_u |          0
          sigma_e |  .01396304
              rho |          0   (fraction of variance due to u_i)
-------------------------------------------------------------------------------
```

CAN Regression Deflator and Steady-State Ratios

```
. reg lndeflatorratio lny lnemploymentratio lngdpgrowthratio , r

Linear regression                               Number of obs     =         31
                                                F(3, 27)          =       3.40
                                                Prob > F          =     0.0319
                                                R-squared         =     0.3301
                                                Root MSE          =     .01504
```

lndeflatorratio	Coef.	Robust Std. Err.	t	P>|t|	[95% Conf.	Interval]
lny	.0187054	.0089645	2.09	0.046	.0003118	.0370991
lnemploymentratio	.3279479	.2376616	1.38	0.179	-.1596935	.8155893
lngdpgrowthratio	-.3122852	.207915	-1.50	0.145	-.7388916	.1143212
_cons	.0189965	.0034276	5.54	0.000	.0119636	.0260294

```
. reg lndeflatorratio lny1 lnemploymentratio lngdpgrowthratio , r

Linear regression                               Number of obs     =         31
                                                F(3, 27)          =       3.54
                                                Prob > F          =     0.0277
                                                R-squared         =     0.3294
                                                Root MSE          =     .01505
```

lndeflatorratio	Coef.	Robust Std. Err.	t	P>|t|	[95% Conf.	Interval]
lny1	.0168462	.0078419	2.15	0.041	.000756	.0329363
lnemploymentratio	.3283341	.2355438	1.39	0.175	-.1549619	.8116301
lngdpgrowthratio	-.3143824	.2071108	-1.52	0.141	-.7393388	.110574
_cons	.0215807	.0039335	5.49	0.000	.0135099	.0296515

USA Regression Deflator and Steady-State Ratios

```
. reg lndeflatorratio lny lnemploymentratio , r

Linear regression                               Number of obs     =         31
                                                F(2, 28)          =       5.12
                                                Prob > F          =     0.0128
                                                R-squared         =     0.2439
                                                Root MSE          =     .00692
```

lndeflatorratio	Coef.	Robust Std. Err.	t	P>|t|	[95% Conf.	Interval]
lny	-.0171707	.0059808	-2.87	0.008	-.0294217	-.0049197
lnemploymentratio	.1913456	.0909742	2.10	0.045	.0049934	.3776977
_cons	.0178673	.0013935	12.82	0.000	.0150129	.0207217

```
. reg lndeflatorratio lny1 lnemploymentratio , r

Linear regression                               Number of obs     =         31
                                                F(2, 28)          =       5.69
                                                Prob > F          =     0.0085
                                                R-squared         =     0.2526
                                                Root MSE          =     .00688

------------------------------------------------------------------------------------
                  |               Robust
  lndeflatorratio |      Coef.   Std. Err.      t    P>|t|     [95% Conf. Interval]
------------------+-----------------------------------------------------------------
             lny1 |  -.0172556     .006218   -2.78   0.010    -.0299927   -.0045186
lnemploymentratio |   .1892124    .0929456    2.04   0.051     -.001178    .3796028
            _cons |   .0149553    .0019305    7.75   0.000      .011001    .0189097
------------------------------------------------------------------------------------
```

CAN USA Panel Employment and Steady-State ratios

```
. xtreg lnemploymentratio lny lndeflatorratio lngdpgrowthratio , r

Random-effects GLS regression                   Number of obs      =        62
Group variable: country                         Number of groups   =         2

R-sq:                                           Obs per group:
     within  = 0.3928                                         min =         31
     between = 1.0000                                         avg =       31.0
     overall = 0.3848                                         max =         31

                                                Wald chi2(1)       =         .
corr(u_i, X)   = 0 (assumed)                    Prob > chi2        =         .

                                   (Std. Err. adjusted for 2 clusters in country)
---------------------------------------------------------------------------------
                  |               Robust
lnemploymentra~o |      Coef.   Std. Err.      z    P>|z|     [95% Conf. Interval]
-----------------+---------------------------------------------------------------
              lny |   .0056559   .0003079    18.37   0.000     .0050524    .0062593
  lndeflatorratio |   .7305746   .0462084    15.81   0.000     .6400078    .8211413
 lngdpgrowthratio |    .648416   .0274863    23.59   0.000     .5945439    .7022881
            _cons |  -.0146608   .0038659    -3.79   0.000    -.0222377   -.0070838
-----------------+---------------------------------------------------------------
          sigma_u |          0
          sigma_e |  .01839263
              rho |          0   (fraction of variance due to u_i)
---------------------------------------------------------------------------------

. xtreg lnemploymentratio lny1 lndeflatorratio lngdpgrowthratio , r

Random-effects GLS regression                   Number of obs      =        62
Group variable: country                         Number of groups   =         2

R-sq:                                           Obs per group:
     within  = 0.3925                                         min =         31
     between = 1.0000                                         avg =       31.0
     overall = 0.3848                                         max =         31

                                                Wald chi2(1)       =         .
corr(u_i, X)   = 0 (assumed)                    Prob > chi2        =         .

                                   (Std. Err. adjusted for 2 clusters in country)
---------------------------------------------------------------------------------
                  |               Robust
lnemploymentra~o |      Coef.   Std. Err.      z    P>|z|     [95% Conf. Interval]
-----------------+---------------------------------------------------------------
             lny1 |    .005067   .0005855     8.65   0.000     .0039194    .0062146
  lndeflatorratio |   .7308515   .0471269    15.51   0.000     .6384845    .8232185
 lngdpgrowthratio |    .649925   .0318144    20.43   0.000     .5875699    .7122802
            _cons |  -.0138865   .0040067    -3.47   0.001    -.0217394   -.0060336
-----------------+---------------------------------------------------------------
          sigma_u |          0
          sigma_e |  .01839159
              rho |          0   (fraction of variance due to u_i)
---------------------------------------------------------------------------------
```

CAN USA Panel GDP Growth and Steady-State ratios
GER GBR Panel Deflator and Steady-State Ratios

```
. xtreg lngdpgrowthratio lny lnemploymentratio lndeflatorratio , r

Random-effects GLS regression                   Number of obs     =         62
Group variable: country                         Number of groups  =          2

R-sq:                                           Obs per group:
     within  = 0.4139                                         min =         31
     between = 1.0000                                         avg =       31.0
     overall = 0.3475                                         max =         31

                                                Wald chi2(1)      =          .
corr(u_i, X)   = 0 (assumed)                    Prob > chi2       =          .

                                 (Std. Err. adjusted for 2 clusters in country)
-------------------------------------------------------------------------------
                  |               Robust
 lngdpgrowthratio |      Coef.   Std. Err.      z    P>|z|     [95% Conf. Interval]
------------------+------------------------------------------------------------
              lny |   .0232899   .0039029     5.97   0.000     .0156403    .0309395
lnemploymentratio |   .2365946   .0503843     4.70   0.000     .1378431    .3353461
  lndeflatorratio |   -.196679   .0038669   -50.86   0.000     -.204258   -.1891001
            _cons |   .0157066   .0031626     4.97   0.000      .009508    .0219052
------------------+------------------------------------------------------------
          sigma_u |          0
          sigma_e |  .01055712
              rho |          0   (fraction of variance due to u_i)
-------------------------------------------------------------------------------
```

```
. xtreg lngdpgrowthratio lny1 lnemploymentratio lndeflatorratio , r

Random-effects GLS regression                   Number of obs     =         62
Group variable: country                         Number of groups  =          2

R-sq:                                           Obs per group:
     within  = 0.4125                                         min =         31
     between = 1.0000                                         avg =       31.0
     overall = 0.3411                                         max =         31

                                                Wald chi2(1)      =          .
corr(u_i, X)   = 0 (assumed)                    Prob > chi2       =          .

                                 (Std. Err. adjusted for 2 clusters in country)
-------------------------------------------------------------------------------
                  |               Robust
 lngdpgrowthratio |      Coef.   Std. Err.      z    P>|z|     [95% Conf. Interval]
------------------+------------------------------------------------------------
             lny1 |   .0205989   .0031933     6.45   0.000     .0143401    .0268577
lnemploymentratio |   .2394602   .0553085     4.33   0.000     .1310575    .3478629
  lndeflatorratio |  -.1962627   .0071002   -27.64   0.000    -.2101789   -.1823465
            _cons |   .0189344   .0037968     4.99   0.000     .0114928     .026376
------------------+------------------------------------------------------------
          sigma_u |          0
          sigma_e |   .0105599
              rho |          0   (fraction of variance due to u_i)
-------------------------------------------------------------------------------
```

GER Regression Employment and Steady-State ratios

```
. xtreg lndeflatorratio lny lnemploymentratio , r

Random-effects GLS regression                   Number of obs     =         62
Group variable: country                         Number of groups  =          2

R-sq:                                           Obs per group:
     within  = 0.0701                                         min =         31
     between = 1.0000                                         avg =       31.0
     overall = 0.1366                                         max =         31

                                                Wald chi2(1)      =          .
corr(u_i, X)   = 0 (assumed)                    Prob > chi2       =          .

                                 (Std. Err. adjusted for 2 clusters in country)
-------------------------------------------------------------------------------
                  |               Robust
  lndeflatorratio |      Coef.   Std. Err.      z    P>|z|     [95% Conf. Interval]
------------------+------------------------------------------------------------
              lny |  -.0114149   .0030391    -3.76   0.000    -.0173714   -.0054585
lnemploymentratio |  -.4346685    .068176    -6.38   0.000     -.568291   -.3010459
            _cons |   .0216146   .0013825    15.63   0.000     .0189048    .0243243
------------------+------------------------------------------------------------
          sigma_u |          0
          sigma_e |  .01603857
              rho |          0   (fraction of variance due to u_i)
-------------------------------------------------------------------------------

. . xtreg lndeflatorratio lny1 lnemploymentratio , r

Random-effects GLS regression                   Number of obs     =         62
Group variable: country                         Number of groups  =          2

R-sq:                                           Obs per group:
     within  = 0.0749                                         min =         31
     between = 1.0000                                         avg =       31.0
     overall = 0.1423                                         max =         31

                                                Wald chi2(1)      =          .
corr(u_i, X)   = 0 (assumed)                    Prob > chi2       =          .

                                 (Std. Err. adjusted for 2 clusters in country)
-------------------------------------------------------------------------------
                  |               Robust
  lndeflatorratio |      Coef.   Std. Err.      z    P>|z|     [95% Conf. Interval]
------------------+------------------------------------------------------------
             lny1 |  -.0114998    .003337    -3.45   0.001    -.0180401   -.0049594
lnemploymentratio |  -.4230604   .0584812    -7.23   0.000    -.5376814   -.3084394
            _cons |   .0200932   .0007572    26.54   0.000     .0186092    .0215772
------------------+------------------------------------------------------------
          sigma_u |          0
          sigma_e |  .01612841
              rho |          0   (fraction of variance due to u_i)
-------------------------------------------------------------------------------
```

```
. reg lnemploymentratio lny lndeflatorratio lngdpgrowthratio , r
```

Linear regression			
	Number of obs	=	31
	F(3, 27)	=	14.62
	Prob > F	=	0.0000
	R-squared	=	0.5560
	Root MSE	=	.00691

lnemploymentra~o	Coef.	Robust Std. Err.	t	P>|t|	[95% Conf.	Interval]
lny	.0240719	.007871	3.06	0.005	.0079219	.0402218
lndeflatorratio	-.3730288	.116976	-3.19	0.004	-.6130437	-.1330138
lngdpgrowthratio	.4926311	.1080423	4.56	0.000	.2709467	.7143156
_cons	.0006101	.0038068	0.16	0.874	-.0072007	.0084209

GBR Regression Employment and Steady-State ratios

```
. . reg lnemploymentratio lny1 lndeflatorratio lngdpgrowthratio , r
```

Linear regression			
	Number of obs	=	31
	F(3, 27)	=	13.24
	Prob > F	=	0.0000
	R-squared	=	0.5527
	Root MSE	=	.00694

lnemploymentra~o	Coef.	Robust Std. Err.	t	P>|t|	[95% Conf.	Interval]
lny1	.0207899	.0072128	2.88	0.008	.0059905	.0355894
lndeflatorratio	-.3563978	.1193777	-2.99	0.006	-.6013407	-.111455
lngdpgrowthratio	.5008119	.1127838	4.44	0.000	.2693986	.7322252
_cons	.0033599	.0031468	1.07	0.295	-.0030968	.0098166

```
. . reg lnemploymentratio lny lngdpgrowthratio , r
```

Linear regression			
	Number of obs	=	31
	F(2, 28)	=	2.77
	Prob > F	=	0.0795
	R-squared	=	0.3107
	Root MSE	=	.01001

lnemploymentra~o	Coef.	Robust Std. Err.	t	P>|t|	[95% Conf.	Interval]
lny	.0308791	.0177306	1.74	0.093	-.0054404	.0671986
lngdpgrowthratio	.2934129	.1267583	2.31	0.028	.0337602	.5530655
_cons	.0165378	.006824	2.42	0.022	.0025595	.0305161

GER Regression GDP Growth and Steady-State ratios

Note that the *p*-values of lny (0.444) and lny1 (0.392) are significantly higher than 20%, the equation generated for per capita GDP, Germany will be rejected.

```
. reg lnemploymentratio lny1 lngdpgrowthratio , r

Linear regression                               Number of obs     =         31
                                                F(2, 28)          =       2.84
                                                Prob > F          =     0.0755
                                                R-squared         =     0.3428
                                                Root MSE          =     .00978
```

lnemploymentra~o	Coef.	Robust Std. Err.	t	P>|t|	[95% Conf.	Interval]
lny1	.0278009	.0151097	1.84	0.076	-.0031499	.0587517
lngdpgrowthratio	.2997256	.1266397	2.37	0.025	.0403159	.5591353
_cons	.0188089	.0077268	2.43	0.022	.0029813	.0346364

```
. reg lngdpgrowthratio lny lnemploymentratio , r

Linear regression                               Number of obs     =         31
                                                F(2, 28)          =       2.72
                                                Prob > F          =     0.0830
                                                R-squared         =     0.3537
                                                Root MSE          =     .00939
```

lngdpgrowthratio	Coef.	Robust Std. Err.	t	P>|t|	[95% Conf.	Interval]
lny	-.0106901	.013762	-0.78	0.444	-.0388803	.0175001
lnemploymentratio	.7023433	.3120357	2.25	0.032	.0631672	1.341519
_cons	.0104513	.0025364	4.12	0.000	.0052557	.015647

GBR Regression GDP Growth and Steady-State ratios

Note that the *p*-values of lny (0.615) and lny1 (0.534) are significantly higher than 20%, the equation generated for per capita GDP, GBR will be rejected.

```
.  reg lngdpgrowthratio lny1 lnemploymentratio , r

Linear regression                               Number of obs     =         31
                                                F(2, 28)          =       2.79
                                                Prob > F          =     0.0789
                                                R-squared         =     0.3614
                                                Root MSE          =     .00933
```

lngdpgrowthratio	Coef.	Robust Std. Err.	t	P>|t|	[95% Conf.	Interval]
lny1	-.011384	.0130918	-0.87	0.392	-.0382013	.0154334
lnemploymentratio	.7097758	.3126355	2.27	0.031	.0693709	1.350181
_cons	.0091998	.0020238	4.55	0.000	.0050542	.0133454

```
. reg lngdpgrowthratio lny lnemploymentratio , r

Linear regression                               Number of obs     =         31
                                                F(2, 28)          =       3.63
                                                Prob > F          =     0.0396
                                                R-squared         =     0.2217
                                                Root MSE          =     .01606

------------------------------------------------------------------------------------
                  |               Robust
 lngdpgrowthratio |      Coef.   Std. Err.      t    P>|t|     [95% Conf. Interval]
------------------+-----------------------------------------------------------------
              lny |    -.02189    .0430407    -0.51   0.615     -.110055     .066275
lnemploymentratio |   .7551485    .4194738     1.80   0.083    -.1041047    1.614402
            _cons |  -.0037334    .0232465    -0.16   0.874    -.0513517    .0438848
------------------------------------------------------------------------------------
```

AUS Regression Deflator and Steady-State Ratios

```
. reg lngdpgrowthratio lny1 lnemploymentratio , r

Linear regression                               Number of obs     =         31
                                                F(2, 28)          =       3.52
                                                Prob > F          =     0.0433
                                                R-squared         =     0.2377
                                                Root MSE          =     .01589

------------------------------------------------------------------------------------
                  |               Robust
 lngdpgrowthratio |      Coef.   Std. Err.      t    P>|t|     [95% Conf. Interval]
------------------+-----------------------------------------------------------------
             lny1 |  -.0231903    .0368357    -0.63   0.534    -.0986448    .0522641
lnemploymentratio |   .7924147    .4370135     1.81   0.081    -.1027668    1.687596
            _cons |  -.0076075    .0255641    -0.30   0.768    -.0599732    .0447581
------------------------------------------------------------------------------------

. . reg lndeflatorratio lny , r

Linear regression                               Number of obs     =         31
                                                F(1, 29)          =       2.69
                                                Prob > F          =     0.1115
                                                R-squared         =     0.0786
                                                Root MSE          =     .01662

------------------------------------------------------------------------------
             |               Robust
lndeflator~o |      Coef.   Std. Err.      t    P>|t|     [95% Conf. Interval]
-------------+----------------------------------------------------------------
         lny |   .0322628    .0196552     1.64   0.112    -.0079366    .0724623
       _cons |   .0343765    .0068028     5.05   0.000     .0204632    .0482898
------------------------------------------------------------------------------
```

NZL Regression Deflator and Steady-State Ratios

```
. reg lndeflatorratio lny1 , r

Linear regression                               Number of obs     =         31
                                                F(1, 29)          =       2.98
                                                Prob > F          =     0.0948
                                                R-squared         =     0.0688
                                                Root MSE          =     .01671
```

lndeflator~o	Coef.	Robust Std. Err.	t	P>|t|	[95% Conf.	Interval]
lny1	.0224	.0129682	1.73	0.095	-.004123	.048923
_cons	.0372063	.0082547	4.51	0.000	.0203236	.054089

Note that even though the *p*-value of lny1 (0.271) is higher than 20%, the equation generated from regression is used as the *p*-value is significantly lower relative to the result from panel regression.

```
. reg lndeflatorratio lny lngdpgrowthratio , r

Linear regression                               Number of obs     =         31
                                                F(2, 28)          =       1.59
                                                Prob > F          =     0.2212
                                                R-squared         =     0.0975
                                                Root MSE          =      .0123
```

lndeflatorratio	Coef.	Robust Std. Err.	t	P>|t|	[95% Conf.	Interval]
lny	-.0239775	.0162609	-1.47	0.151	-.0572864	.0093315
lngdpgrowthratio	.2102566	.1232754	1.71	0.099	-.0422617	.4627749
_cons	.0172754	.0028521	6.06	0.000	.011433	.0231177

AUS NZL Panel Employment and Steady-State Ratios

Note that even though the *p*-values of lny (0.232) and lny1 (0.289) are higher than 20%, panel is used as the *p*-value is significantly lower relative to the result from linear regression.

```
. . reg lndeflatorratio lny1 lngdpgrowthratio , r

Linear regression                               Number of obs     =         31
                                                F(2, 28)          =       0.88
                                                Prob > F          =     0.4255
                                                R-squared         =     0.0668
                                                Root MSE          =     .01251
```

lndeflatorratio	Coef.	Robust Std. Err.	t	P>|t|	[95% Conf.	Interval]
lny1	-.0195811	.0174548	-1.12	0.271	-.0553356	.0161734
lngdpgrowthratio	.2045116	.157459	1.30	0.205	-.1180286	.5270518
_cons	.0140119	.0059352	2.36	0.025	.0018542	.0261696

AUS NZL Panel GDP Growth and Steady-State Ratios

```
. . xtreg lnemploymentratio lny lngdpgrowthratio , r

Random-effects GLS regression                   Number of obs      =        62
Group variable: country                         Number of groups   =         2

R-sq:                                           Obs per group:
     within  = 0.0266                                         min =         31
     between = 1.0000                                         avg =       31.0
     overall = 0.0293                                         max =         31

                                                Wald chi2(1)       =         .
corr(u_i, X)   = 0 (assumed)                    Prob > chi2        =         .

                                  (Std. Err. adjusted for 2 clusters in country)
------------------------------------------------------------------------------------
                  |               Robust
lnemploymentra~o  |      Coef.   Std. Err.      z    P>|z|     [95% Conf. Interval]
------------------+-----------------------------------------------------------------
              lny |   .0115794     .00969     1.19   0.232    -.0074126    .0305715
 lngdpgrowthratio |  -.0366854   .0134633    -2.72   0.006     -.063073   -.0102979
            _cons |    .021644    .000933    23.20   0.000     .0198153    .0234727
------------------+-----------------------------------------------------------------
          sigma_u |          0
          sigma_e |  .01504056
              rho |          0   (fraction of variance due to u_i)
------------------------------------------------------------------------------------
```

```
. . xtreg lnemploymentratio lny1 lndeflatorratio lngdpgrowthratio , r

Random-effects GLS regression                   Number of obs      =        62
Group variable: country                         Number of groups   =         2

R-sq:                                           Obs per group:
     within  = 0.0323                                         min =         31
     between = 1.0000                                         avg =       31.0
     overall = 0.0324                                         max =         31

                                                Wald chi2(1)       =         .
corr(u_i, X)   = 0 (assumed)                    Prob > chi2        =         .

                                  (Std. Err. adjusted for 2 clusters in country)
------------------------------------------------------------------------------------
                  |               Robust
lnemploymentra~o  |      Coef.   Std. Err.      z    P>|z|     [95% Conf. Interval]
------------------+-----------------------------------------------------------------
             lny1 |   .0100842    .009506     1.06   0.289    -.0085472    .0287156
  lndeflatorratio |   .0042188   .0004661     9.05   0.000     .0033053    .0051323
 lngdpgrowthratio |  -.0400732   .0095358    -4.20   0.000     -.058763   -.0213834
            _cons |   .0235819   .0028498     8.28   0.000     .0179964    .0291673
------------------+-----------------------------------------------------------------
          sigma_u |          0
          sigma_e |  .01512476
              rho |          0   (fraction of variance due to u_i)
------------------------------------------------------------------------------------
```

```
. xtreg lngdpgrowthratio lny lndeflatorratio , r

Random-effects GLS regression                   Number of obs      =        62
Group variable: country                         Number of groups   =         2

R-sq:                                           Obs per group:
     within  = 0.1153                                         min =        31
     between = 1.0000                                         avg =      31.0
     overall = 0.0782                                         max =        31

                                                Wald chi2(1)       =         .
corr(u_i, X)   = 0 (assumed)                    Prob > chi2        =         .

                                   (Std. Err. adjusted for 2 clusters in country)
---------------------------------------------------------------------------------
                 |               Robust
lngdpgrowthra~o  |      Coef.   Std. Err.      z    P>|z|     [95% Conf. Interval]
-----------------+---------------------------------------------------------------
             lny |   .0480402   .0177765     2.70   0.007     .0131989    .0828815
 lndeflatorratio |   .3852627   .0418245     9.21   0.000     .3032883    .4672372
           _cons |   .0170733   .0091137     1.87   0.061    -.0007892    .0349358
-----------------+---------------------------------------------------------------
         sigma_u |          0
         sigma_e |  .03975848
             rho |          0   (fraction of variance due to u_i)
---------------------------------------------------------------------------------

. xtreg lngdpgrowthratio lny1 lndeflatorratio , r

Random-effects GLS regression                   Number of obs      =        62
Group variable: country                         Number of groups   =         2

R-sq:                                           Obs per group:
     within  = 0.1513                                         min =        31
     between = 1.0000                                         avg =      31.0
     overall = 0.0940                                         max =        31

                                                Wald chi2(1)       =         .
corr(u_i, X)   = 0 (assumed)                    Prob > chi2        =         .

                                   (Std. Err. adjusted for 2 clusters in country)
---------------------------------------------------------------------------------
                 |               Robust
lngdpgrowthra~o  |      Coef.   Std. Err.      z    P>|z|     [95% Conf. Interval]
-----------------+---------------------------------------------------------------
            lny1 |   .0439352   .0160457     2.74   0.006     .0124862    .0753843
 lndeflatorratio |   .3633925   .0465411     7.81   0.000     .2721736    .4546114
           _cons |    .026614   .0135639     1.96   0.050     .0000291    .0531988
-----------------+---------------------------------------------------------------
         sigma_u |          0
         sigma_e |  .03879267
             rho |          0   (fraction of variance due to u_i)
---------------------------------------------------------------------------------
```

Appendix 6.2 ***General Regression and Panel Regression Equations for the Economies***

Table A6.1 General Regression Equations for ASIA, AMERICAS, EUROPE, and PACIFIC

GENERAL EQUATIONS (Regression)	*ASIA (JPN and KOR)*	*AMERICAS (CAN and USA)*	*EUROPE (GER and GBR)*	*PACIFIC (AUS and NZL)*
Inflation, π	JPN: $Ln(\pi) = 0.024 + 0.037ln(k^{*}/k) + 0.367ln(N)$ KOR: $Ln(\pi) = 0.004 - 0.019ln(k^{*}/k) - 0.182ln(N) + 0.954ln(GDP)$	CAN: $Ln(\pi) = 0.019 + 0.019ln(k^{*}/k) + 0.328ln(N) - 0.312ln(GDP)$ USA: $Ln(\pi) = 0.018 - 0.018ln(k^{*}/k) + 0.191ln(N)$	N.A.	AUS: $Ln(\pi) = 0.034 + 0.032ln(k^{*}/k)$ NZL: $Ln(\pi) = 0.017 - 0.024ln(k^{*}/k) + 0.210ln(GDP)$
	JPN: $Ln(\pi) = 0.028 + 0.035ln(k^{**}/k) + 0.360ln(N)$ KOR: $Ln(\pi) = 0.027 - 0.056ln(k^{**}/k) - 0.319ln(N) + 0.844ln(GDP)$	CAN: $Ln(\pi) = 0.022 + 0.017ln(k^{**}/k) + 0.328ln(N) -0.314ln(GDP)$ USA: $Ln(\pi) = 0.015 - 0.017ln(k^{**}/k) + 0.190ln(N)$	N.A.	AUS: $Ln(\pi) = 0.037 + 0.022ln(k^{**}/k)$ NZL: $Ln(\pi) = 0.014 - 0.020ln(k^{**}/k) + 0.205ln(GDP)$
Employment, N	JPN: $Ln(N) = 0.019 + 0.025ln(k^{*}/k) + 0.165ln(\pi) + 0.174ln(GDP)$	N.A.	GER: $Ln(N) = 0.0006 + 0.024ln(k^{*}/k) - 0.373ln(\pi) + 0.493ln(GDP)$ GBR: $Ln(N) = 0.017 + 0.031ln(k^{*}/k) + 0.293ln(GDP)$	N.A.
	JPN: $Ln(N) = 0.022 + 0.025ln(k^{**}/k) + 0.159ln(\pi) + 0.176ln(GDP)$ KOR: $Ln(N) = 0.039 - 0.067ln(k^{**}/k) - 0.242ln(\pi) + 0.345ln(GDP)$	N.A.	GER: $Ln(N) = 0.003 + 0.021ln(k^{**}/k) - 0.356ln(\pi) + 0.501ln(GDP)$ GBR: $Ln(N) = 0.019 + 0.028ln(k^{**}/k) + 0.300ln(GDP)$	N.A.
GDP per capita, GDP	N.A.	N.A.	N.A.	N.A.
	N.A.	N.A.	N.A.	N.A.

Table A6.2 General Panel Regression Equations for ASIA, AMERICAS, EUROPE, and PACIFIC

GENERAL EQUATIONS (Panel)	*ASIA (JPN, KOR)*	*AMERICAS (CAN, USA)*	*EUROPE (GER, GBR)*	*PACIFIC (AUS, NZL)*
Inflation, π	N.A.	N.A.	$Ln(\pi) = 0.022 - 0.011ln(k^{*}/k) - 0.435ln(N)$	N.A.
	N.A.	N.A.	$Ln(\pi) = 0.020 - 0.012ln(k^{**}/k) - 0.423ln(N)$	N.A.
Employment, N	N.A.	$Ln(N) = -0.015 + 0.006ln(k^{*}/k) + 0.731ln(\pi) + 0.648ln(GDP)$	N.A.	$Ln(N) = 0.022 + 0.012ln(k^{*}/k) - 0.037ln(GDP)$
	N.A.	$Ln(N) = -0.014 + 0.005ln(k^{**}/k) + 0.731ln(\pi) + 0.650ln(GDP)$	N.A.	$Ln(N) = 0.024 + 0.010ln(k^{**}/k) + 0.004ln(\pi) - 0.040ln(GDP)$
GDP per capita, GDP	$Ln(GDP) = 0.017 + 0.015ln(k^{*}/k) + 0.409ln(\pi) + 0.240ln(N)$	$Ln(GDP) = 0.016 + 0.023ln(k^{*}/k) - 0.197ln(\pi) + 0.237ln(N)$	N.A.	$Ln(GDP) = 0.017 + 0.048ln(k^{*}/k) - 0.385ln(\pi)$
	$Ln(GDP) = 0.018 + 0.013ln(k^{**}/k) + 0.431ln(\pi) + 0.267ln(N)$	$Ln(GDP) = 0.019 + 0.021ln(k^{**}/k) - 0.196ln(\pi) + 0.239ln(N)$	N.A.	$Ln(GDP) = 0.026 + 0.044ln(k^{**}/k) - 0.363ln(\pi)$

Table A6.3 Equations (2009 and 2021) for Japan and Korea from Panel and Regression Analysis

GENERAL EQUATIONS (2009 and 2021)	*ASIA (JAP)*	*ASIA (KOR)*
Inflation, π	$Ln(\pi)_{2009} = 0.020 + 0.037ln(k^{*}/k)$	$Ln(\pi)_{2009} = 0.036 - 0.019ln(k^{*}/k)$
	$Ln(\pi)_{2021} = 0.024 + 0.037ln(k^{*}/k)$	$Ln(\pi)_{2021} = 0.039 - 0.019ln(k^{*}/k)$
	$Ln(\pi)_{2009} = 0.024 + 0.035ln(k^{**}/k)$	$Ln(\pi)_{2009} = 0.032 - 0.056ln(k^{**}/k)$
	$Ln(\pi)_{2021} = 0.028 + 0.035ln(k^{**}/k)$	$Ln(\pi)_{2021} = 0.056 - 0.056ln(k^{**}/k)$
Employment, N	$Ln(N)_{2009} = 0.018 + 0.025ln(k^{*}/k)$	*N.A.*
	$Ln(N)_{2021} = 0.023 + 0.025ln(k^{*}/k)$	
	$Ln(N)_{2009} = 0.020 + 0.025ln(k^{**}/k)$	*N.A.* *As there was no equation for* k^{*}*, comparison to* k^{**} *would not be meaningful*
	$Ln(N)_{2021} = 0.026 + 0.025ln(k^{**}/k)$	
GDP per capita, GDP (Panel)	$Ln(GDP)_{2009} = 0.012 + 0.015ln(k^{*}/k)$	$Ln(GDP)_{2009} = 0.031 + 0.015ln(k^{*}/k)$
	$Ln(GDP)_{2021} = 0.004 + 0.015ln(k^{*}/k)$	$Ln(GDP)_{2021} = 0.030 + 0.015ln(k^{*}/k)$
	$Ln(GDP)_{2009} = 0.016 + 0.013ln(k^{**}/k)$	$Ln(GDP)_{2009} = 0.030 + 0.013ln(k^{**}/k)$
	$Ln(GDP)_{2021} = 0.017 + 0.013ln(k^{**}/k)$	$Ln(GDP)_{2021} = 0.032 + 0.013ln(k^{**}/k)$

Table A6.4 Equations (2009 and 2021) for Canada and the USA from Panel and Regression Analysis

GENERAL EQUATIONS (2009 and 2021)	*AMERICAS (CAN)*	*AMERICAS (USA)*
Inflation, π	$Ln(\pi)_{2009} = 0.014 + 0.019ln(k^{*}/k)$	$Ln(\pi)_{2009} = 0.011 - 0.018ln(k^{*}/k)$
	$Ln(\pi)_{2021} = 0.046 + 0.019ln(k^{*}/k)$	$Ln(\pi)_{2021} = 0.024 - 0.018ln(k^{*}/k)$
	$Ln(\pi)_{2009} = 0.016 + 0.017ln(k^{**}/k)$	$Ln(\pi)_{2009} = 0.008 - 0.017ln(k^{**}/k)$
	$Ln(\pi)_{2021} = 0.039 + 0.017ln(k^{**}/k)$	$Ln(\pi)_{2021} = 0.021 - 0.017ln(k^{**}/k)$
Employment, N (Panel)	$Ln(N)_{2009} = -0.030 + 0.006ln(k^{*}/k)$	$Ln(N)_{2009} = -0.008 + 0.006ln(k^{*}/k)$
	$Ln(N)_{2021} = 0.062 + 0.006ln(k^{*}/k)$	$Ln(N)_{2021} = 0.044 + 0.006ln(k^{*}/k)$
	$Ln(N)_{2009} = -0.029 + 0.005ln(k^{**}/k)$	$Ln(N)_{2009} = -0.007 + 0.005ln(k^{**}/k)$
	$Ln(N)_{2021} = 0.063 + 0.005ln(k^{**}/k)$	$Ln(N)_{2021} = 0.045 + 0.005ln(k^{**}/k)$
GDP per capita, GDP (Panel)	$Ln(GDP)_{2009} = 0.017 + 0.023ln(k^{*}/k)$	$Ln(GDP)_{2009} = 0.006 + 0.023ln(k^{*}/k)$
	$Ln(GDP)_{2021} = 0.020 + 0.023ln(k^{*}/k)$	$Ln(GDP)_{2021} = 0.015 + 0.023ln(k^{*}/k)$
	$Ln(GDP)_{2009} = 0.020 + 0.021ln(k^{**}/k)$	$Ln(GDP)_{2009} = 0.009 + 0.021ln(k^{**}/k)$
	$Ln(GDP)_{2021} = 0.023 + 0.021ln(k^{**}/k)$	$Ln(GDP)_{2021} = 0.018 + 0.021ln(k^{**}/k)$

Table A6.5 Equations (2009 and 2021) for Germany and the United Kingdom from Panel and Regression Analysis

GENERAL EQUATIONS (2009 and 2021)	*EUROPE (GER)*	*EUROPE (GBR)*
Inflation, π (Panel)	$Ln(\pi)_{2009} = 0.021 - 0.011ln(k^{*}/k)$	$Ln(\pi)_{2009} = 0.029 - 0.011ln(k^{*}/k)$
	$Ln(\pi)_{2021} = 0.021 - 0.011ln(k^{*}/k)$	$Ln(\pi)_{2021} = 0.023 - 0.011ln(k^{*}/k)$
	$Ln(\pi)_{2009} = 0.019 - 0.012ln(k^{**}/k)$	$Ln(\pi)_{2009} = 0.027 - 0.012ln(k^{**}/k)$
	$Ln(\pi)_{2021} = 0.019 - 0.012ln(k^{**}/k)$	$Ln(\pi)_{2021} = 0.021 - 0.012ln(k^{**}/k)$
Employment, N	$Ln(N)_{2009} = 0.00006 + 0.024ln(k^{*}/k)$	$Ln(N)_{2009} = 0.017 + 0.031ln(k^{*}/k)$
	$Ln(N)_{2021} = 0.003 + 0.024ln(k^{*}/k)$	$Ln(N)_{2021} = 0.029 + 0.031ln(k^{*}/k)$
	$Ln(N)_{2009} = 0.005 + 0.021ln(k^{**}/k)$	$Ln(N)_{2009} = 0.019 + 0.028ln(k^{**}/k)$
	$Ln(N)_{2021} = 0.006 + 0.021ln(k^{**}/k)$	$Ln(N)_{2021} = 0.031 + 0.028ln(k^{**}/k)$
GDP per capita, GDP	*N.A.*	*N.A.*
	N.A.	*N.A.*

Table A6.6 Equations (2009 and 2021) for Australia and New Zealand for Panel and Regression Analysis

GENERAL EQUATIONS (2009 and 2021)	*PACIFIC (AUS)*	*PACIFIC (NZL)*
Inflation, π	$Ln(\pi)_{2009} = 0.034 + 0.032ln(k^*/k)$	$Ln(\pi)_{2009} = 0.018 - 0.024ln(k^*/k)$
	$Ln(\pi)_{2021} = 0.034 + 0.032ln(k^*/k)$	$Ln(\pi)_{2021} = 0.015 - 0.024ln(k^*/k)$
	$Ln(\pi)_{2009} = 0.037 + 0.022ln(k^{**}/k)$	$Ln(\pi)_{2009} = 0.025 - 0.020ln(k^{**}/k)$
	$Ln(\pi)_{2021} = 0.037 + 0.022ln(k^{**}/k)$	$Ln(\pi)_{2021} = 0.022 - 0.020ln(k^{**}/k)$
Employment, N (Panel)	$Ln(N)_{2009} = 0.022 + 0.012ln(k^*/k)$	$Ln(N)_{2009} = 0.022 + 0.012ln(k^*/k)$
	$Ln(N)_{2021} = 0.020 + 0.012ln(k^*/k)$	$Ln(N)_{2021} = 0.023 + 0.012ln(k^*/k)$
	$Ln(N)_{2009} = 0.024 + 0.010ln(k^{**}/k)$	$Ln(N)_{2009} = 0.024 + 0.010ln(k^{**}/k)$
	$Ln(N)_{2021} = 0.022 + 0.010ln(k^{**}/k)$	$Ln(N)_{2021} = 0.023 + 0.010ln(k^{**}/k)$
GDP per capita, GDP (Panel)	$Ln(GDP)_{2009} = -0.002 + 0.048ln(k^*/k)$	$Ln(GDP)_{2009} = 0.007 + 0.048ln(k^*/k)$
	$Ln(GDP)_{2021} = 0.006 + 0.048ln(k^*/k)$	$Ln(GDP)_{2021} = 0.011 + 0.048ln(k^*/k)$
	$Ln(GDP)_{2009} = 0.008 + 0.044ln(k^{**}/k)$	$Ln(GDP)_{2009} = 0.011 + 0.044ln(k^{**}/k)$
	$Ln(GDP)_{2021} = 0.016 + 0.044ln(k^{**}/k)$	$Ln(GDP)_{2021} = 0.009 + 0.044ln(k^{**}/k)$

Appendix 6.3 Snapshots (2009 and 2021) of the Macroeconomic Variables for the Economies

- JAP $Ln(\pi)_{2009} = 0.020 + 0.037ln(k^*/k); Ln(\pi)_{2009} = 0.024 + 0.035ln(k^{**}/k)$

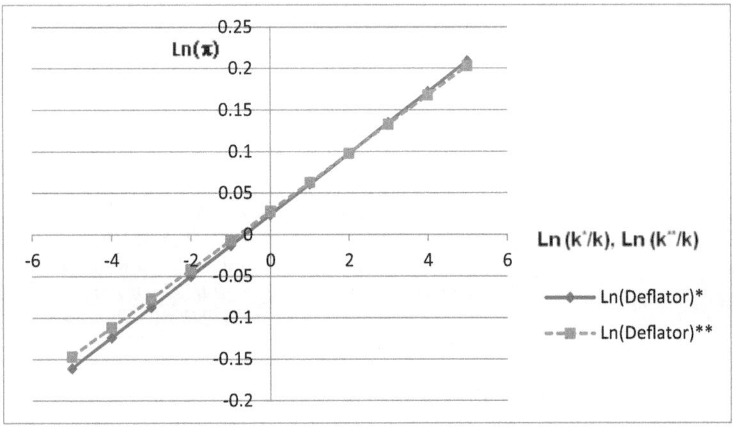

Figure A6.1 Japan's Inflation and Steady-State Ratio in 2009.

- JAP $Ln(\pi)_{2021} = 0.024 + 0.037ln(k^*/k); Ln(\pi)_{2021} = 0.028 + 0.035ln(k^{**}/k)$

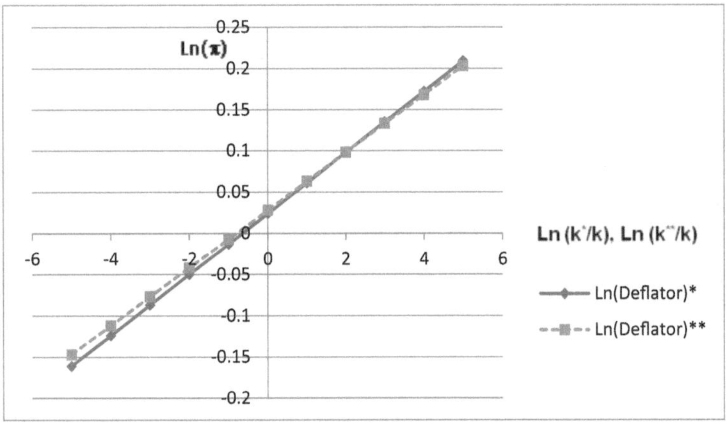

Figure A6.2 Japan's Inflation and Steady-State Ratio in 2021.

- JAP $Ln(N)_{2009} = 0.018 + 0.025ln(k^{*}/k)$; $Ln(N)_{2009} = 0.020 + 0.025ln(k^{**}/k)$

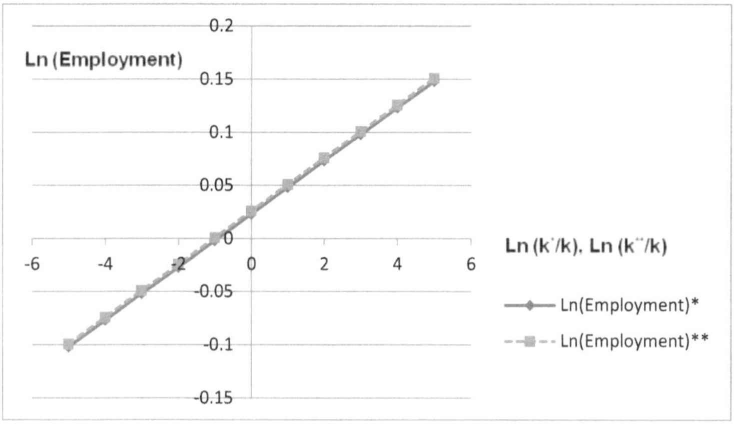

Figure A6.3 Japan's Employment and Steady-State Ratio in 2009.

- JAP $Ln(N)_{2021} = 0.023 + 0.025ln(k^{*}/k)$; $Ln(N)_{2021} = 0.026 + 0.025ln(k^{**}/k)$

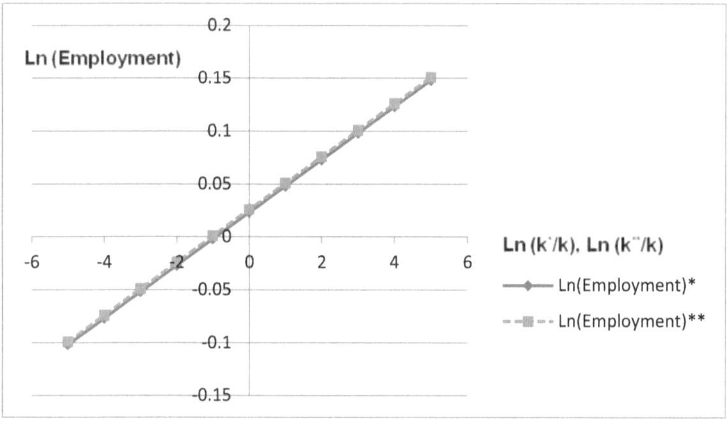

Figure A6.4 Japan's Employment and Steady-State Ratio in 2021.

- JAP $Ln(GDP)_{2009} = 0.012 + 0.015ln(k^{*}/k); Ln(GDP)_{2009} = 0.016 + 0.013ln(k^{**}/k)$

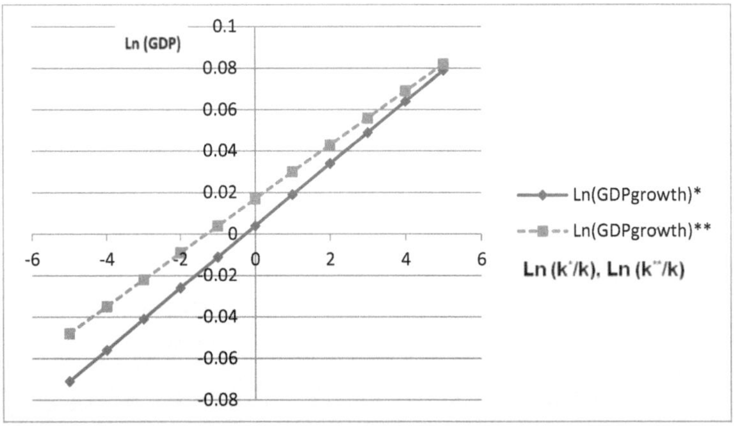

Figure A6.5 Japan's GDP Growth and Steady-State Ratio in 2009.

- JAP $Ln(GDP)_{2021} = 0.004 + 0.015ln(k^{*}/k); Ln(GDP)_{2021} = 0.017 + 0.013ln(k^{**}/k)$

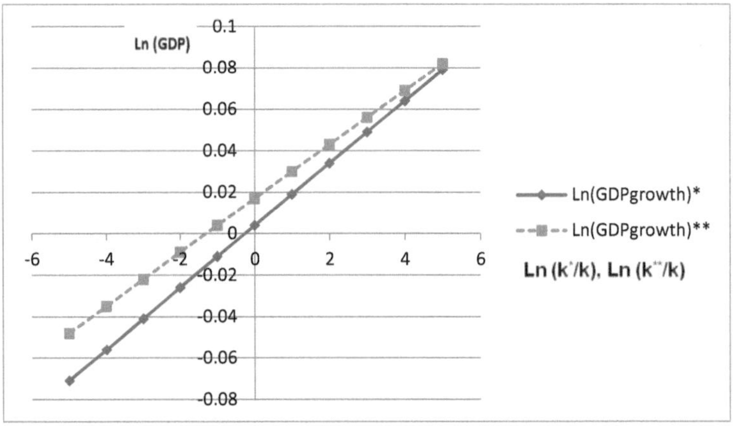

Figure A6.6 Japan's GDP Growth and Steady-State Ratio in 2021.

- KOR $Ln(\pi)_{2009} = 0.036 - 0.019 ln(k^{*}/k)$; $Ln(\pi)_{2009} = 0.032 - 0.056 ln(k^{**}/k)$

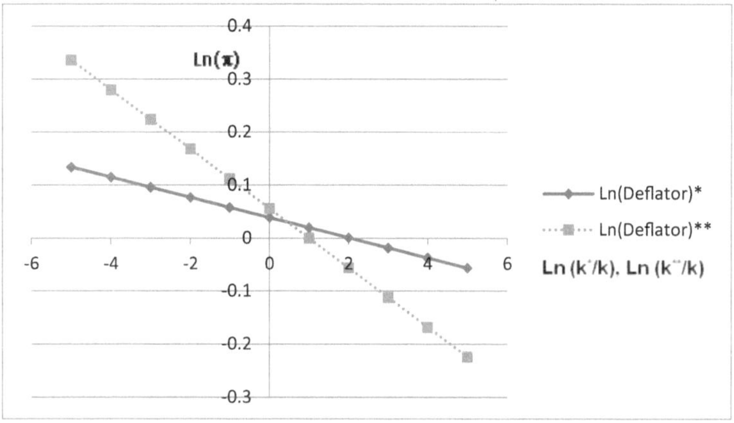

Figure A6.7 Korea's Inflation and Steady-State Ratio in 2009.

- KOR $Ln(\pi)_{2021} = 0.039 - 0.019 ln(k^{*}/k)$; $Ln(\pi)_{2021} = 0.056 - 0.056 ln(k^{**}/k)$

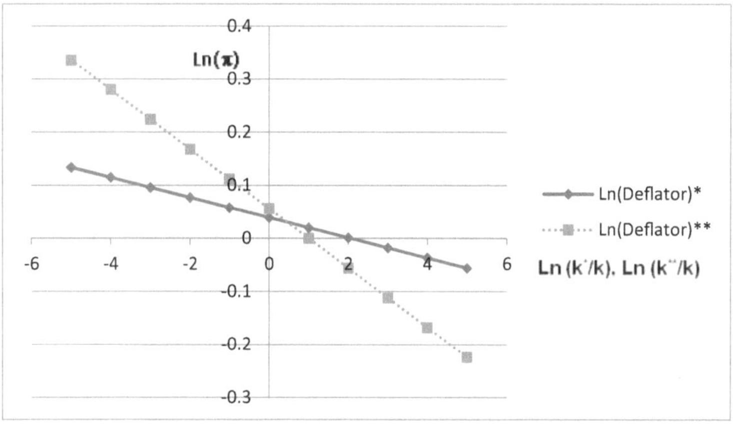

Figure A6.8 Korea's Inflation and Steady-State Ratio in 2021.

- KOR $Ln(GDP)_{2009} = 0.031 + 0.015ln(k^{*}/k)$; $Ln(GDP)_{2009} = 0.030 + 0.013ln(k^{**}/k)$

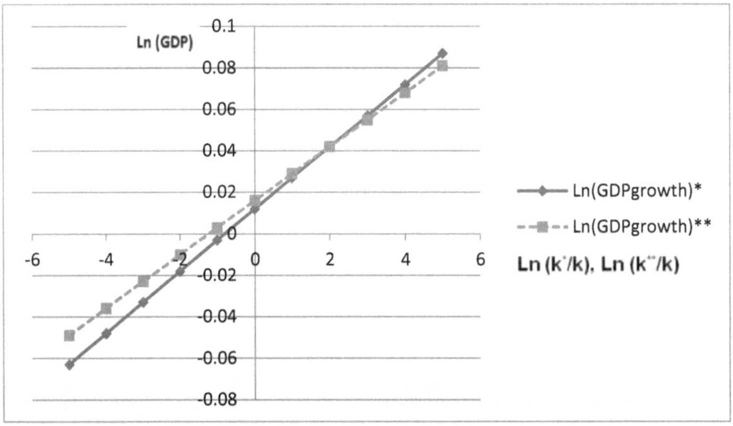

Figure A6.9 Korea's GDP Growth and Steady-State Ratio in 2009.

- KOR $Ln(GDP)_{2021} = 0.030 + 0.015ln(k^{*}/k)$; $Ln(GDP)_{2021} = 0.032 + 0.013ln(k^{**}/k)$

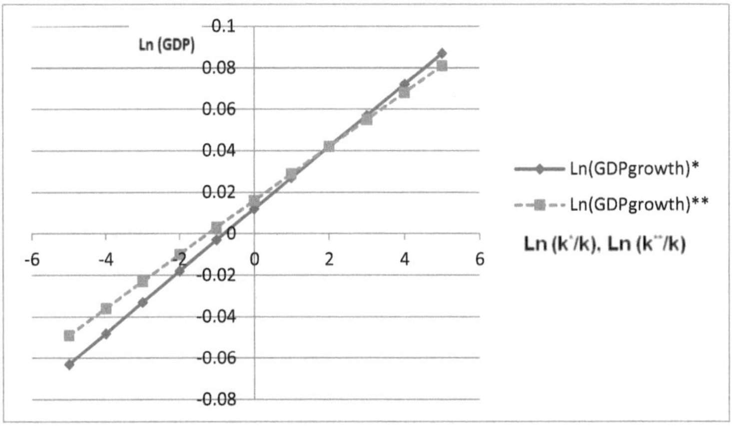

Figure A6.10 Korea's GDP Growth and Steady-State Ratio in 2021.

- CAN $Ln(\pi)_{2009} = 0.014 + 0.019ln(k^{*}/k); Ln(\pi)_{2009} = 0.016 + 0.017ln(k^{**}/k)$

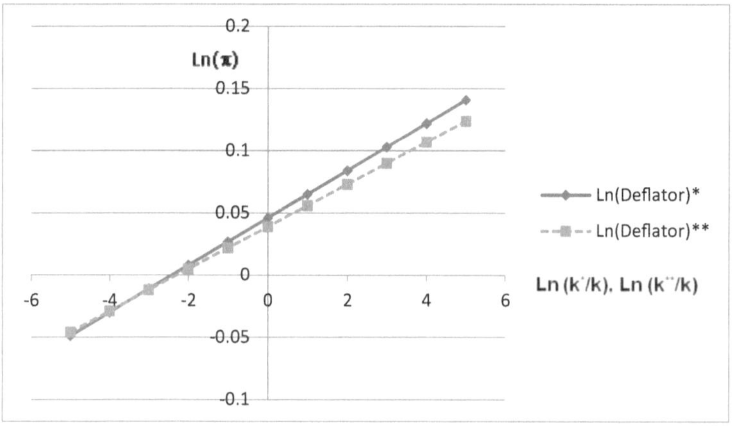

Figure A6.11 Canada's Inflation and Steady-State Ratio in 2009.

- CAN $Ln(\pi)_{2021} = 0.046 + 0.019ln(k^{*}/k); Ln(\pi)_{2021} = 0.039 + 0.017ln(k^{**}/k)$

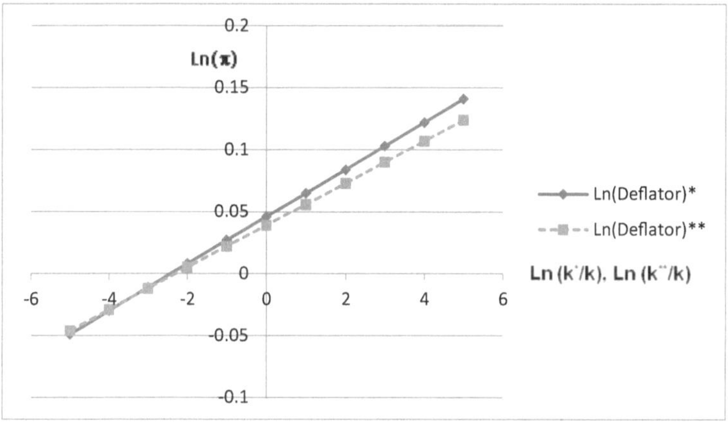

Figure A6.12 Canada's Inflation and Steady-State Ratio in 2021.

- CAN $Ln(N)_{2009} = -0.030 + 0.006ln(k^{*}/k); Ln(N)_{2009} = -0.029 + 0.005ln(k^{**}/k)$

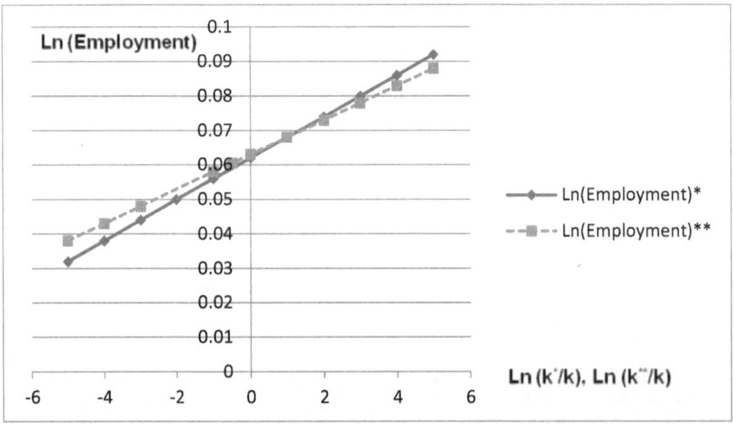

Figure A6.13 Canada's Employment and Steady-State Ratio in 2009.

- CAN $Ln(N)_{2021} = 0.062 + 0.006ln(k^{*}/k); Ln(N)_{2021} = 0.063 + 0.005ln(k^{**}/k)$

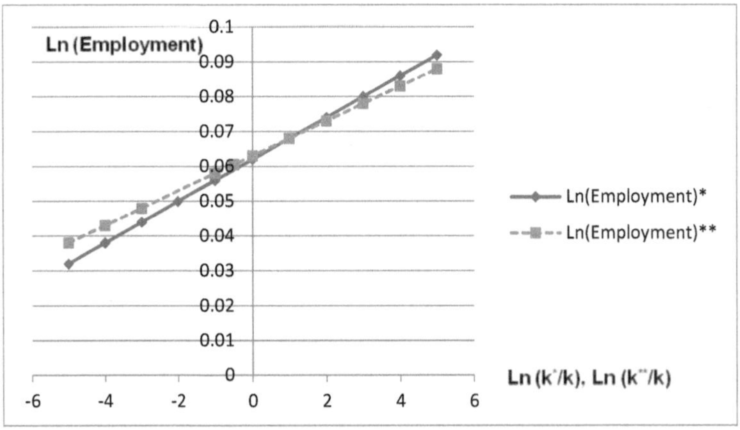

Figure A6.14 Canada's Employment and Steady-State Ratio in 2021.

- CAN $Ln(GDP)_{2009} = 0.017 + 0.023ln(k^{*}/k); Ln(GDP)_{2009} = 0.020 + 0.021ln(k^{**}/k)$

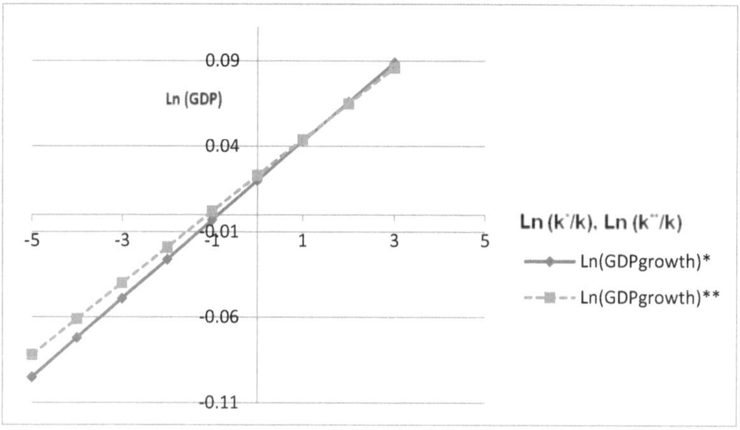

Figure A6.15 Canada's GDP Growth and Steady-State Ratio in 2009.

- CAN $Ln(GDP)_{2021} = 0.020 + 0.023ln(k^{*}/k); Ln(GDP)_{2021} = 0.023 + 0.021ln(k^{**}/k)$

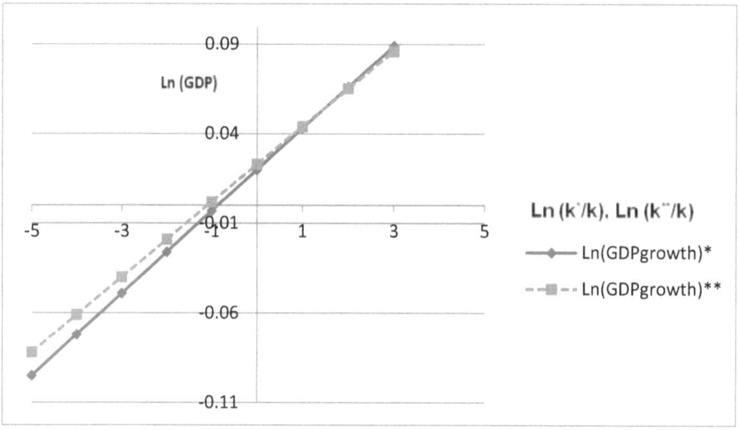

Figure A6.16 Canada's GDP Growth and Steady-State Ratio in 2021.

- USA $Ln(\pi)_{2009} = 0.011 - 0.018ln(k^{*}/k)$; $Ln(\pi)_{2009} = 0.008 - 0.017ln(k^{**}/k)$

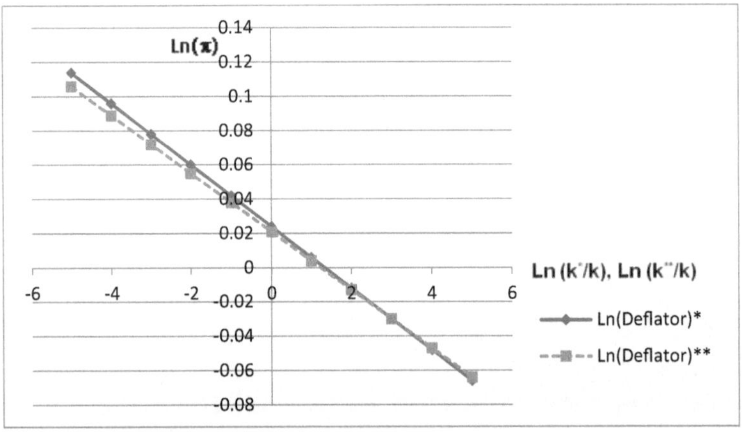

Figure A6.17 USA's Inflation and Steady-State Ratio in 2009.

- USA $Ln(\pi)_{2021} = 0.024 - 0.018ln(k^{*}/k)$; $Ln(\pi)_{2021} = 0.021 - 0.017ln(k^{**}/k)$

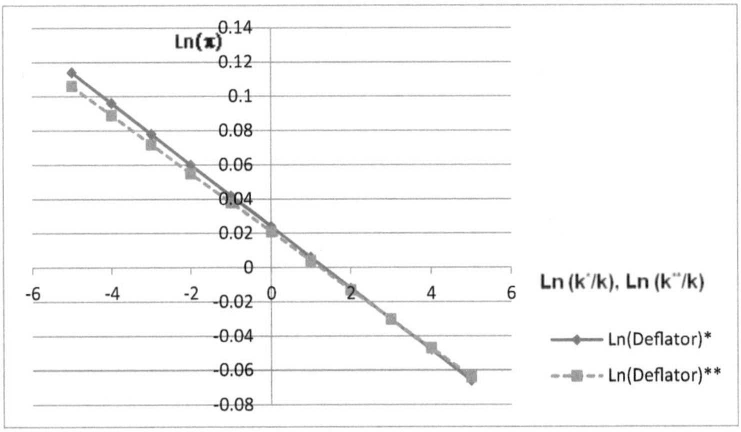

Figure A6.18 USA's Inflation and Steady-State Ratio in 2021.

- USA $Ln(N)_{2009} = -0.008 + 0.006ln(k^*/k)$; $Ln(N)_{2009} = -0.007 + 0.005ln(k^{**}/k)$

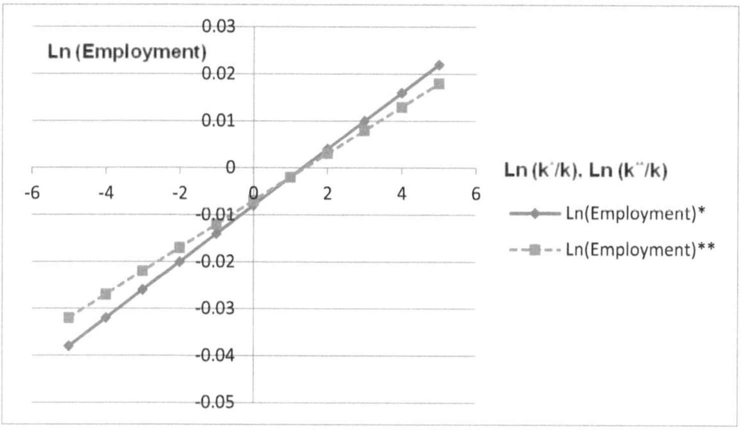

Figure A6.19 USA's Employment and Steady-State Ratio in 2009.

- USA $Ln(N)_{2021} = 0.044 + 0.006ln(k^*/k)$; $Ln(N)_{2021} = 0.045 + 0.005ln(k^{**}/k)$

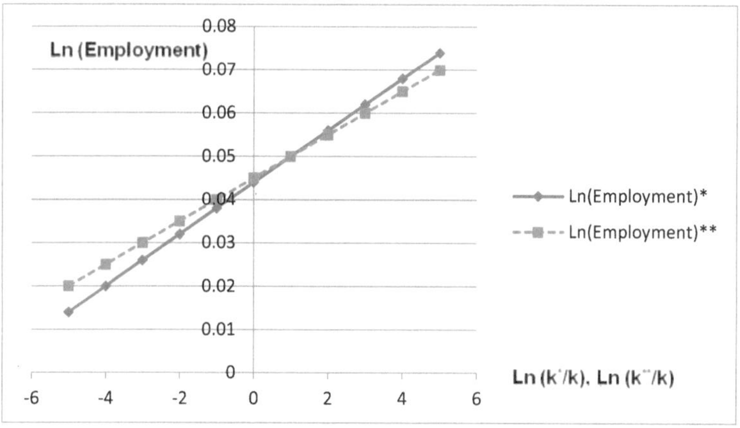

Figure A6.20 USA's Employment and Steady-State Ratio in 2021.

- USA $Ln(GDP)_{2009} = 0.006 + 0.023ln(k^*/k)$; $Ln(GDP)_{2009} = 0.009 + 0.021ln(k^{**}/k)$

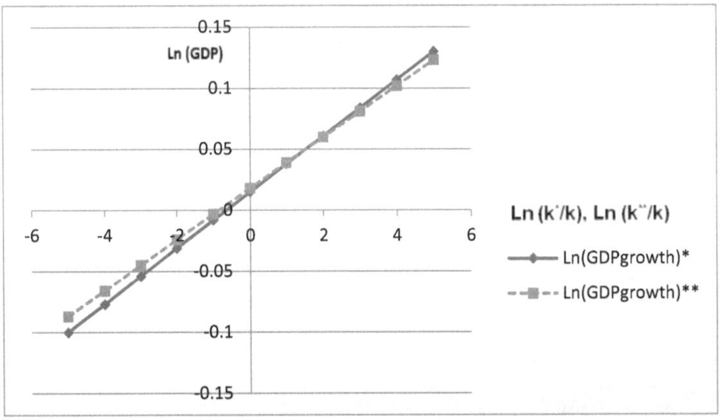

Figure A6.21 USA's GDP Growth and Steady-State Ratio in 2009.

- USA $Ln(GDP)_{2021} = 0.015 + 0.023ln(k^*/k)$; $Ln(GDP)_{2021} = 0.018 + 0.021ln(k^{**}/k)$

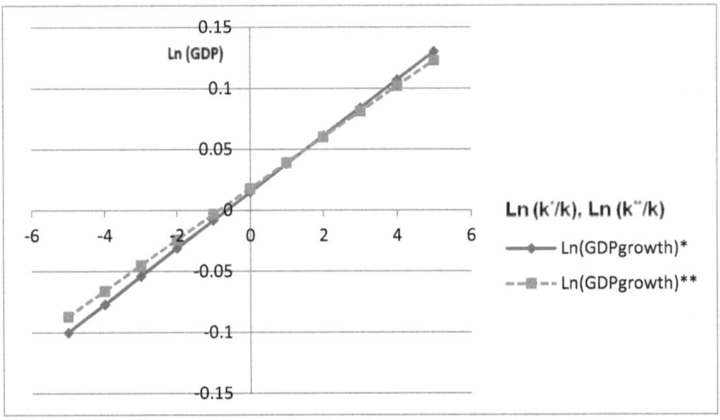

Figure A6.22 USA's GDP Growth and Steady-State Ratio in 2021.

- GER $Ln(\pi)_{2009} = 0.021 - 0.011ln(k^*/k); Ln(\pi)_{2009} = 0.019 - 0.012ln(k^{**}/k)$

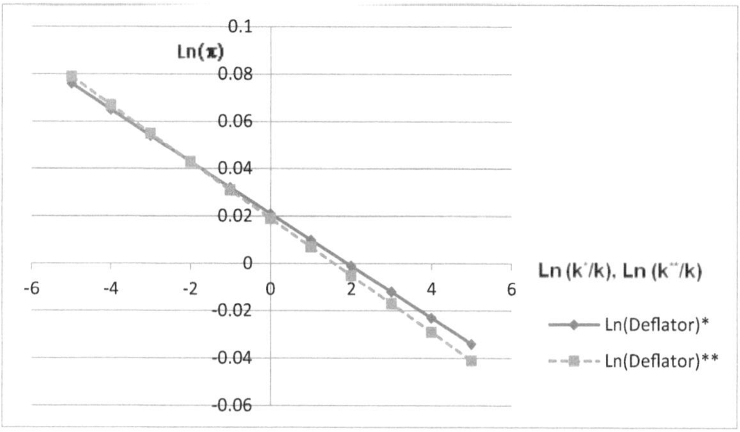

Figure A6.23 Germany's Inflation and Steady-State Ratio in 2009.

- GER $Ln(\pi)_{2021} = 0.021 - 0.011ln(k^*/k); Ln(\pi)_{2021} = 0.019 - 0.012ln(k^{**}/k)$

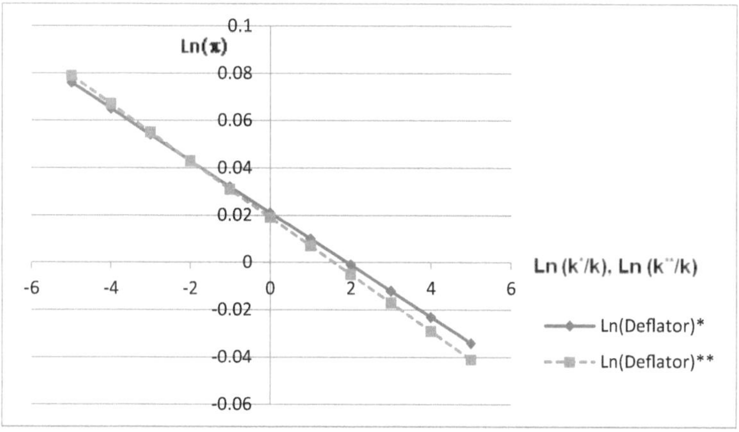

Figure A6.24 Germany's Inflation and Steady-State Ratio in 2021.

- GER $Ln(N)_{2009} = 0.00006 + 0.024ln(k^*/k); Ln(N)_{2009} = 0.005 + 0.021ln(k^{**}/k)$

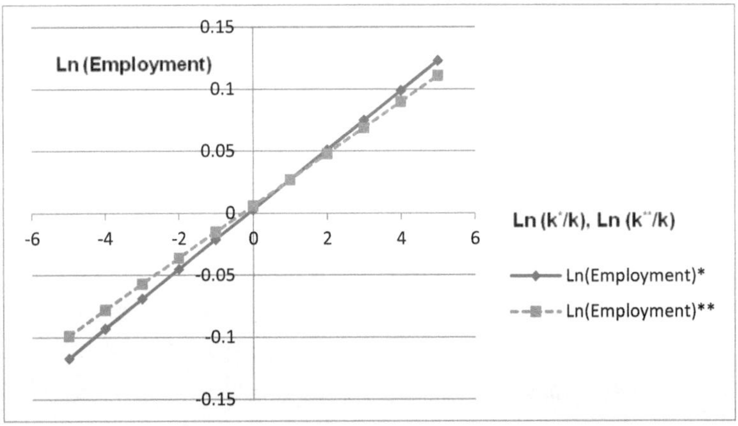

Figure A6.25 Germany's Employment and Steady-State Ratio in 2009.

- GER $Ln(N)_{2021} = 0.003 + 0.024ln(k^*/k); Ln(N)_{2021} = 0.006 + 0.021ln(k^{**}/k)$

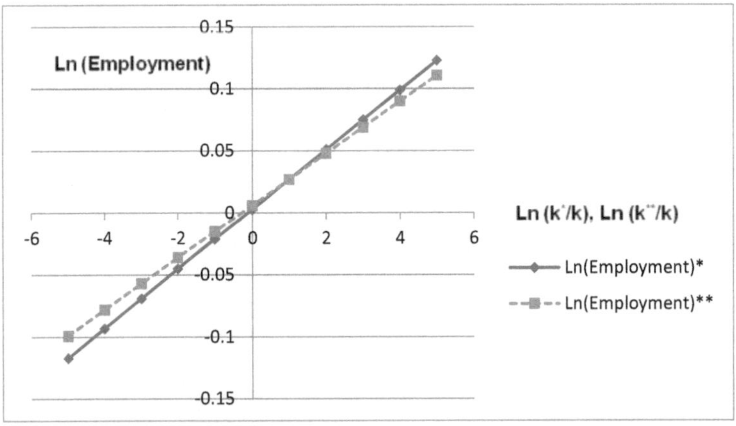

Figure A6.26 Germany's Employment and Steady-State Ratio in 2021.

- GBR $Ln(\pi)_{2009} = 0.029 - 0.011ln(k^{*}/k)$; $Ln(\pi)_{2009} = 0.027 - 0.012ln(k^{**}/k)$

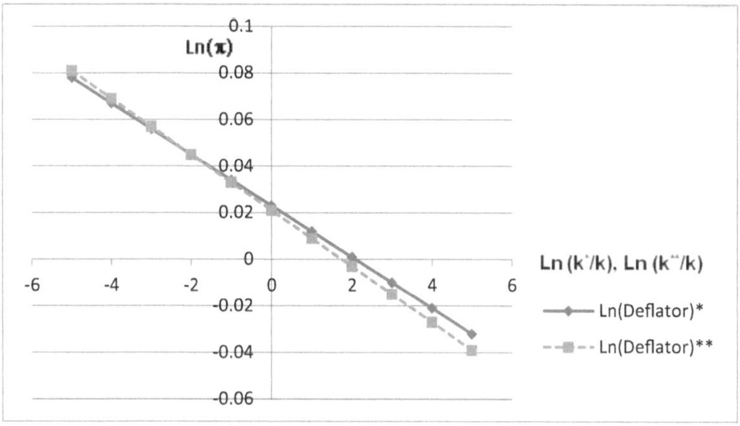

Figure A6.27 United Kingdom's Inflation and Steady-State Ratio in 2009.

- GBR $Ln(\pi)_{2021} = 0.023 - 0.011ln(k^{*}/k)$; $Ln(\pi)_{2021} = 0.021 - 0.012ln(k^{**}/k)$

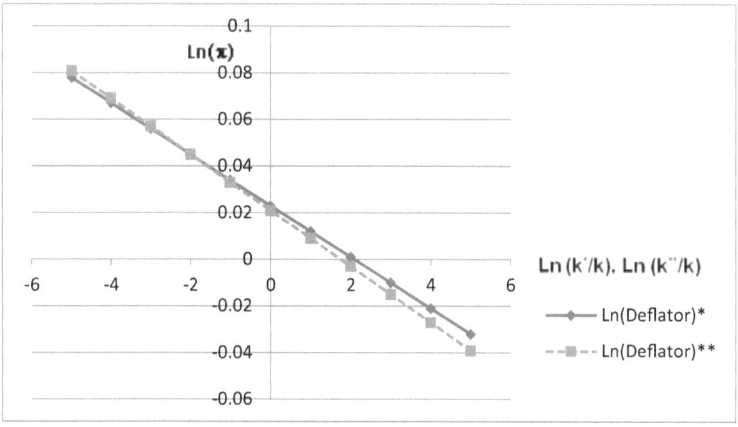

Figure A6.28 United Kingdom's Inflation and Steady-State Ratio in 2021.

- GBR $Ln(N)_{2009} = 0.017 + 0.031ln(k^{*}/k); Ln(N)_{2009} = 0.019 + 0.028ln(k^{**}/k)$

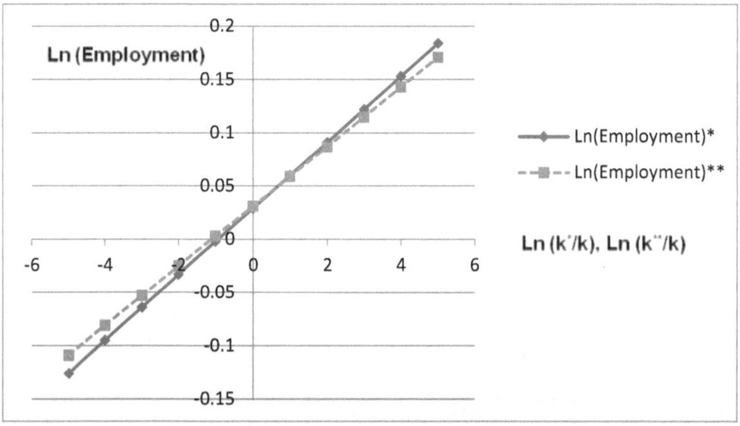

Figure A6.29 United Kingdom's Employment and Steady-State Ratio in 2009.

- GBR $Ln(N)_{2021} = 0.029 + 0.031ln(k^{*}/k); Ln(N)_{2021} = 0.031 + 0.028ln(k^{**}/k)$

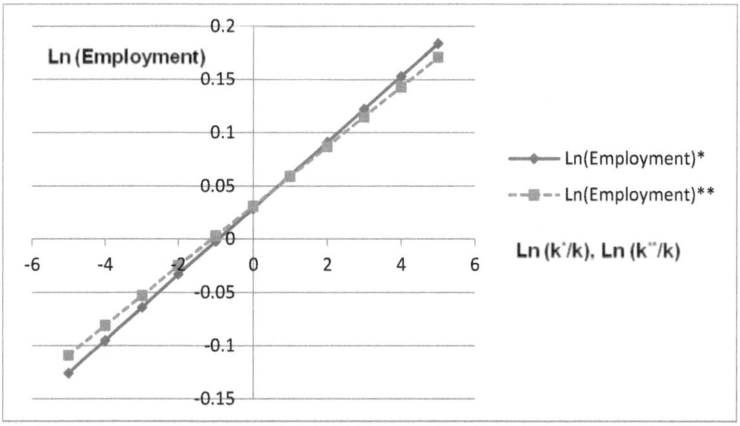

Figure A6.30 United Kingdom's Employment and Steady-State Ratio in 2021.

- AUS $Ln(\pi)_{2009} = 0.034 + 0.032ln(k^{*}/k)$; $Ln(\pi)_{2009} = 0.037 + 0.022ln(k^{**}/k)$

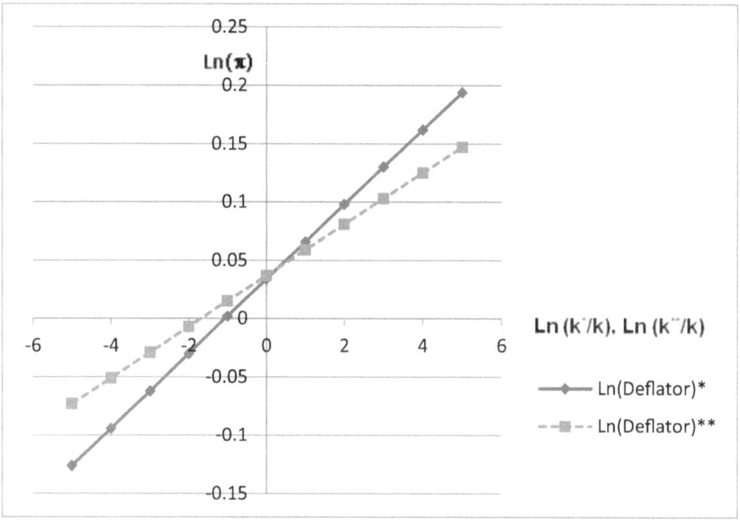

Figure A6.31 Australia's Inflation and Steady-State Ratio in 2009.

- AUS $Ln(\pi)_{2021} = 0.034 + 0.032ln(k^{*}/k)$; $Ln(\pi)_{2021} = 0.037 + 0.022ln(k^{**}/k)$

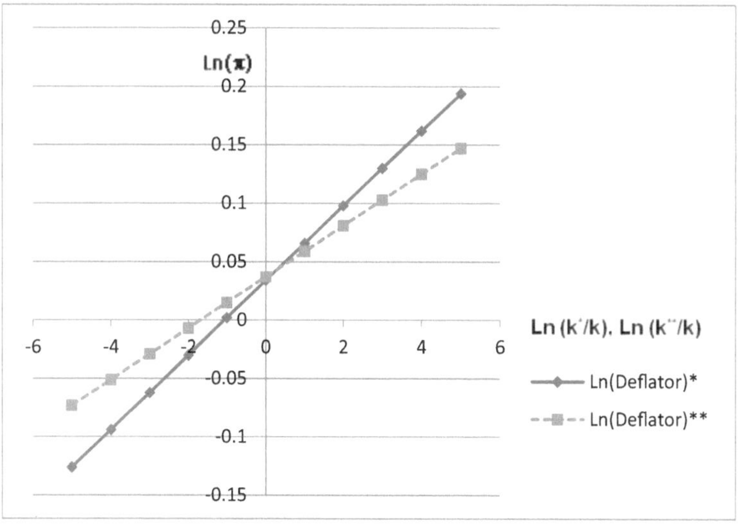

Figure A6.32 Australia's Inflation and Steady-State Ratio in 2021.

- AUS $Ln(N)_{2009} = 0.022 + 0.012ln(k^{*}/k)$; $Ln(N)_{2009} = 0.024 + 0.010ln(k^{**}/k)$

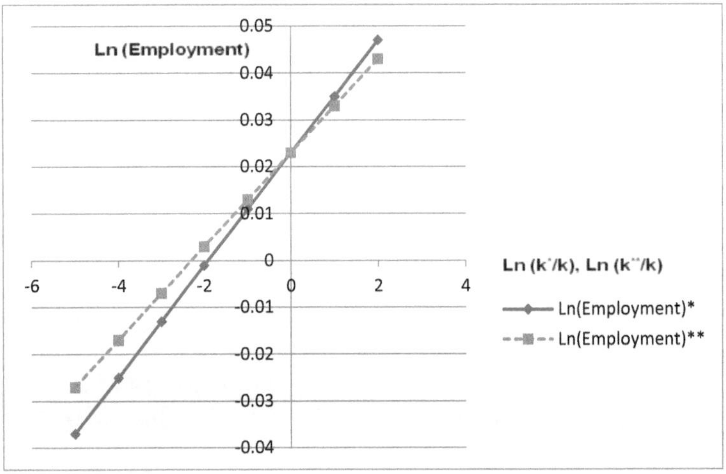

Figure A6.33 Australia's Employment and Steady-State Ratio in 2009.

- AUS $Ln(N)_{2021} = 0.020 + 0.012ln(k^{*}/k)$; $Ln(N)_{2021} = 0.022 + 0.010ln(k^{**}/k)$

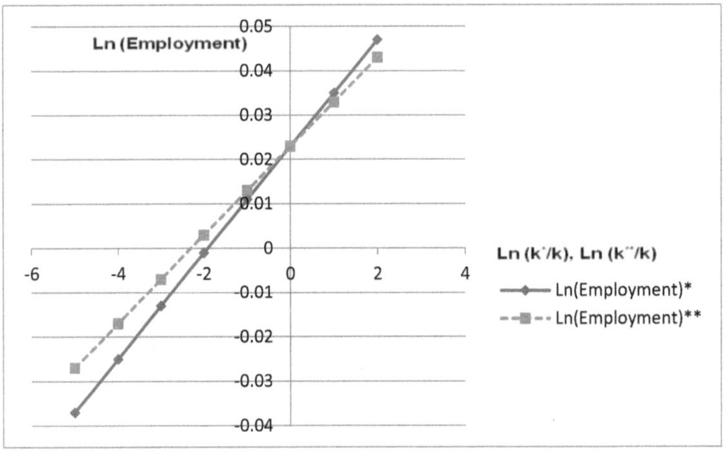

Figure A6.34 Australia's Employment and Steady-State Ratio in 2021.

- AUS $Ln(GDP)_{2009} = -0.002 + 0.048ln(k^*/k)$; $Ln(GDP)_{2009} = 0.008 + 0.044ln(k^{**}/k)$

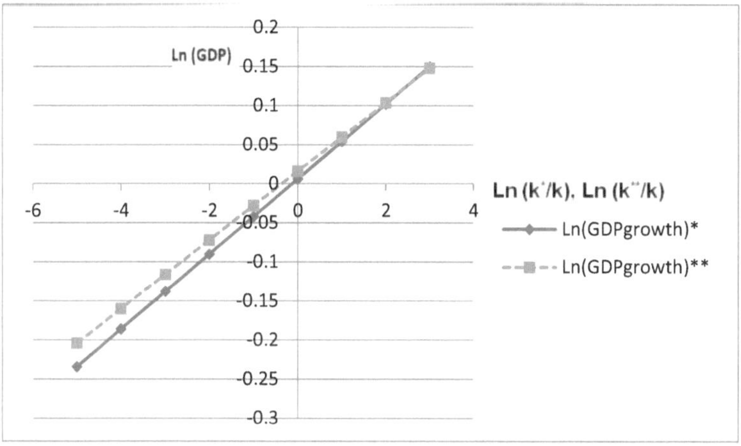

Figure A6.35 Australia's GDP Growth and Steady-State Ratio in 2009.

- AUS $Ln(GDP)_{2021} = 0.006 + 0.048ln(k^*/k)$; $Ln(GDP)_{2021} = 0.016 + 0.044ln(k^{**}/k)$

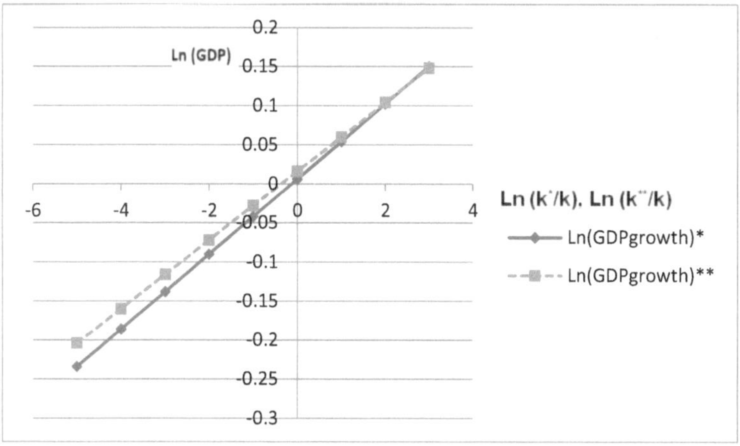

Figure A6.36 Australia's GDP Growth and Steady-State Ratio in 2021.

- NZL $Ln(\pi)_{2009} = 0.018 - 0.024ln(k^{*}/k)$; $Ln(\pi)_{2009} = 0.025 - 0.020ln(k^{**}/k)$

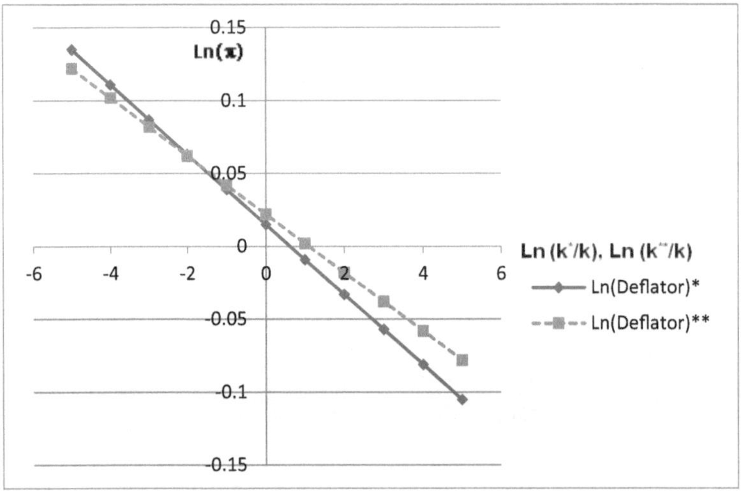

Figure A6.37 New Zealand's Inflation and Steady-State Ratio in 2009.

- NZL $Ln(\pi)_{2021} = 0.015 - 0.024ln(k^{*}/k)$; $Ln(\pi)_{2021} = 0.022 - 0.020ln(k^{**}/k)$

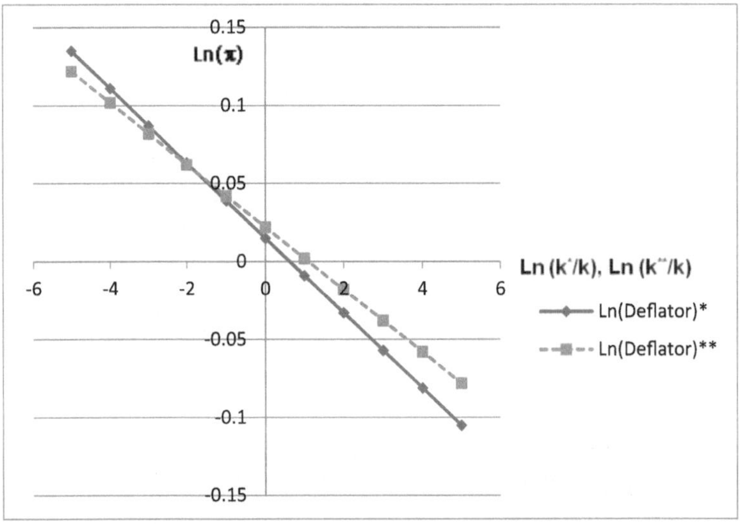

Figure A6.38 New Zealand's Inflation and Steady-State Ratio in 2021.

- NZL $Ln(N)_{2009} = 0.022 + 0.012ln(k^{*}/k)$; $Ln(N)_{2009} = 0.024 + 0.010ln(k^{**}/k)$

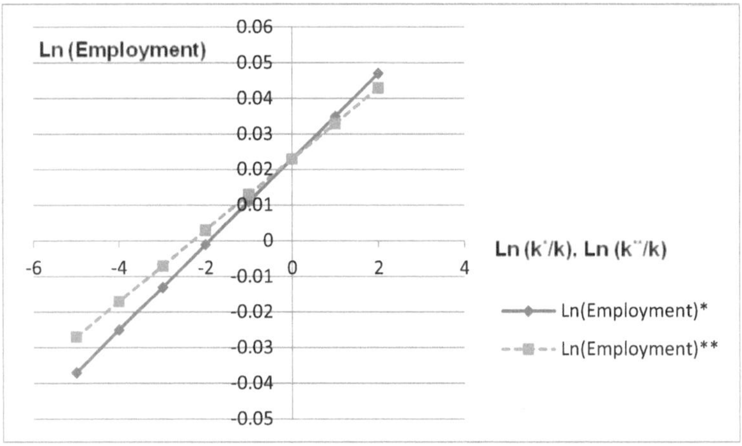

Figure A6.39 New Zealand's Employment and Steady-State Ratio in 2009.

- NZL $Ln(N)_{2021} = 0.023 + 0.012ln(k^{*}/k)$; $Ln(N)_{2021} = 0.023 + 0.010ln(k^{**}/k)$

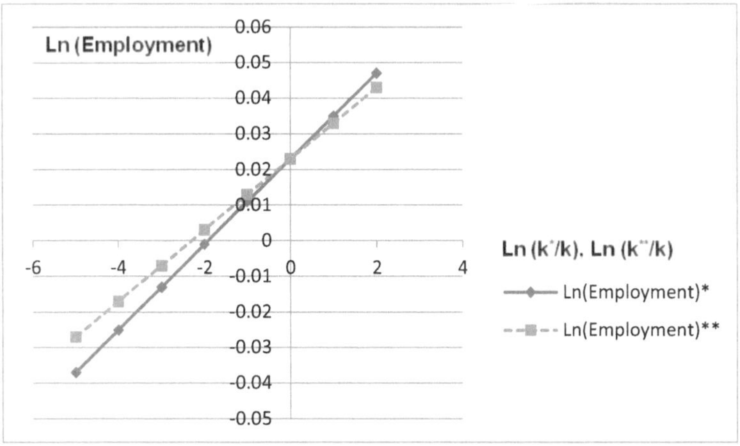

Figure A6.40 New Zealand's Employment and Steady-State Ratio in 2021.

- NZL $Ln(GDP)_{2009} = 0.007 + 0.048ln(k^{*}/k)$; $Ln(GDP)_{2009} = 0.011 + 0.044ln(k^{**}/k)$

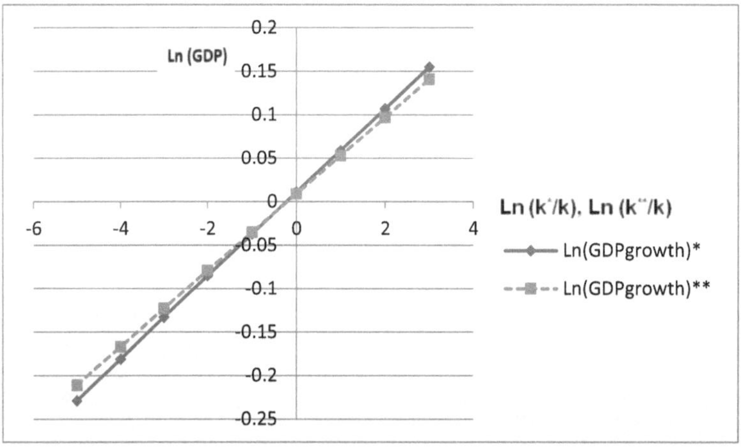

Figure A6.41 New Zealand's GDP Growth and Steady-State Ratio in 2009.

- NZL $Ln(GDP)_{2021} = 0.011 + 0.048ln(k^{*}/k)$; $Ln(GDP)_{2021} = 0.009 + 0.044ln(k^{**}/k)$

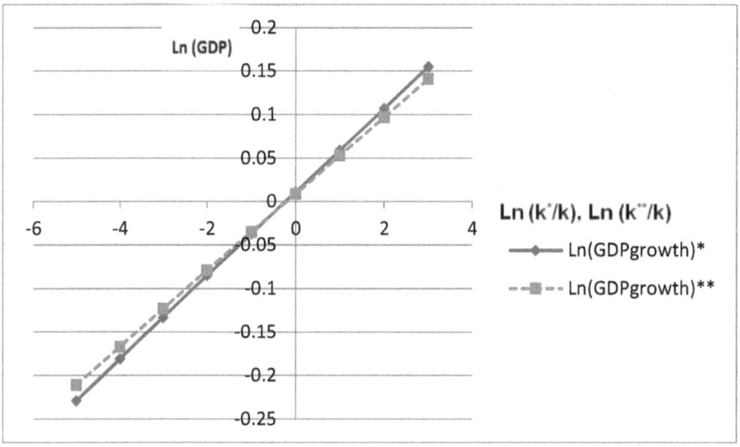

Figure A6.42 New Zealand's GDP Growth and Steady-State Ratio in 2021.

7 Sustainable Development and Public Policy

A Summary of the Research and Future Studies

7.1 Introduction

The final chapter concludes by presenting the implications of the results involving sustainable development and public policy with directions for future studies. It was established in Chapter 5 that the standard macroeconomic model overstates the steady-state equilibrium of an economy; in other words, the capacity of an economy might not be correctly represented. This was highlighted in Chapter 6 with different policy ranges for Australia's inflation, Japan's GDP growth, and Korea's inflation. The policy range would of course differ between the standard macroeconomic model and the environmental-macroeconomics (EM) model. The contention here is that the standard macroeconomic model provides a mistaken policy range. Furthermore, should policy recommendations be made based on a mistaken domain, the proposed policy might not be effective in achieving the desired outcome.

Prior chapters have shown with evidence that current practices of policy formulation must change by recourse to the adoption of EM frameworks. It is nigh impossible to cost the depreciation and price the utilisation of the environment as the natural ecosystem displays characteristics of a public good. Thus, policies to preserve the ecosystem will never be achieved lest the policy community first recognises the principal conflict between economic growth and ecosystem preservation. This calls for sustainable development so that the environment would be appreciated and prioritised. Good public policies must be crafted to safeguard the environment by engaging the public in creation and production, that is, policy co-creation and co-production. The public owns public goods as much as the policymakers do; and muddling delays urgent help that must be rendered to the ecosystem.

In this concluding chapter, sustainable development and public policy will be discussed first. Public policy can aid sustainable development with policy co-creation and co-production. This is followed by a summary of the research and directions for future research. The summary of the research reviews what has been discussed in each of the chapters in this book along with significant findings from the analysis that was performed. Directions for future study are discussed in the section before the conclusion.

DOI: 10.4324/9781003002550-7

7.2 Sustainable Development and Public Policy

In one of the earliest known pieces on carbon dioxide emissions, Callendar (1938) documented how production of carbon dioxide from man-made (artificial) combustion led to increase in mean temperature. Since that writing, artificial production of carbon dioxide over the past decades had been fuelled by economic growth, globalisation, and urbanisation; and this has resulted in warmer temperatures and intensified extreme weather. However, this phenomenon we now know as climate change was only integrated into long-run macroeconomic models in 2018 by Nordhaus (2019) (a co-recipient of the 2018 Nobel Prize). Discussions on environmental external effects and policy measures continue to progress (Halkos and Managi, 2023), as well as integration of environmental economics into traditional macroeconomic models (see Harris and Roach, 2021). This book adds to the above debate with effects and measures of climate change (carbon dioxide) and sustainable development (long-run policymaking) [topics that remain least developed, see González-Ramírez et al. (2021) in the environmental economics pedagogy]. As there are lags in policy effect and impacts benefiting future generations, the sustainable development element must be empathised. However, for policies to be effective and impactful, an accurate policy range for public policy must first be accurately identified in macroeconomic models. This book has illustrated an incorrect policy range should the standard macroeconomic model be used; instead, the EM model should be adopted as it identifies a right policy range.

Sustainable development was discussed in Section 2.3; this section will focus more on how sustainable development can be achieved with public policy (as well as stabilisation policies). In theory (Glasbergen et al., 2007), sustainable development and public policy can be explained with perspectives from actor (Belletti et al., 2017), instrument, political, and multi-stakeholder (Wamsler, 2017). And in practice (Lemons and Brown, 2013), the role of science (Funtowicz et al., 1998), ethics, economics, and law can explain biodiversity conservation, climate change, and resource protection; though ultimately, it is the local government (Preuss, 2009) with the greatest influence. Stabilisation policies in the form of monetary and fiscal policies are often driven top-down via federal financial institutions, given that the economic and financial security of an economy is at stake. Although there are monetary and fiscal policies with green elements of carbon tax and subsidies on green goods (Bailey, 2020; Benkhodja et al., 2023) and green bonds (Monasterolo and Raberto, 2018), these may not be correctly prescribed when the environment is not afforded recognition in the standard macroeconomic model.

Policymaking involves multiple stakeholders in an increasingly complicated set of relationships. Success of a policy is often evaluated based on the idea of maximising overall well-being of the community from public services. Public action must be transparent and built on a participatory process. Yet, little is understood about the influence of the community on policymaking. That is, the role of the community has not been clearly defined in existing models of the policymaking process. Community involvement may transform service offerings, but of equal consequence and interest in the present era is that the community itself is transformed by the service offering. The role of community (or service users) in designing and implementing public service offerings has been broadly defined as co-creation and co-production. Co-creation involves citizens at the initiation (content and service delivery) or design (formulation) stage of policymaking. Related concepts include public participation, collaborative governance, and community involvement (Voorberg et al., 2014). Community involvement in these areas has often been assumed to be a virtue in itself which implies that co-creation as a process is a goal in itself. Co-production, on the other hand, refers to an arrangement where citizens are involved in implementation; and such arrangements have been argued to reduce uncertainty for the users (Fledderus et al., 2015) and strengthen the production of services. These efforts are positioned to strengthen social cohesion (Brandsen and Honingh, 2016) and to contribute to the quality (Brandsen and Pestoff, 2006) of public services offered.

When an economy is a subset of a larger natural ecosystem (Daly, 2007), there ought to be transparency (Humphreys et al., 2007) and public opinion on how a public good is managed. Public education must be credited for the awareness on economic development in a sustainable manner (Hessing et al., 2005), where many environmental policies are now co-created and co-produced with multiple stakeholders creating policies that traditionally would have been possible only from a top-down decision. Co-creation offers a platform for comments, direct feedback, and rebuttal (Karpouzoglou et al., 2016) whilst co-production had been studied and sharpened (Parks et al., 1981) and can reduce information asymmetry (McMillan et al., 2014) and perception of climate risk (Braunschweiger and Ingold, 2023). Policy-science dialogues conditioned on knowledge co-production processes (Frantzeskaki and Kabisch, 2016) had been credited for effective and inclusive decision-making from a bottom-up participative approach (Howarth and Monasterolo, 2017) and with group grounding (Palermo and Hernandez, 2020) in mind. An applied participatory analysis (Wamsler, 2017) can contrast current practices on how and why different stakeholders are involved or excluded and feed these processes back into both theory and practice. And the illusion of inclusion (Few et al., 2006) in climate change adaptation can be addressed when the scope and limitations of public involvement are made explicit at the start. This allows the participation process to transform power relations and be perceived as a form of empowerment (McMillan et al., 2014), offers environmental strategy (Tan, 2017), and builds culture for public participation (Wang et al., 2020).

Effective stabilisation policies demand that macroeconomic goals of output, employment, and inflation operate within an acceptable range which can be measured with short-run snapshots of an economy. However, sustainable development of the economy can only be determined by long-run time series. In a standard macroeconomic model, there is no appreciation for environment as a capital which falsifies the policy domain and therefore, ineffective stabilisation policies. For instance, how relevant is the misery index (that sums only seasonally adjusted unemployment and inflation rate) when the environment is not acknowledged as a factor of production in a growing economy. And how could tax reforms be less distorted and more efficient when grandfathering of resource firms is encouraged. Preferably, taxes should be administered on abnormal profits of resource firms and carbon dioxide emissions; and taxes should be reduced on innovative initiatives and carbon dioxide reductions. And land tax would encourage land to be used more efficiently and make clear its sovereignty as a natural asset. For sustainable development to occur, the environment must be internalised in a standard macroeconomic model such as that of the EM model. Although a valuation of the environment (Tan, 2016) may offer policy clarity, the environment remains a public good. This would suggest that the public be engaged (Helm, 2005) and bestowed participatory rights to how an economy develops in a sustainable manner – for an economy remains a subset of the larger natural ecosystem (Daly, 2007).

7.3 Summary of the Research

The main thrust of this research is to demonstrate methods for deriving a set of stabilisation policies that addresses not only output, employment, and inflation but also sustainability. In this section, a brief discussion of each chapter and of significant findings from the analysis will be presented.

Chapter 1 provided a synopsis of the standard macroeconomic framework and policy practices that stem from the utilisation of such a framework. Chapter 2 stressed the debate between growth versus development with the natural ecosystem as a bedrock for stabilisation policies. In an effort to continue growing, economies pedestalise economic progress where attention is skewed towards economic performance with an intentional oblivion to the environment. The difference between economic growth and economic development needs to be distinguished for a healthy review on sustainable development. As the environment is both a source and a sink, care ought to be taken for it to be accorded as a capital in macroeconomic modelling.

Chapter 3 reviewed the literature on environmental accounting and environmental macroeconomics. This review highlighted the challenges posed by standard macroeconomic frameworks when environmental capital (KN) was not internalised. As such, recommendations for the development of advanced macroeconomic modelling must be considered for sustainable policies to be formulated. This chapter provided recommendations for the proposed EM framework following the illustration of an introductory EM framework which was empirically tested. However, enhancements are required for this model before it can be operationalised. These enhancements were accomplished in Chapters 4 and 5, beginning with the measurement of KN in Chapter 4.

Chapter 4 focused on the measurement of KN by factoring KN into the factor utilisation model. The empirical evidence was made with reference to eight selected Organisation for Economic Co-operation and Development (OECD) economies, namely, Australia, Canada, Germany, Japan, Korea, New Zealand, the United Kingdom, and the USA between the years 1990 and 2021. An association between the utilisation of KN and the three macroeconomic goals of output, employment, and inflation was demonstrated via the income gap. It was shown that an economy is more efficient when the income gap (which measures the capacity that is available in an economy) rises with a low level of KN utilisation.

Chapter 5 offered a comparison of the eight selected OECD economies' steady state between the standard macroeconomic model and the EM model. Pricing and valuing the environment as a capital has its debates which presents challenges for recognising environment as a capital in the standard macroeconomic framework. The approach in Chapter 4 was included in this chapter with empirical evidence of the steady states for the two models presented. It was found that the capacity of an economy can be overstated in the absence of KN. Such oversight (with no allowance rendered for KN) could have an effect on the steady state of an economy with respect to its macroeconomic goals of output, employment, and inflation.

Chapter 6 presented a methodology for analysing how macroeconomic goals are related by steady states. An explanatory relationship between the macroeconomic variables and the steady-state ratios was formalised using panel and linear regressions. This formalised relationship is operationalised with years 2009 and 2021 data for both the standard macroeconomic and EM models. There were selected economies and their macroeconomic variables with considerable differences in their policy ranges. The respective economies and their macroeconomic variables were Australia (inflation), Japan (GDP growth), and Korea (inflation). This finding was consistent for both 2009 and 2021 snapshots post GFC and the COVID-19 pandemic exogenous shocks.

At the time when this book was written, the global economy had just rode itself out of the COVID-19 pandemic whilst the ghost of geopolitical tensions continues to dog economic recovery. Inflation continues to rise in 2022 and is expected to increase at an increasing rate which is an encouraging sign that the cycle of tightening is not far. This will mean that economic growth is near with more ravelling of natural resources to quench the thirst for growth from policymakers. Environmental policies lost a redemption opportunity after the GFC. There is hope that this will not be a lost opportunity after the COVID-19 pandemic with greater public engagement and less muddled participatory processes.

One would expect a macroeconomic variable to display similar traits across the economies in terms of their relationships with the steady-state ratios [(k^*/k), (k^{**}/k)]. However, this type of similarity was not observed. The observation from the snapshots showed that inflation in Australia was positively related to its steady-state ratios whilst inflation in Korea displayed an inverse relationship. A different observation was made of the relationship between

GDP growth and steady-state ratios where it was a positive relationship in both Australia and Japan.

To recapitulate Chapter 6, the relationship between GDP growth and steady-state ratios for Japan in the standard macroeconomic model was below that of the EM model. This result implies that, to achieve a given reduction in GDP growth for Japan, the steady-state ratio must be increased by a greater amount in the EM model than in the standard macroeconomic model. The rate of change in GDP growth in the standard macroeconomic model in Japan was steeper relative to that of the EM model. Hence, in the case of Japan, to achieve a given increase in GDP growth, the increase in the steady-state ratio has to be greater in the EM model.

The rate of change of inflation with respect to the steady-state ratios in the standard macroeconomic model in Australia was greater than that of the EM model. However, the rate of change of inflation and steady-state ratios for Korea in the standard macroeconomic model was less than that of the EM model. Regardless of the nature of the relationships between inflation and the steady-state ratios and the gradients for the two models, it was observed that the effort to curb inflation was understated in the standard macroeconomic model for both Australia and Korea, simply because any increase or decrease in the steady-state ratios is greater for the EM model compared to the standard macroeconomic model.

The type of relationship (positive or inverse) between the macroeconomic variables and the steady-state ratios determines whether policymakers should increase or decrease the steady-state ratios. Consider the case of inflation for Australia and Korea. Inflation in Australia was positively related and was inversely related in Korea with respect to the steady-state ratios. Policymakers prefer to reduce inflation to keep inflation in a manageable range. Thus, the steady-state ratio should be decreased for Australia and increased in Korea.

7.4 Future Studies

The limitations of the study are as follows and offer scope for future studies.

The proxy selected for the depreciation of environmental capital (D_{KN}) is carbon dioxide (CO_2). CO_2 was chosen because the selected World Development Indicators (WDI) databank allows for the conversion of all other greenhouse gases (GHG) into CO_2 terms. This conversion allows for completeness in terms of capturing all CO_2 emissions. In addition, there are substantial emissions data dating back to 1970. If D_{KN} was not proxied to CO_2 alone and was extended to capture other considerations of KN, the output of the analysis might have been different. For example, if D_{KN} was extended to include deforestation, soil erosion, and water pollution, then the size of KN might be considerably larger. However, if these were the proxies for D_{KN}, the difficulty would be to obtain a universally agreed measurement method for environmental degradation. But what is not so easily comprehended is the interaction between drivers of climate change and effects of weather patterns. A possible enhancement that could be made to the model and greatly reduce ambiguities about future climate states is to move away from the Cobb–Douglas framework to an endogenous framework such as the Romer model which considers different types of factor utilisation with constant or variable elasticity of substitution.

Standard macroeconomic analysis factor utilisation frameworks serve as the basis for developing the aggregate supply (AS) framework. A possible extension is to develop the AS and combine it with the aggregate demand (AD) to effect a general equilibrium analysis. Such analysis can be differentiated between the standard macroeconomic model and the EM model.

The snapshots selected for the analysis were for the years 2009 and 2021. The years 2009 and 2021 were selected as they were the immediate years after the 2007–2008 GFC and COVID-19 pandemic. There is a possibility that this analysis could have been skewed as a result of the exogenous shocks. There are two options around this. Firstly, to conduct an analysis during exogenous events such as the 1990 oil shock, 1997 Asian Financial Crisis (AFC), and the dot-com bust in 2000 to ascertain if there are further consistencies and the extent of volatility. Secondly, it might be wise for the analysis to be compared with years where for the year preceding that there were no major exogenous shocks. Hence, a recommendation would be to select "stable" years with less volatility. This comparison could help to generalise a predictive model for future time periods.

And last but not least, developing economies (as opposed to OECD economies) may not have the solace to decide if GDP is accountable from expenditure or income approach. Therefore, the discussion on whether it was income from revenue or income from the sale of natural assets (or an allowance for environmental degradation) would not have been a priority for developing economies. This is certainly scope for future work, subject to accuracy and availability of time-series data and suggested proxies.

7.5 Conclusion

Policy discussions and debates abound when an economy is operating at, beyond, or close to its steady-state equilibrium. There is a portfolio of policies available to policymakers, for example, monetary policy and fiscal policy (two of the more accessible approaches). The debate usually centres on who should bear the responsibility for steering an economy forward, specifically the Reserve Bank for monetary policy versus the Central Government for fiscal policy. However, these debates will add no value *if* the policy range has not been correctly identified by the appropriate macroeconomic model – from the outset. This book argues that the EM model should be the macroeconomic model that is used for economies when determining the steady state of an economy as well as how the steady state affects the policy variables.

References

Bailey, D. (2020), "Re-thinking the fiscal and monetary political economy of the green state", *New Political Economy*, 25(1), pp. 5–17.

Belletti, G., Marescotti, A., Touzard, J. M. (2017), "Geographical indications, public goods, and sustainable development: The roles of actors' strategies and public policies", *World Development*, 98, pp. 45–57.

Benkhodja, M. T., Ma, X., Razafindrabe, T. (2023), "Green monetary and fiscal policies: The role of consumer preferences", *Resource and Energy Economics*, 73, 101370.

Brandsen, T., Honingh, M. E. (2016), "Distinguishing different types of coproduction: A conceptual analysis based on the classical definitions", *Public Administration Review*, 76(3), pp. 427–435.

Brandsen, T., Pestoff, V. (2006), "Co-production, the third sector and the delivery of public services: An introduction", *Public Management Review*, 8(4), pp. 493–501.

Braunschweiger, D., Ingold, K. (2023), "What drives local climate change adaptation? A qualitative comparative analysis", *Environmental Science & Policy*, 145, pp. 40–49.

Callendar, G. S. (1938), "The artificial production of carbon dioxide and its influence on temperature", *Quarterly Journal of the Royal Meteorological Society*, 64(275), pp. 223–240.

Daly, H. E. (2007), *Ecological Economics and Sustainable Development, Selected Essays of Herman Daly*, Edward Elgar Northampton, United States of America.

Few, R., Brown, K., Tompkins, E. L. (2006), "Public participation and climate change adaptation", Tyndall Centre for Climate Change Research Working Paper, 95.

Fledderus, J., Brandsen, T., Honingh, M. E. (2015), "User co-production of public service delivery: An uncertainty approach", *Public Policy and Administration*, 30(2), pp. 145–164.

Frantzeskaki, N., Kabisch, N. (2016), "Designing a knowledge co-production operating space for urban environmental governance—Lessons from Rotterdam, Netherlands and Berlin, Germany", *Environmental Science & Policy*, 62, pp. 90–98.

Funtowicz, S., Ravetz, J., O'Connor, M. (1998), "Challenges in the use of science for sustainable development", *International Journal of Sustainable Development*, 1(1), pp. 99–107.

Glasbergen, P., Biermann, F., Mol, A. P. (eds) (2007), *Partnerships, Governance and Sustainable Development: Reflections on Theory and Practice*, Edward Elgar Publishing, The United Kingdom.

González-Ramírez, J., Caviglia-Harris, J., Whitehead, J. C. (2021), "Teaching environmental and natural resource economics: A review of the economic education literature", *International Review of Environmental and Resource Economics*, 15(3), pp. 235–369.

Halkos, G., Managi, S. (2023), "New developments in the disciplines of environmental and resource economics", *Economic Analysis and Policy*, 77, pp. 513–522.

Harris, J. M., Roach, B. (2021), *Environmental and Natural Resource Economics: A Contemporary Approach – Fifth Edition*, Routledge, The United Kingdom.

Helm, D. (2005), "Economic instruments and environmental policy", *The Economic and Social Review*, 36(3), pp. 205–228.

Hessing, M., Howlett, M., Summerville, T. (2005), *Canadian Natural Resource and Environmental Policy: Political Economy and Public Policy*, 2nd Edition, UBC Press, Vancouver, Canada.

Howarth, C., Monasterolo, I. (2017), "Opportunities for knowledge co-production across the energy-food-water nexus: Making interdisciplinary approaches work for better climate decision making", *Environmental Science & Policy*, 75, pp. 103–110.

Humphreys, M., Sachs, J., Stiglitz, J. (eds) (2007), *Escaping the Resource Curse*, Columbia University Press, New York, United States of America.

Karpouzoglou, T., Zulkafli, Z., Grainger, S., Dewulf, A., Buytaert, W., Hannah, D. M. (2016), "Environmental virtual observatories (EVOs): Prospects for knowledge co-creation and resilience in the information age", *Current Opinion in Environmental Sustainability*, 18, pp. 40–48.

Lemons, J., Brown, D. A. (eds) (2013), *Sustainable Development: Science, Ethics, and Public Policy*, Springer Science & Business Media, Rotterdam, The Netherlands.

McMillan, R., Spronk, S., Caswell, C. (2014), "Popular participation, equity, and co-production of water and sanitation services in Caracas, Venezuela", *Water International*, 39(2), pp. 201–215.

Monasterolo, I., Raberto, M. (2018), "The EIRIN flow-of-funds behavioural model of green fiscal policies and green sovereign bonds", *Ecological Economics*, 144, pp. 228–243.

Nordhaus, W. (2019), "Climate change: The ultimate challenge for economics", *American Economic Review*, 109(6), pp. 1991–2014.

Palermo, V., Hernandez, Y. (2020), "Group discussions on how to implement a participatory process in climate adaptation planning: A case study in Malaysia", *Ecological Economics*, 177, 106791.

Parks, R. B., Baker, P. C., Kiser, L., Oakerson, R., Ostrom, E., Ostrom, V., Percy, S., Vandivort, M. B., Whitaker, G. P., Wilson, R. (1981), "Consumers as coproducers of public services: Some economic and institutional considerations", *Policy Studies Journal*, 9(7), pp. 1001–1011.

Preuss, L. (2009), "Addressing sustainable development through public procurement: The case of local government", *Supply Chain Management: An International Journal*, 14(3), pp. 213–223.

Tan, S. (2016), "Framework for valuing the utilisation of the environment", *International Journal of Social Economics*, 43(6), pp. 619–642.

Tan, S. (2017), "Strategy for environmental sustainability for island-state Singapore – Engaging the public", *Asian Journal of Public Affairs*, 9(2), pp. 1–18.

Voorberg, W. H., Bekkers, V. J. J. M., Tummers, L. G. (2014), "A systematic review of co-creation and co-production: Embarking on the social innovation journey", *Public Management Review*, 17(9), pp. 1333–1357.

Wamsler, C. (2017), "Stakeholder involvement in strategic adaptation planning: Transdisciplinarity and co-production at stake?", *Environmental Science & Policy*, 75, pp. 148–157.

Wang, Y., Cao, H., Yuan, Y., Zhang, R. (2020), "Empowerment through emotional connection and capacity building: Public participation through environmental non-governmental organizations", *Environmental Impact Assessment Review*, 80, 106319.

Index